Social Work Practice with Transgender and Gender Variant Youth

Second edition

Edited by Gerald P. Mallon

Routledge
Taylor & Francis Group

LONDON AND NEW YORK

First edition published 2000 as *Social Services with Transgendered Youth* by The Haworth Press, Inc.

This edition published 2009
by Routledge
2 Park Square, Milton Park, Abingdon, Oxon OX14 4RN

Simultaneously published in the USA and Canada
by Routledge
270 Madison Ave, New York, NY 10016

Routledge is an imprint of the Taylor and Francis Group, an informa business

Typeset in Sabon by Greengate Publishing Services, Tonbridge, Kent
Printed and bound in Great Britain by CPI Antony Rowe, Chippenham, Wiltshire

British Library Cataloguing in Publication Data
A catalogue record for this book is available from the British Library

Library of Congress Cataloging in Publication Data
Social work practice with transgender and gender variant youth / edited by Gerald P. Mallon.—2nd ed.
p. cm.
1. Transgender youth—Psychology. 2. Transgender youth—Mental health services. 3. Social work with transgender youth. 4. Transgender people—Services for—United States. I. Mallon, Gerald P.
HQ77.9.S64 2009
362.7083–dc22
2008034081

ISBN 10: 0-415-99481-0 (hbk)
ISBN 10: 0-415-99482-9 (pbk)

ISBN 13: 978-0-415-99481-1 (hbk)
ISBN 13: 978-0-415-99482-8 (pbk)

Social Work Practice with Transgender and Gender Variant Youth
Second edition

Through personal narratives and case studies, *Social Work Practice with Transgender and Gender Variant Youth* explores the childhood and adolescent experiences of transgender and gender variant young people.

Addressing the specific challenges of transgender and gender variant youth from diverse races, cultures, social classes, and religious backgrounds, this compelling book offers practice guidance that will help social workers and the youths' families learn more about the reality of transgender and gender variant youths' lives. Some of the areas discussed in this work include:

- individual practice with transgender and gender variant children;
- group work practice with transgender and gender variant adolescents;
- family-centered practice with the families of transgender youth;
- internal and external stress factors for the transgender youth.

This fully updated second edition also features a new discussion of the legal issues that transgender and gender variant youth face, and a concluding section focusing on recommendations for clinical treatment with trans and gender variant youth.

The book discredits negative stereotypes surrounding these youths and offers a positive and alternative insight into their experiences. Additionally, the chapters openly address questions that practitioners may have about gender identity as well as offering concrete and practical recommendations about competent and positive trans-affirming practice with this population. *Social Work Practice with Transgender and Gender Variant Youth* will interest academics, advocates for youth, and social service practitioners.

Gerald P. Mallon is Professor and Executive Director of the National Resource Center for Fam ency Planning at the Hunter College Scho ity, USA.

For Teresa DeCrescenzo

Contents

Notes on contributors

About the editor

Gerald P. Mallon, DSW, is Professor at the Hunter College Social Work in New York City.

For more than 33 years, Dr. Mallon has been a child welfare practitioner, advocate, and researcher. He is the author or editor of 20 books and numerous peer-reviewed publications in professional journals. His most recent publications include *Social Work Practice with Lesbian, Gay, Bisexual, and Transgender People*; *Lesbian and Gay Foster and Adoptive Parents: Recruiting, Assessing, and Supporting an Untapped Resource for Children and Youth*; and *Child Welfare for the Twenty-first Century: A Handbook of Practices, Policies, and Programs*, coedited with Peg Hess.

Dr. Mallon earned his doctorate in Social Welfare from the City University of New York at Hunter College and holds an MSW from Fordham University and a BSW from Dominican College.

Dr. Mallon has lectured extensively in the United States, Ireland, Australia, Indonesia, Canada, Cuba, and the United Kingdom.

Correspondence may be sent to 129 East 79th Street, Suite 801, New York, New York 10021 or via email at gmallon@hunter.cuny.edu.

Contributors

Flor Bermudez is the Youth in Out-of-home Care Attorney based in the New York Office at Lambda Legal. She may be contacted via email at fbermudez@lambdalegal.org.

W. Christian Burgess, LMSW, is the Director, School Programs at Safe Horizon, New York. He may be contacted via email at wburgess@safehorizons.org.

Ken Cooper, LCSW, is Assistant Director of Adult Day Services at Service Program for Old People in New York City. He may be contacted via email at kcooper@spop.org.

Carrie Davis, LCSW, is Director of Mental Health Services at the Lesbian, Gay, Bisexual, and Transgender Center of New York. She may be contacted via email at carrie@gaycenter.org.

Teresa DeCrescenzo, LCSW, is Founder and President of GLASS in West Hollywood, California. She may be contacted via email at TerryD50@aol.com.

Wendell D. Glenn, MSW, is Director of GLASS Oakland Programs, Oakland, California. He may be contacted via email at wendellg@glassla.org.

Sarah E. Herbert, MD, is a Clinical Assistant Professor, PSYCH:Psychiatry, Professor Emeritus, PSYCH:Psychiatry, and a staff physician at Emory Hospital in Atlanta, Georgia. She may be contacted via email at sherber@emory.edu.

Gus Klein, LMSW, is a social worker in San Francisco, California. He may be contacted via email at augustklein@gmail.com.

Sofia Pazos, LCSW, is a social worker at the Hudson Guild in New York. She may be contacted via email at qgirl@earthlink.net.

Susan Sommer is Senior Counsel based in the New York headquarters of Lambda Legal. She may be contacted via email at ssommer@lambdalegal.org.

Stephanie K. Swann, Ph.D., is a Clinical Professor at the University of Georgia, School of Social Work, and a therapist in private practice in Atlanta, Georgia. She may be contacted via email at skswann@uga.edu.

Cole Thaler is the National Transgender Rights Attorney based in the Southern Regional Office of Lambda Legal. He may be contacted via email at cthaler@lambdalegal.org.

Acknowledgments

The original idea for writing this book came from discussions I had with Ray Berger, who was at the time this was first published the editor of the *Journal of Gay and Lesbian Social Services* and who is, although he in now retired, a great person to work with. His tireless quest to help practitioners and scholars to think about and write about gay, lesbian, bisexual, and transgender persons allowed me and many others to write articles and edit journal special issues that speak to the needs of persons whose voices have been marginalized. Eloise Cook from Routledge is responsible for my revisiting this work and for encouraging me to publish this second edition and shepherd me through the process. Her assistance has been invaluable.

My immediate thanks are due next to those practitioners and scholars who agreed to author the chapters that go to make up this volume. In asking each of these professionals to participate in this project, it was important for me that they be trained social work practitioners and educators. I am proud that many of the authors have been my former students at the Hunter School of Social Work or at another school of social work where I taught earlier in my career. All of these students had written in my classes so passionately about transgender persons that when I asked them to submit papers for this volume, their enthusiasm and their eagerness for contributing to this volume made this a very stimulating project for me to be involved in. Their willingness in reediting these papers written more than a decade ago was also a wonderful opportunity to reconnect.

Although I am grateful to all the authors who contributed, I must pay special homage to two of the authors. The first is Wendell Glenn from the Gay and Lesbian Social Services (GLASS) in Los Angeles. Wendell has been my mentor and my very best teacher about the lives of transgendered youth. One afternoon in a Taco Restaurant on Santa Monica Boulevard and Robertson, in West Hollywood, he changed my life. Wendell's courage and honesty in sharing his story with me allowed me, for the first time, to really understand what it means for some people to identify as transgendered. Wendell's deep commitment to transgendered youth and his ability to convey their experiences to me helped to free me from my own ignorance and judgment. I will always be indebted to him for sharing this knowledge with me and for contributing to opening my mind and my heart to being a better practitioner.

Second, special thanks are also due to Carrie Davis, CSW, from the Lesbian, Gay, Bisexual, and Transgender Center in New York City. Carrie is one of the brightest social workers whom I have had the pleasure of knowing these past 33 years. Carrie's commitment to working with trans persons in New York, and her gift for educating other social workers about how they could and should work more effectively with trans persons, are remarkable. I am delighted that I could include contributions by Carrie in this second edition so that she can share her vast knowledge of practice with trans persons with other professionals.

My thanks are also extended, as always to friends and family who supplied me with relationships that have sustained me and have given me a life outside of my work.

Finally, I would like to thank my colleague and good friend Teresa DeCrescenzo. More than two decades ago, when no one else was brave enough to do so, Terry opened the Gay and Lesbian Social programs in Los Angeles – the first group home programs for LGBT youth in the country. Terry and her partner, the late Betty Berzon, have a long history of deep commitment to the LGBT community in general and specifically to LGBT youth in need of a place to call home. Through the many joys and sometimes struggles of our lives and our careers, Terry has always been there for me whenever I have needed an ear or someone who knew what I was experiencing, and through it all, Terry has always been my good and loyal friend. For this reason and for others that are rooted in deep feelings and not always possible to express in words, this book is dedicated to her.

A word about language

The terms "transman" or "male-bodied" refers to female-to-male (FTM or F2M) transgender people, and "transwoman" or "female-bodied" refers to male-to-female (MTF or M2F) transgender people. There are some who note that terms such as "FTM" and "MTF" are subjugating language that reinforces the binary gender stereotype. In this book contributors utilized many terms to discuss the lives and realities of trans and gender variant youth, each did so with respect and with a full understanding of the current language and knowledge at the time this book went to press.

Introduction to practice with transgender and gender variant youth

Carrie Davis

This chapter introduces knowledge which supports practice that social workers need to establish beginning competency in working with transgender and gender nonconforming youth. The concepts and variables explored in this collection require a common language. Traditional clinical social work language can often be "out of step" with the vernacular of trans communities themselves, which sometimes makes translation of ideas and concepts into practice more challenging. Trans communities have developed an inventive, expressive, and diverse language of preferred identities, terms, knowledge, and pronouns. Whenever possible, this chapter emphasizes the language, terminology, and vocabulary of trans culture, with a specific focus on trans youth, rather than the language or terminology used by social services providers.

Trans language

The trans community, as Burdge (2007, p. 243) notes, has generated a unique language with which to communicate its reality. Undoubtedly, keeping up with this changing lexicon can be challenging. Language, furthermore, is a critical component in the recognition of subjugated knowledge (Anderson, 2000; Aranda and Street, 2001; Hartman, 1990, 1992; Holbrook, 1995). Trans language is an evolutionary vocabulary that changes intergenerationally, geographically, and within a political context. Trans language is somewhat fluid and continually evolving. Some trans terms have emerged organically from within the community; others have been developed by science or academia.

Transvestite and transsexual people were first assigned global meaning in a medical and historical context during the first quarter of the twentieth century. The clinical distinction that developed between transvestite and transsexual further enhanced the perception of these as psychopathological identities. In the light of this pathologizing, trans people have begun to utilize their voices to make claim to, or reclaim, these terminologies (Davis, 2008). The creation and use of the word "transgender" in the

1960s is one example. Although obvious, it bears stating that all-gender pronouns address some aspect of sexism and complement and complicate the complexity of identity.

In seeking to understand our own subjugated knowledge, we as practitioners must remain aware that this knowledge is also produced and later interpreted under the oppressive influence of the prevailing and dominant global knowledge (Kondrat, 1995) – one steeped in an irrational fear of gender difference or cultural transphobia, as well as sexism, racism, classism, bigenderism, and so forth.

For this reason, it is not uncommon for trans communities themselves also to use subjugating language. We routinely hear references to "real," "genetic" and/or "bio(logical)" men or women. Clearly, these conflict with both the knowledge trans people have about their own lives, and our developing understanding of gender. Every individual, trans or non-trans, is real, genetic, and biological. When misused, terms such as these create a double standard applied by non-trans people and also by trans people themselves and enforce the existing cultural hierarchy, which structures and subjugates trans people as less real and less natural than non-trans people.

Given the dichotomy between a subjugating knowledge such as that authored outside the trans communities and the knowledge derived from trans individuals, it is not surprising that the relationship between the trans communities and non-trans communities have often been uncertain, and sometimes suspicious. In this manner, social service providers and researchers focusing their efforts on trans people for much of the past century have exacerbated the contradictory and uneasy power association between the marginalization of trans people by nontrans people.

Definitions

Social workers should keep in mind, before launching into a discussion about definitions, that in some cases trans youth – at least initially, before they emerge into their trans consciousness themselves – may not know or have access to these definitions. Nevertheless, language is important and assists social workers in developing a higher level of comfort in working with trans youth. Based on previous work (Davis, 2008), what follows is a quick review of Trans 101 definitions as they are near the start of the twenty-first century. To that end, gender comprises several different elements:

Sex refers to biological, anatomical, or organic sexual markers such as vagina, ovaries, eggs, estrogen levels, and menstruation for females, and penis, testis, sperm, and testosterone levels for males. We tend to think of these as very clear distinctions, yet the truth is more fluid. Variations in our sex include chromosomal variations, changing hormonal levels as we age, biological changes due to illness (such as hysterectomy, mastectomy), changes related to choice, and the varied anatomical differences faced by intersex individuals born with characteristics of both sexes (who are typically forced to undergo genital surgery at birth to make them "normal," long before they have the opportunity to confirm their own gender).

Gender role can be defined as social and perceived expectations of gendered acts or expressions. Examples include cultural notions that boys play with trucks, girls play with dolls; boys wear pants, girls wear skirts; boys date girls, girls date boys. Gender role changes over time and from cultural subgroup to cultural subgroup.

Gender had been conceived of as distinct from sex, or sexual identity, as early as the 1860s, but it is only relatively recently that a lucid conception of gender identity as distinct from understandings of sexual identity and sexual orientation has begun to evolve. This was articulated as a private, inner sense of maleness or femaleness (Hogan and Hudson, 1998; Money, 1987) and coincided with the emergence of a gay civil rights movement. Money (1987) further developed an understanding of gender which suggests that gender is a complex combination of many factors, including variations and combinations of organic and non-organic markers including chromosomal gender, gonadal gender, prenatal hormonal gender, prenatal and neonatal brain hormonalization, internal accessory organs, external genital appearance, pubertal hormonal gender, assigned gender, and gender identity. Despite this, transgender-identified persons would be conflated with the identities of those identified as lesbian and gay, within what was termed a "gay movement."

Gender identity can be understood as the self-conception of one's gender; it is about how I see myself, how I feel about my gender identity and myself, and may or may not have an organic component. We are still learning more about this.

All three of these, *sex + gender role + gender identity*, combine to create one's *gender*. And while gender has typically been thought of as a binary construct, as man or woman, an alternative paradigm understands gender as a continuum – as an infinite series of individually defined genders, one for each living person.

The next concept is *sexual identity*. In adolescence, puberty is distinguished by physical growth and maturation, and the elaboration of the secondary sexual characteristics. Undeniable as these biological changes are, they are still subject to interpretation and assigned cultural meanings. Developmental theorists often make a strong connection between physical or biological developmental theory and psychosocial concerns. Legislators, clergy, physicians, researchers, and other clinicians have created various methods to quantify and value the sexes. But these imposed markers of sexual identity are often incongruent with each other. Legislated sex not only can vary on the basis of the actual physical constitution of a trans body, but may also have a geopolitical component related to what state, city, or country a trans person may happen to enter, visit, or reside in, and what borders they might cross (Currah and Minter, 2000; Currah *et al.*, 2006; Valentine, 2007). In this framework, an understanding of one's biology as a social construction is reasoned, and sexual identity is understood as a social, not organic, construction (Butler, 1993). Despite this, organic markers have traditionally been used to categorize individuals as either male or female, though other individuals may also be considered intersex at birth. Sexual identity, and/or an understanding of biological sex, are replaced here with an understanding of the sex that the participants had been identified as at birth (assigned sex – typically based on genital appearance and gender of rearing), the sex that individuals understand themselves to be, and the legal sex that individuals currently understood themselves as.

Transition refers to the place one perceives oneself to be in the process, or vector, from living and being perceived as identified at birth (either male or female) to living and being perceived as the trans individual understands themselves. This often includes assessment of transition milestones, sometimes described as living part time, living full time, doing "drags," and so forth. This assessment also considers access to gender-confirming surgery, described as operative or surgical status (non-operative, pre-operative, post-operative, partly operative); and access to gender-confirming hormones (endogenous, cross-gender hormones), described as hormonal status (pre-hormones, using hormones).

The language used to describe *sexual orientation* (sexual, affectional, or romantic attraction) is sometimes elusive when perceived in the context of the trans communities. Terms such as straight, gay, lesbian, and bisexual/pansexual/omnisexual traditionally require agreement about individual conceptions of gender, as well as sexual identity, and are frequently framed around understandings of genitalia. Within the trans communities, these choices and language are often also valued as independent of transition milestones such as access to gender-confirming hormones or surgery.

In this phraseology, trans women attracted to men and trans men attracted to women may identify as straight, while trans women attracted to women identify as lesbian, and trans men attracted to men identify as gay irrespective of genital configuration and/or access to gender-confirming surgeries. This further develops the significance of viewing people with people with transgender histories as sexual minorities. Other choices can include queer, asexual, pansexual, omnisexual, and questioning.

In addition, there are few, if any, affirming and representative terms for individuals who prefer and are attracted to trans people, commonly referred to in the trans women's communities with pejorative terms such as "trannie-chaser." The dearth of representative terminology can confound clinicians, researchers, social scientists, and others who seek to "bag and tag" the trans communities and who attempt to label trans partners as straight, lesbian, gay and bisexual against their will, ignoring the complexities gender and of representative identities.

Though the term *transgender* was not created or used until the late 1970s, transgender-identified people have been present in all cultures and at all times (Feinberg, 2001). When the modern conception of differing sexual orientations began to emerge in the 1860s, people who were seen to express their gender differently were bundled into Karoly Maria Kertbeny's evolving definition of homosexuality (Hogan and Hudson, 1998). This has been an awkward fit, as people of transgender experience have historically sought out a variety of sexual partners, including those of the same or differing sexes.

What others have written and what I am suggesting here is clearly a modern and evolutionary language. Both "transvestite" and "transsexual" were first assigned meaning in a medical context by Magnus Hirschfeld. Transsexual was later given prominence in both Cauldwell's "Psychopathia Transsexualis" (1949) and Benjamin's "Transsexualism and Transvestism as Psycho-somatic and Somato-psychic Syndromes" (1954). The clinical distinction made at this time between transvestite and transsexual further enhances the perception of these as psychopathological identities.

In the light of this, trans people have begun to utilize their voices to make claim to, or reclaim, these terminologies. The reconfiguration by some trans people of the word most commonly read as "transsexual" to read as "transexual" (with a single "s") is a poignant example of the reclamation of trans identities by trans people. Riki Ann Wilchins (1997), one of founders of Transsexual Menace, notes that

> [t]his ... seemed a way of asserting some small amount of control over a naming process that has always been entirely out of my hands – a kind of quiet mini-rebellion of my own. I think transactivist Dallas Denny captured the spirit of the whole enterprise; "Yeah, we'll change it to one 's' until they all start using it. Then we'll go back to two, or maybe to three."
>
> (p. 15)

Popularized by Virginia Prince in the late 1970s, "transgender" (or "transgenderist") originally referred to someone who did not desire gender-confirming medical intervention and/or who considered that they fell "between" genders. Prince and others conceived transgender as a challenge to older terms that hinted at pathology or medicalized identity such as terms like "transsexual" and "transvestite."

Transgender, created by people with trans histories to refer to trans people, is now generally considered an umbrella term encompassing many different identities. It is commonly used to describe an individual who is seen as gender different. Outside the transgender communities, people identified as transgender are usually perceived through a dichotomous lens and are commonly described as transgressing gender norms, gender variant, or gender deviant. This traditional misreading is predicated on a conception of transgender within a pathologically oriented perspective framed in a language layered in heterosexist, sexist, bigenderist, and trans-phobic context and meaning.

In this definition, gender difference is not regulated. A person who is identified, or self-identifies, as transgender may, or may not, live full time in a sex different from the sex that they were assigned at birth – sometimes referred to as the "opposite sex." Being seen as transgender may, or may not, have anything to do with whether that individual has had any sort of gender-confirming surgery (GCS), also commonly known "sex reassign-ment" surgery (SRS). Individuals who are seen as gender different or gender questioning may, or may not, personally identify themselves as transgender.

In this way, care needs to be taken not to label or identify anyone as transgender who does not perceive themselves that way. This is particu-larly true for trans youth who may not have access to these terms and who may in fact initially refer to themselves as "gay," "lesbian," or "bisexual."

By using the words "transgender" and/or "trans," this chapter looks for a common language, communities, and purposes and is not seeking to erase any of the diverse identities of those individuals who identify them-selves and/or are seen as androgyne, bi-gendered, butch queen, CD, cross-dresser, drag king, drag queen, female-to-male, femme queen, FTM, gender-bender, gender-blender, gender challenged, gender fucked, gender gifted, gender nonconforming, gender queer, male-to-female, MTF, new man, woman, non-op, non-operative transsexual, passing man, passing woman, phallic woman, post-op, post-operative transsexual, pre-op, pre-operative transsexual, sex change, she-male, stone butch, TG, third sex, trannie/tranny, trannie-fag, trans, trans-butch, transsexual/transsexual, transgender, transgenderist, transie, trans man, trans person, transexed, transexed man, transexed woman, transsexual man, transsexual woman, transvestic-fetishist, transvestite, trans woman, tryke, TS, two-spirited, and the like. The framework provided by "transgender" as an umbrella term then serves as a transitory and common idiom, useful to connect communities and purposes.

Development of a trans identity for trans youth

Imagine if some non-trans children were randomly reared in a gender role opposite to that of their sexual identity – boys as girls, girls as boys (see

Colapinto's 2001 work for a discussion of this). For many children, that event would be highly troubling and traumatic. The public, as well as mental healthcare providers, would most certainly consider this an abuse perpetrated by these children's caretakers. Yet on some level this is what all transgender-identified children, youth, and adults encounter until they finally muster the reserves to express their actual gender identity (see Chapter 5 by Mallon and DeCrescenzo for a full discussion of the issues facing transgender children).

Coming out for trans youth begins with an increasing awareness that one is different, the sense that how one sees oneself in terms of gender and how others perceive one do not match up. In these early stages, trans individuals may be forced to compartmentalize their lives, to hide the true parts of themselves, to remain closeted at all costs – to manage their gender. Coming out is a continuous process. While it begins with acknowledging the truth of one's identity to oneself, every trans individual finds themselves continually confronted with the risks and possibilities of coming out to family, friends, religious groups, teachers and classmates, employers and coworkers, and medical and mental health professionals.

Certainly, it seems reasonable to recognize that perceiving one's identity as non-normative, or in this way being restricted from expressing, having to repress, or being unable to recognize one's gender in childhood, as well as adolescence and adulthood, is in itself traumatic and, possibly, abusive.

This would then posit that the first, and perhaps most overlooked, abuse trans people experience is at the hands of (often loving) parents and caregivers in childhood. Many, if not most, trans people as children consciously or unconsciously struggle with the understanding that their gender identities are considered socially and parentally inappropriate or deviant. Since children who display differing gender roles and identities are usually punished harshly and rarely parentally reinforced, the bonds of attachment and trust between child and caregiver are certainly going to be affected.

Trans youth are consciously or unconsciously aware that gender-different behavior rarely brings about a nurturing and caretaking response from parents and other caregivers (Brooks, 2000). This can elicit a pattern of blame and guilt. Related as a protective dissociation, this could be seen as one of the first adaptive tools trans people might utilize to endure the trauma of being unable to actualize their gender identity.

Gender management

To survive this form of gender trauma, trans youth typically employ adaptive and maladaptive strategies of gender management. These are usually functional, though often only temporarily, and can engender acute confusion, anxiety, and despair, often characterized as depression. Family members may overtly or covertly participate in this process of negotiation and denial. Gender management can include:

- *Repression or erasure of gender identity* by consciously or subconsciously deciding to pass quietly and invisibly in the birth-assigned gender and sex. This may involve extensive defenses, often aspects of sublimation.
- *Negation of gender identity and gender reconstruction* by consciously or subconsciously denying one's gender and adopting behavior and expression that confirm the gender assumptions made by others about one's identity and birth-assigned gender and sex. This often includes admission to gender-polarized groups and engaging in what is coded as hypergendered behavior such as joining the military, parenting children, and so forth.
- *Modification of gender identity* to fit within cultural norms where possible – adopting "moderately" masculine- or feminine-vectored behavior so as to express an aspect of one's gender but still be able to fit as well as possible.

Imagine how difficult it would be to a youth to have to manage, rather than explore, one's gender identity, through childhood, through adolescence, and possibly through adulthood. Imagine the absence of control and the feelings of helplessness this might engender. This is the context most trans youth must negotiate at a critical point in their lives when adolescent development alone can be a challenging period.

"Transitioning"

LGB persons sometimes have the ability to "pass," but many trans-identified individuals do not have that privilege. Coming out for trans youth calls forth tremendous personal resources; maintaining one's own sense of identity in the face of invisibility, oppression, and discrimination challenges one's inner strength and determination. At the same time, one can never overestimate the stress of the closet. Having to hide one's identity always takes a toll spiritually, emotionally, socially, and sometimes physically.

"Transitioning" brings its own stresses and emerging strengths. Think for a minute about the challenges of shifting identities. Consider as you read this for yourselves; how would you manage a transition of this magnitude? Imagine the struggle you might endure, even now, as an adult, with all the resources you have at your disposal; imagine the loss of privilege.

Now consider the same situation at age 15. What forces would confront you? How would your family and friends respond? What about your school and your place of worship? What about money and economic influence? Consider how all these forces and more would seek to erase who you are and deny your sense of self. Now consider how you might respond.

It is clear that gender difference and gender transition have the power to lead to feelings of disconnectedness from the trans person's own family and from their family of origin due to ignorance and lack of acceptance. Trans youth can find themselves feeling disconnected from family affirmation and supports.

Though we know identification with one's cultural group is a significant component in the development of an individual's self-concept, many trans people delay in developing a trans self-concept – which is a devastating disconnection.

Trans youth lack suitable and positive trans role models. In the dominant culture, positive trans role models are rare. Trans people, when visible, are typically portrayed in a pejorative sense. In addition, some trans-identified people may have never met another trans person.

In addition, peer networks can be tenuous for most trans people. Peer rejection and/or isolation is one of the most dangerous aspects of a trans identity.

While trans people often experience multiple disconnections from community, trans youth of color may experience even greater disconnectedness, often feeling cut off from their racial or ethnic communities or forced to choose between their ethnic communities and whatever trans community they have begun to connect with.

Transgender space

Transgender and gender nonconforming individuals, particularly trans youth, typically pose a challenge to public space and how it is made available via the use and misuse of gender (Namaste, 2000). In this way, transgender youth can be at risk within ordinary public space, which refuses to overtly incorporate what could be termed trans space. Trans youth soon come to understand that trans spaces, and the trans communities that inhabit these spaces, are difficult to discover, are exceedingly fragile, and are often migratory. Those who do uncover some element of trans space, whether it be social, physical, online/electronic, or temporal, are always aware of the invisible borders, as well as the extremely hostile territory, that surround them at all times.

Anzaldúa (1999) describes space such as this as a "borderland." Borderlands are resonant cultural zones of conflict and exchange populated by border citizens living both on the threshold and within the threshold of that space – the borderland. Such "borderlands are physically present whenever two or more cultures edge each other, where people of different races occupy the same territory, where under, lower, middle and upper classes touch, where space between two individuals shrinks with intimacy" (Anzaldúa, 1999, p. 19). In this way, the search for enduring trans space becomes a search for an enduring trans community.

Trans space may not be readily visible or appropriate for youth. Social spaces may include clubs and bars, performance spaces, and outdoor spaces such as parks or sex-work strolls. Because of a dearth of safe public trans space, providers who serve trans communities often become *de facto* trans spaces, whether or not they are equipped for social or community purposes. Some trans space may be electronic and reside online – in websites, message boards, or chat rooms. Trans space may also be perceived as temporal; it varies with the day of the week and the time of day. Trans space is often subjected to police scrutiny and may close or shift its boundaries without warning. Like much of Western culture, trans spaces are usually segregated by gender (where trans men and trans women often occupy different space), class, race and ethnicity, and age. Like the dominant, non-trans culture, trans communities are ethnically heterogeneous. The experiences and histories of trans women of color are noticeably different from the experiences and histories of white trans women. The construction of an African-American or Latino/a person's experiences of, and struggle against, multiple oppressions needs to be considered within the context of the possible construction of the existence of the trans person of color as irreconcilable with the struggle against racism, sexism, and heterosexism. In this model, the power of stereotypical images of trans people as prostitutes, as mentally ill, as men in dresses and women in suits, and as confused gay or lesbian people, cannot be discounted. The resulting erasure of the identities of trans people of color and the silencing of their voices often preclude the consideration and inclusion of their concerns.

Somatic characteristics

Somatic characteristics may play a role in the provision and access to services, especially those related to "passability." Passing refers to the ability to be perceived and identified as a non-transgender person. The ability to pass as non-trans is seen as directly related to economic and social privilege. Aspects of passing for trans persons include facial features, height, weight, body morphology, surgical status, hand and foot size, hair, body and facial hair, and so forth. In this regard, the trans communities are very heterogeneous, with some members passing very easily as non-trans people and others being seen routinely as trans people. Jessica Xavier (1999) describes passing and its significance to the transgender communities:

> Passing affords all [trans people] physical safety in public spaces, and for those of us living full-time, job security and access to the social, economic and professional pathways of the nontransgendered. Thus the vast majority of MTFs [male-to-females] and many if not most FTMs [female-to-males] become careful observers of those with birth privilege in their chosen genders.

Age

Transgender youth typically confront minimal age requirement barriers for access to services, requirements for parental consent, and medical ethics issues. It is generally acknowledged that "the effectiveness of a healthcare intervention may best be measured in terms of the quality of life of the patient" (Wren, 2000). Early hormonal treatment and/or gender confirmation surgery has been shown to significantly improve the lives of trans adolescents, avoiding sometimes immutable physical changes that are the result of a puberty associated with that individuals presumed biological sex, not their identified gender. In addition, trans youth who are able to access medical care to resolve some of their intense gender concerns may be better able to complete some of the developmental tasks of adolescence, enter into satisfying peer and interpersonal relationships, and continue in school like other youth their age (Cohen-Kettenis and van Goozen, 1997; Gooren and Delemarre-van de Waal, 1996; Wren, 2000).

Despite the value of the early affirmation of self-identity and respect for self-determination that intervention can offer, minor children typically cannot access medical care without parental consent. The instances where they can, such as sexually transmitted diseases, pregnancy, and substance abuse treatment, are usually narrowly defined. In addition, emancipated minor status is not universal, subject to interpretation, and difficult for youth to accomplish easily (Russo, 1999; Swann and Herbert, 1999).

Minors encounter unique barriers to care that are presumed to end when they achieve majority status – typically at age 18. Despite this, barriers to care are perceived to extend to trans individuals in early adulthood. Education may also play a factor in barriers to care. As such, the ability to stay in school, financial means, type of schooling, and so forth are considered. Financial means is a factor in all health care and includes income, health insurance, and so forth. Aspects of support affect access to and efficacy of care. Support comprises parental consent as well as levels of support from family, community, trans families and friends, positive role models, and so forth.

Ethics

Professional ethical concerns also play a role in determining treatment for trans youth. The unique situations presented by trans and gender nonconforming people often do not neatly fit into ethical codes. Ethical codes for organizations such as the American Academy of Child Psychiatry (AACP), the American Psychological Association (APA), and the National Association of Social Workers (NASW) either place responsibility for youth with their respective parents or guardians, are ambiguous, or are silent on the matter (Swann and Herbert, 1999). Though the NASW recently published a policy position supporting the needs of trans communities, the issues and concerns of trans youth were conspicuously absent (Lev and Moore, 2000).

Medical providers and clinics are often cautious when working with trans youth. "'Every day, I feel torn between wanting to empower my patients and wanting to be sure not to harm them,' says Jayne Jordan, a physician's assistant in the [Michael Callen-Audre Lorde Community Health] Center's transgender medicine program" (Russo, 1999). In addition, not all youth that identify as transgender, gender different and gender questioning during adolescence will continue to identify themselves as transgender or transsexual in adulthood (American Psychiatric Association, 1997; Cohen-Kettenis and van Goozen, 1997). The legal ramifications of providing such care to minors in a litigious society are not well understood yet. So, while research may indicate the value of early medical treatment and care for trans youth, legal and ethical concerns and possible conflicts may erect potent barriers to that care. The role of social workers and other mental health providers can be integral to the interdisciplinary provision of services in these instances. Social workers may be able to offer information and support to youth, parents, and providers in these cases and often ameliorate legal concerns.

Absence of services

Trans people, especially trans youth, confront a critical shortage of services. In most areas, this includes a near-total absence of trans-positive providers offering medical and social services, and services concerned with mental health, substance abuse, domestic violence, shelter, HIV/AIDS, hormone-confirming therapy, and trans-masculine-specific services. In addition, trans people encounter few transgender-identified service providers. A scarcity of services in rural, suburban, or no-urban areas serves as a barrier as well as a factor exacerbating the isolation of trans people (Lombardi, 2001; Pazos, 1999).

The impact of harm reduction should also be examined in these situations. Many trans youth are acutely aware of the physical and social problems they will later face by undergoing the masculinizing or feminizing puberty that is associated with their presumed birth or biological sex. When faced with barriers to treatment, trans youth may seek hormones from non-medical or discreditable medical providers who provide them with injectable and non-injectable "street" medications. The actual consistency of these preparations is unknown to the end user and they are rarely taken under medical supervision and monitoring. In addition to the typical physical and mental health risks associated with any form of hormone-confirming therapy, trans people who self-medicate using these substances may be subject to many of the same health risks as intravenous drug users (Denny, 1994, 1995, 2002, 2006; Haymes, 1998; Israel and Tarver, 1997; Lombardi, 2001; Russo, 1999).

Transgender identity as pathology

Identity concerns frequently obscure the identities of trans youth. Despite an increasing awareness of the harmful role that transphobic, judgmental, and discriminatory behavior by healthcare providers plays in the relationship between care providers and transgender-identified people, this behavior is still prevalent.

In addition, trans youth often encounter hostile stares and comments, as well as stigmatizing, pathologizing, and insensitive treatment from staff at all levels of the medical and social services systems. Colucciello (1999) reports that nurses typically are unaware of the complexity of trans identities, making pejorative and dehumanizing comments such as "'Why are they doing this?' and 'I do not know how to address them.'" Grimshaw (1998) warns of nurses who do not use the client's pronoun of choice, refer to clients as "it," or "[avoid] talking to them by always being busy."

Disclosing one's trans identity has many risks, including institutionalization, violence and abuse, harassment and, possibly, homelessness. The therapy or counseling that trans people encounter is often reparative in intent or designed to obstruct or discourage the client's stated goals and self-determination. As such, the problems that transgender youth face are similar to those faced by lesbian, gay, bisexual, and questioning youth, where much of the oppression that is casually related to homophobia is actually a fear of gender nonconformity, or genderphobia. In many instances, discrimination and oppression based on sexual orientation is often indistinguishable from that based on gender or gender identity (Mallon, 1999a). In addition, Gender Identity Disorder in Children is still used to institutionalize gender-different youth – most of whom will eventually identify as lesbian, gay, bisexual, and/or transgender (Minter, 2000; National Gay and Lesbian Task Force, 1996).

The Board of Trustees of the American Psychiatric Association's vote to delete a previously defined mental illness by removing the diagnosis of "homosexuality" from its *Diagnostic and Statistical Manual of Mental Disorders*, second edition (*DSM*-II) in 1973 signaled the invigoration of the gay civil rights movement. Conversely, the APA has resisted the removal or reform of gender dysphoria (which first appeared in the *DSM*-III in 1980), later remodeled in the *DSM*-IV in 1994 as the Gender Identity Disorders (GID): Transvestic Fetishism 302.3, Gender Identity Disorder in Children, 302.6, Gender Identity Disorder Not Otherwise Specified, 302.6, and Gender Identity Disorder in Adolescents or Adults, 302.85 (American Psychiatric Association, 1994). The importance of depathologizing homosexuality has been considered critical in the understanding of lesbian and gay development (Butler, 2006; Dean *et al.*, 2000).

An understanding of a normative transgender identity may not be possible until that identity is uncoupled from its pathological underpinnings. Today, much of the focus on the pathologies exhibited by lesbian and gay people is formally directed toward the developmental concerns, stigmatization, and fear they encounter in an unaccepting and dominant culture. A similar, clinical focus toward the concerns of transgender people may also seem appropriate. Despite this, the belief that "homosexuality is a treatable, pathological condition" is still "widely held" (Olsen and Mann, 1997, p. 153) by medical students and can be assumed to translate to similar attitudes about transgender-identified people, affecting the care available to both communities. The social worker is not innocent in this discourse, and the resistance to GID reform marks a major challenge for social work practice within the transgender communities. These diagnoses continue to stigmatize trans individuals and the trans communities as suffering from mental illness, as well as severely hindering transgender civil rights efforts (National Gay and Lesbian Task Force, 1996; Lombardi, 2001; Minter, 2000; Wilchins, 1997). Blumenstein *et al.* note that "for many transgender people, societal stigma and the tendency for mental health professionals to continue to pathologize the trans-experience, results in secrecy, shame, depression and fear" (2000, p. 183).

Identity erasure

Few screening, intake, and assessment procedures recognize trans identities. The subsequent erasure of the consumer's trans identity renders trans people and their unique concerns invisible, making the connection between trans identity and health needs obscure. In addition, the diversity and complexity inherent in the identities that trans people inhabit, many of which challenge clinical definition, may constitute a factor in care, as well as an access concern. Zevin (2000) notes that request to "transgender is somewhat in between, as the patient defines where they want to be. And to some doctors that has been very disturbing."

As of this writing, many in the healthcare communities use the phrase "transsexual women" to refer to female-to-male individuals, whereas the reverse is true in the trans communities themselves, where such people are referred to as transsexual men, or as trans men. Similarly, many care providers commonly use the phrase "transsexual men" to refer to male-to-female individuals while the trans communities refer to these people as transsexual women, or as trans women. The creation and use of the word "transgender" by people with trans histories to refer to trans people is another example of this friction. Non-clinical identities such as transgender continue to make some in the psychiatric and medical communities, as well as the industries they are a part of, uncomfortable.

Ignorance of transgender identities may also confuse erstwhile allies. While the concerns of lesbian, gay, bisexual, and transgender youth overlap, many clinicians and other providers continue to stigmatize transgender, gender-questioning, and gender-different youth as "gender deviant" and "provocative." The consequence of these transphobic attitudes is the consistent erasure of the identities of transgender individuals. The challenge, then, is to recognize that adolescence is not too early for youth to identify, or be identified, as either trans women or trans men. Dean *et al.* report that "within the health care system, transgendered youth probably encounter ignorance and prejudice similar to and greater than that experienced by lesbian and gay youth" (2000, p. 133). To this end, Haymes (1998) notes that "it is ironic that while the medical profession has advanced to the point of being able to effectively and appropriately treat transgender individuals, there is an internalized system-wide [trans]phobia that prohibits it from embracing the challenge."

Personally established barriers

The economic barriers of oppression

The oppressions that trans youth face have severe economic repercussions. Trans youth may look different, or abnormal, leading to a lack of recognition of a trans morphology (Wilchins, 1997, pp. 33–35). In this way, trans youth can be "spotted," isolated and separated from non-trans people. The violence, harassment, and discrimination associated with a perception of trans youth as exhibiting a form of deviance or pathology can deprive them of legally sanctioned employment. The resulting underemployment or unemployment, poverty, homelessness, and diminished educational opportunities create severe economic hardship.

Adolescents "are the most uninsured and underinsured of all groups" (Gay and Lesbian Medical Association and LGBT health experts, 2001). Yet economic barriers to care exist even when trans youth are covered by health insurance. Almost all health insurance explicitly excludes coverage for any and all transgender-related mental and medical care, on the arbitrary premise that such treatment is experimental in nature (Middleton, 1997). In contrast, psychiatric diagnosis of GID conveys little formal disability protection and is specifically excluded from the protections of the Americans with Disabilities Acts (ADA).

In this context of economic and societal marginalization, sex-work and its derivations – exhibition and entertainment – have been the only historical employment opportunities permissible for many trans women, especially trans youth. This includes working as prostitutes, escorts, strippers, lap dancers, streetwalkers, telephone sex-workers, showgirls, performers, and as models or actresses for masturbatory-oriented print, film, and video materials (Dean *et al.*, 2000; Klein, 1999, Mallon, 1999b). Scant parental support combined with absence of insurance coverage often converge and lead trans youth to sex-work to pay for the exigencies of gender transition. Despite the risk, few trans youth can fund their medical and living costs without engaging in prostitution, stripping, or other forms of sex-work. In addition, the economics of sex-work puts youth at risk for HIV/AIDS and sexually transmitted diseases, exploitation and violence, and chemical dependency.

Isolation

Social isolation may be considered one of the most significant and dangerous aspects of a trans identity (Israel and Tarver, 1997). "Isolation keeps most transgendered youth from seeking essential health and medical care until crises occur" (Dean *et al.*, 2000).

Many trans youth quickly understand that gender-different behavior rarely elicits adult caring, and the result is an attachment problem, especially as shown in the lifelong guilt and blame that trans people experience. One might consider whether inability to live out one's gender role in childhood is, in itself, a childhood trauma. This is what almost all transgender-identified youth typically encounter until they are finally able to express and seek support for their actual gender identity – typically during their post-adolescent development.

Identification with one's cultural group is a significant component in the development of an individual's self-concept. Despite the importance of this, peer networks can be tenuous for most trans youth. While support services and groups for lesbian, gay, bisexual, and questioning youth appear with increasing regularity in schools and community centers, the stigma associated with expressing a trans identity prevents most trans youth from accessing these groups and resources.

In the dominant culture, positive trans role models are rare. Many trans youth have never met another trans person. When trans people do appear in the media, it is often in a pejorative sense. These portrayals usually depict trans people as sex-workers, mentally ill, freaks, self-mutilators, cripples, criminals, and as unlovable. In this context, trans people (1) are sought out and regularly appear on daytime talk "shock" television shows; (2) are often used to jar the conventional viewer's sensibilities in advertising, news, and in films; (3) appear with increasing frequency on street corners and sex-work strolls (Mallon, 1999a), as well as in jails and prisons nationwide; (4) appear in the classified advertising sections of local newspapers, and in pornographic films and magazines (Rodgers, 1995); and (5) appear in anti-trans writings and rhetoric and are labeled as male saboteurs by some vocal personages in the radical lesbian feminist movement, or appear in pro-trans writings and rhetoric and are labeled as heroic gender crusaders by some vocal personages in the postmodern feminist movement (Stone, 1994). The absence of trans peers and a trans social network can reinforce the maladaptive behavior that most trans youth utilize to erase or reconstruct their identities.

Clearly, social work practice with trans youth requires a critical rereading of the relationship between the typically oppressive sources of global knowledge and the subjugated knowledge of the trans communities. The process by which trans-identified individuals and the trans communities recognize and value knowledge lies at social work's core of valuing the "dignity and worth of the person" and the individual's right to "self-determination" (National Association of Social Workers, 1999, pp. 4–5).

In this context, very little has been written about actual social work practice with the transgender communities. Other than Mallon's useful *Social Services with Transgendered Youth* (1999a), Lev's *Transgender Emergence: Therapeutic Guidelines for Working with Gender-variant People and their Families* (2004); and Brill and Pepper's (2008) wonderful work titled *The Transgender Child* what is available is either dated or very limited in scope and various program descriptions, what is available is either dated or very limited in scope (Blumenstein, Davis, Walker, and Warren, 2000).

Conclusions

As the social work profession moves toward developing more affirming practice models for working with transgender youth, professionals must be attuned to the complexity of working with this population and must be committed to their own continued education to work more effectively with trans youth.

It is the hope of this author and the others who have written for this publication that the information contained within these pages is a bold step toward encouraging affirming services for transgender youth and their families.

References

American Psychiatric Association (1973). *Diagnostic and Statistical Manual of Mental Disorders* (2nd ed.). Washington, DC: American Psychiatric Association.

American Psychiatric Association (1980). *Diagnostic and Statistical Manual of Mental Disorders* (3rd ed.). Washington, DC: APA.

American Psychiatric Association (1994) *Diagnostic and Statistical Manual of Mental Disorders* (4th ed.). Washington, DC: APA.

American Psychiatric Association (1997) *Diagnostic and Statistical Manual of Mental Disorders*, (4th ed.TR). Washington DC: APA.

Anderson, J. M. (2000). Writing in subjugated knowledges: Towards a transformative agenda in nursing research and practice. *Nursing Inquiry 7*, 145. Retrieved October 29, 2002 from Academic Search Premier database on the World Wide Web: http://library.hunter.cuny.edu/webres.htm.

Anzaldúa, G. (1987). *Borderlands/La Frontera: The New Mestiza*. San Francisco: Spinsters/Aunt Lute Foundation.

Aranda, S. and Street, A. (2001). From individual to group: Use of narratives in a participatory research process. *Journal of Advanced Nursing 33*(6), 791–797. Retrieved November 13, 2002 from Academic Search Premier database on the World Wide Web: http://library.hunter.cuny.edu/webres.htm.

Benjamin, H. (1954). Transsexualism and transvestism as psycho-somatic and somato-psychic syndromes. *American Journal of Psychotherapy 8*, 219–230.

Blumenstein, R., Davis, C., Walker, L., and Warren, B. (2000). New York City Gender Identity Project: a model community-based program. In T. O'Keefe (Ed.) *Sex, Gender and Sexuality: 21st Century Transformations*. London: Extraordinary People Press.

Brill, S. and Pepper, R. (2008). *The Transgender Child: A Handbook for Families and Professionals*. San Francisco, CA: Cleis Press.

Brooks, F. (2000). Beneath contempt: The mistreatment of non-traditional/gender atypical boys. *Journal of Gay and Lesbian Social Services 12*(1/2), 107–115.

Butler, J. (1993). *Bodies That Matter: On the Discursive Limits of "Sex"*. New York: Routledge.

Butler, J. (2006). Undiagnosing gender. In P. Currah, R. M. Juang, and S. P. Minter (Eds.). *Transgender Rights*. Minneapolis, MN: University of Minnesota Press.

Burdge, B. J. (2007). Bending gender, ending gender: Theoretical foundations for social work practice with the transgender community. *Social Work 52*(3), 243–250.

Cauldwell, D. (1949). Psychopathia transexualis. *Sexology 16*, 274–280.

Cohen-Kettenis, P. T. and van Goozen, S. H. M. (1997). Sex reassignment of adolescent transsexuals: A follow-up study. *Journal of the American Academy of Child and Adolescent Psychiatry 36*, 263–271.

Colapinto, J. (2001). *As Nature Made Him: The Boy who was Raised as a Girl*. New York: HarperCollins.

Colucciello, M. T. (1999). Relationship between critical thinking, dispositions, and learning styles. *Journal of Professional Nursing, 15*(5), 294–301.

Currah, P. and Minter, S. (2000). *Transgender Equality: A Handbook for Activists and Policymakers*. New York and San Francisco: Policy Institute of the National Gay and Lesbian Task Force and National Center for Lesbian Rights.

Currah, P., Juang, R. M., and Minter, S. P. (Eds.) (2006). *Transgender Rights*. Minneapolis: University of Minnesota Press.

Davis, C. (2008). Social work practice with transgender and gender non-conforming persons. In G. P. Mallon (Ed.) *Social Work Practice with LGBT People* (pp. 83–111). New York: Routledge.

Dean, L., Meyer, I., Robinson, K., Sell, R., Sember, R., Silenzio, V., *et al.* (2000) Lesbian, gay, bisexual, and transgender health: Findings and concerns. *Journal of the Gay and Lesbian Medical Association* 4(3), 105–151. Retrieved April 9, 2001 from the World Wide Web: http://www.glma.org/pub/jglma/vol4/3/index.html.

Denny, D. (1994) *Gender Dysphoria: A Guide to Research*. New York: Garland.

Denny, D. (1995). Transgendered youth at risk for exploitation, HIV, hate crimes. *Healing Well*. Retrieved October 9, 2001, from the World Wide Web: http://www.gender.org/aegis/index.html.

Denny, D. (2002). The politics of a diagnosis and a diagnosis of politics: The university-affiliated gender clinics, and how they failed to meet the needs of transsexual people. *Transgender Tapestry 98; The Journal 2*(3), 3–8.

Denny, D. (2006). Transgender communities of the United States in the late twentieth century. In P. Currah, R. M. Juang, and S. P. Minter (Eds.) *Transgender Rights*. Minneapolis: University of Minnesota Press.

Feinberg, L. (2001) Trans health crisis: For us it's life or death. *American Journal of Public Health 91*, 897–900.

Gay and Lesbian Medical Association and LGBT health experts (2001, April) *Companion Document for Lesbian, Gay, Bisexual, and Transgender (LGBT) Health*. San Francisco: Gay and Lesbian Medical Association. Retrieved October 8, 2001 from the World Wide Web: http://www.glma.org/policy/hp2010/index.html.

Gooren, L. J. G. and Delemarre-van de Waal, H. (1996). Memo on the feasibility of endocrine interventions in juvenile transsexuals. *Journal of Psychology and Human Sexuality 8*, 69–74.

Grimshaw, J. (1998). Closing the gap between nursing rsearch and practice. *Evidenced Based Nursing*, 1(3), 71–74.

Hartman, A. (1990). Many ways of knowing [editorial]. *Social Work 35*(1), 3–4. Retrieved October 26, 2002 from Academic Search Premier database on the World Wide Web: http://library.hunter.cuny.edu/webres.htm.

Hartman, A. (1992, November). In search of subjugated knowledge [editorial]. *Social Work 37*(6), 483–484. Retrieved October 26, 2002 from Academic Search Premier database on the World Wide Web: http://library.hunter.cuny.edu/webres.htm.

Haymes, R. (1998). Towards healthier transgender youth. *Crossroads: The Newsletter of the National Youth Advocacy Coalition 6*, 14–15. Retrieved February 14, 2001 from the World Wide Web: http://www.youthresource.com/feat/trans/art_health.htm.

Hogan, S. and Hudson, L. (1998). *Completely Queer: The Gay and Lesbian Encyclopedia*. New York: Henry Holt.

Holbrook, T. (1995). Finding subjugated knowledge: Personal document research. *Social Work 40*(6), 746–751.

Imre, R. W. (1984). The nature of social work. *Social Work 29*, 41–45. Retrieved October 26, 2002 from Academic Search Premier database on the World Wide Web: http://library.hunter.cuny.edu/webres.htm.

Imre, R. W. (1991). What do we need to know for good practice? [editorial]. *Social Work 36*(3), 198–200. Retrieved October 26, 2002 from Academic Search Premier database on the World Wide Web: http://library.hunter.cuny.edu/webres.htm.

Israel, G. E., and Tarver, D. E. (1997). *Transgender Care: Recommended Guidelines, Practical Information, and Personal Accounts*. Philadelphia: Temple University Press.

Kazemek, F. E., Wellik, J., and Zimmerman, P. (2002). Across the generations. *Journal of Adolescent and Adult Literacy 45*(7). Retrieved October 18, 2002 from Academic Search Premier database on the World Wide Web: http://library.hunter.cuny.edu/webres.htm.

Klein, B. (1999). Group work practice with male to female transgendered sex workers. In G.P. Mallon (Ed.) *Social Services with Transgendered Youth* (pp. 95–109). New York: Haworth.

Kondrat, M. E. (1995). Concept, act, and interest in professional practice: Implications of an empowerment perspective. *Social Service Review 69*(3), 405–428. Retrieved November 9, 2002 from Academic Search Premier database on the World Wide Web: http://library.hunter.cuny.edu/webres.htm.

Lev, A. I. and Moore, B. (2000). *Social Work Embraces Transgender*, in Focus, NASW--MASS Chapter Newsletter.

Lev, A. I. (2004). *Transgender Emergence: Therapeutic Guidelines for Working with Gender-variant People and their Families*. Binghamton, NY: Haworth Press.

Lombardi, E. (2001). Enhancing transgender health care. *American Journal of Public Health 91*(6), 869–972.

Mallon, G. (Ed.) (1999a). *Social Services with Transgendered Youth*. New York: Haworth Press.

Mallon, G. P. (1999b). Knowledge for practice with transgendered persons. *Journal of Gay and Lesbian Social Services, 10*(3/4), 1–18. (Co-published simultaneously in G. P. Mallon (Ed.) *Social Services with Transgendered Youth*. New York: Haworth Press.)

Middleton, L. (1997). Insurance and the reimbursement of transgender health care. In B. Bullough, V. L. Bullough, and J. Elias (Eds). *Gender Blending* (pp. 455–465). Amherst: Prometheus Books.

Minter, S. (2000). *Representing Transsexual Clients: An Overview of Selected Legal Issues*. San Francisco: National Center for Lesbian Rights, Retrieved December 10, 2001 from the World Wide Web: http://www.nclrights.org/publications/pubs_tgclients.html.

Money, J. (1987). Propaedeutics of diecious G-I/R: Theoretical foundations for understanding dimorphic gender-identity/role. In J.M. Reinisch, L.A. Rosenblum, and S.A. Sanders (Eds.) *Masculinity/Femininity: Basic Perspectives*, (pp. 22–43). New York: Oxford University Press.

Namaste, V. K. (2000). *Invisible Lives*. Chicago: University of Chicago Press.

National Association of Social Workers (1999). *Code of Ethics*. Washington, DC: National Association of Social Workers.

National Gay and Lesbian Task Force (1996, December 13). *Statement on Gender Identify Disorder*. Washington, DC: National Gay and Lesbian Task Force. Retrieved May 25, 2008 from the World Wide Web: http://www.thetask force.org/.

Olsen C. G. and Mann B. L. (1997). Medical student attitudes on homosexuality and implications for health care. *Journal of the Gay Lesbian Medical Association*, 1, 149–154.

Pazos, S. (1999). Practice with female to male transgendered youth. In G.P. Mallon (Ed.) *Social Services with Transgendered Youth* (pp. 65–82). New York: Haworth.

Rogers, J. (2000). Getting real at ISU: A campus transition. In K. Howard and A. Stevens, (Eds.), *Out and About on Campus: Personal Accounts by Lesbian, Gay, Bisexual, and Transgendered College Students* (pp. 12–18). Los Angeles: Alyson.

Russo, M. (1999). *Teen transsexuals: When do children have a right to decide their gender?* Retrieved May 4, 2007 from the World Wide Web: www.salon.com/health/sex/urge/1999/08/28/transsexualteens/index.html

Stone, S. (1994). The empire strikes back: A posttranssexual manifesto (3rd version). Retrieved March 24, 2001, from the World Wide Web: http://www.actlab.utexas.edu/~sandy. First version available in J. Epstein and K. Straub (Eds.) *Body Guards: The Cultural Politics of Gender Ambiguity*. New York: Routledge.

Swann, S. K. and Herbert, S. E. (1999). Ethical issues in the treatment of gender dysphoric adolescents. In G. P. Mallon (Ed.), *Social Work with Transgendered Adolescents* (pp. 19–34). New York: Haworth Press.

Valentine, D. (2007). *Imagining Transgender: An Ethnography of a Category*. Durham, NC: Duke University Press.

Wilchins, R. A. (1997). *Read My Lips: Sexual Subversion and the End of Gender*. Ithaca, NY: Firebrand Books.

Wren, B. (2000). Early physical intervention for young people with atypical gender identity disorder. *Clinical Psychology and Psychiatry 5*, 220–231.

Xavier, J. (1999). Passing as stigma management. *Transsexual Women's Resource*. Retrieved May 4, 2007 from the World Wide Web: www.annelawrence.com/passing.

Zevin, B. (Speaker) (2000). Demographics of the transgender clinic at San Francisco's Tom Waddell Health Center. Proceedings of the Transgender Care Conference, May 5, 2000. San Francisco: *HIV InSite*, University of California San Francisco. Retrieved November 8, 2001 from the World Wide Web: http://hivinsite.ucsf.edu/InSite.jsp?doc=2098.4742.

Chapter 1

Knowledge for practice with transgender and gender variant youth

Gerald P. Mallon

Introduction

About 15 years ago, a young client said to me: "You have it all wrong, Gary, I am not gay, I am transgender. I may have the biological body of a male, but inside, I am a woman. I am heterosexual, and I am a female." So said my 17-year-old client to me one day, and I thought after he told me this, "You are nuts. If you have a penis, then you are a male, and no matter what you'd like to be, or see yourself as, you are a male." How ignorant and how uninformed I was about transgender persons. I didn't realize that, as activist Riki Anne Wilchins said (Goldberg, 1999, p. B2), "it's not about what's between my legs."

Those who did not understand their circumstances or their nature had called lesbian, gay, and bisexual persons crazy, but transgender persons have been even more misunderstood. If most social work practitioners are ill-prepared to deal with gay, bisexual, and lesbian persons – and in many cases they are – then certainly they are unprepared to respond to the needs of transgender persons. As a practitioner with more than 33 years of experience, many of them with lesbian, gay, bisexual, and questioning clients, I initially felt very inadequate in my attempts to meet the needs of clients who identified as transgender. Apart from its significance as a practice dilemma, this case also illustrates an important truth about transgender persons in contemporary society: that most people, even very experienced practitioners, have little or no accurate knowledge about the lives of transgender persons.

An ecological approach

The person:environment perspective, loosely utilized throughout this text as a framework for practice, has been a central influence on the profession's theoretical base and has usefulness and relevance as an approach to social work practice with transgender persons. Gitterman and Germain (1996, p. 19) underscore the point that disempowerment, which threatens the health, social well-being, and life of those who are oppressed, imposes enormous adaptive tasks on transgender persons. An understanding of the destructive relationships that exist between transgender persons and an environment that is focused on "either/or" male or female gender constructions is integral to the process of developing practice knowledge about working with trangendered persons as clients. The purpose of this chapter, then, is to define, identify, and describe the knowledge base of practice with transgender persons and to review social work's response to the needs of this population.

What the social worker is supposed to do should dictate the boundaries of the profession's knowledge base, noted Meyer (1982). If social workers are supposed to be able to work with transgender persons, then a knowledge base for practice with them must be within those boundaries. An organized knowledge base is crucial to any profession. Anyone, notes Mattaini (1995, p. 59), "can act." The professional, however, is expected to act deliberately, taking the steps that are most likely to be helpful, least intrusive, and consistent with the person's welfare. Making a conscious determination about those choices requires an extensive knowledge base.

Sources of knowledge

My chapter in *Social Work Practice with Lesbian, Gay, Bisexual, and Transgender Persons* (Mallon, 2008), which focused on the acquisition of knowledge for social work practice for lesbian, gay, bisexual, and trans people, identifies several key sources of knowledge, which in a modified version herein provide a framework for this chapter's discussion of knowledge for practice with transgender persons. Sources that I identified include (1) practice wisdom derived from narrative experiences of the profession and professional colleagues, (2) the personal experiences of the practitioner, (3) a knowledge of history and current events, (4) a knowledge of the professional literature, (5) research issues that inform practice, (6) theoretical and conceptual analyses, and (7) information that is provided by the case itself. All of these, understood within an ecological framework of person:environment, with a consciousness of the reality of oppression in the lives of transgender persons, is called upon to inform social work practice with transgender persons, and each contributes to the development of the knowledge base of practice with this population.

Practice wisdom

Practice wisdom can be viewed as that which is derived from the narrative experiences of the profession, both from professional colleagues and from clients. Although narrative experiences may have drawbacks, in that one person's experience is not generalizable to the experiences of many, listening to the life stories of clients and permitting them to tell their story in their own words is central to the experience of social work practice (Mason-Schrock, 1996).

Interest in narrative theory has grown in recent years, and the use of life stories in practice has in some organizations replaced elaborate, formalized intake histories. Life stories, which tend to be rich in detail, are usually obtained early in the work with a client and can be not only a useful means toward gathering important data to enhance one's knowledge base, but also useful in establishing a rapport and a trusting relationship with a transgender client. As the client tells and the worker listens empathetically, in the telling and the listening the story gains personal and cultural meanings. This process, particularly with transgender persons who have been oppressed, marginalized, and silenced, can also be a healing process. It is, as Gitterman and Germain (1996, p. 145) put it, "our human way of finding meaning in life events, of explaining our life experience to ourselves and others, so that we can move on."

Social work practitioners, however, should be cautious about utilizing practice wisdom, especially when most social workers have probably had very limited experience with transgender persons. That said, listening to life stories can inform practice in a meaningful way. If one listens to – really listens to – the narratives with the third ear, and then connects the themes with past practice-based data obtained from previous practice, it can help to make sense of the situation and to guide one's practice (Parlee, 1996).

In addition to listening to the life stories of clients, and the practice experiences of practitioners, social workers practicing with transgender persons can rely on rules that have been handed down by experienced practitioners to others – rules that appear to work. Although practice with transgender persons is a very new area of practice, heuristic practice, which can be described as principles to guide patterns of professional behavior, and that which has shaped and refined practice may also serve as models for other workers. The acquisition of group-specific language to guide practice, and a knowledge of the myths and stereotypes about transgender persons, can be extremely useful forms of heuristic practice. Such fragments of practice wisdom can be valuable as a guide for practitioners interested in enhancing their practice knowledge base in working with transgender persons.

Personal experience

The personal experience of practitioners is the second powerful force that guides knowledge development. Although social workers are guided not only by their own personal experiences but by a professional code of ethics, most social workers base some of their knowledge about clients by integrating and synthesizing events gathered from their own life experiences. Within the guidelines provided by the profession's code of ethics, basic interpersonal and problem-solving skills that social workers have developed throughout their lives are an important means toward informing one's practice (Moore, 1999).

It is a myth that most people do not know anyone who is transgender, but, unquestionably, social workers who have a close friend or a family member who is openly dealing with gender issues may have additional personal experiences that can assist them in guiding their practice with this population. Additionally, social workers who are themselves transgender will undoubtedly have additional insights into transgender clients. However, being transgender alone does not provide a practitioner with a complete and full knowledge for practice with transgender clients. Individuals who are transgender identified themselves may be at various stages of their own sexual identity development, and their knowledge may be at best incomplete. Professional practice requires that practitioners conduct themselves in ways that are consistent with professional values and ethics.

Issues of self-disclosure become significant when a social worker has had personal experiences or shares something in common with a client, in this case a transgender identity. A transgender practitioner may find it helpful to disclose their orientation with a client who is struggling with whether or not to come out, but in other cases the worker's disclosure could inhibit the client from sharing genuine feelings (Gartrell, 1994). Although self-disclosure can be useful in many cases, and while practitioners are using self-disclosure more than they did in the past, social workers need, at a minimum, close supervision and consultation to process these issues. Although personal experiences are key in knowledge development, social workers must always be in touch with their own feelings (Greene, 1994) and must remember that self-disclosure always has to do with the well-being of the client, not the practitioner.

History and current events

Since practice is embedded in the broader social context of life, a knowledge of the social policies and shifting social forces is important for knowledge development and for working with transgender persons. Since historical events are most often documented in the news media, including newspapers, information from multiple media sources can be important sources of information (Park, 1998). News stories and talk shows in the mass media are often less than objective and in many cases replete with inaccuracies; however, for many, these are the only sources of knowledge about gay men and lesbians and an important basis to work from, even in a professional context.

The media, especially some in the talk show circuit, have all made a great deal of money by sensationalizing the stories of individuals who are somewhere on the transgender spectrum. Some social workers may feel that these shows provide a baseline of information about transgender persons, but for the most part they only impart misinformation and perpetuate myths.

The Internet, more than any other avenue, has provided very important sources of information about trans persons and at the same time has permitted those persons at early stages of disclosure of a trans identity to explore their gender identity in a private and anonymous manner within the confines of their own homes. Not only has the information superhighway grown exponentially during the past several years (and since the first edition of this book), but the Internet, for many, may be the first place to begin a search about the plethora of issues pertaining to trans persons. Although there are undoubtedly inaccuracies on the Internet, one huge benefit for those seeking access to knowledge about trans individuals is that the Web has a reach that exceeds geography. Consequently, persons in remote rural areas have the same access to information about and communication with trans persons around the world as those in more urban centers, whereas in the past such data was to be found only in urban environs. Granted, one must have access to a computer to make such connections, but libraries, schools, and Internet cafés can provide individuals with such access in many communities.

A review of appropriate websites about trans and gender different persons is beyond the scope of this publication, as there are literally tens of thousands, and maybe more, that exist on the topic. The reader may find appropriate sites by using one of the numerous search engines (Google, Yahoo, WebCrawler, Lycos, Excite, and others) and by keying in code words and phrases such as "transgender," "gender orientation," "gender different" and "gender variant."

Social work's history with transgender persons can best be described as a marginal relationship. Despite the fact that the Delegate Assembly of the National Association of Social Workers (NASW, 2000) proposed to adopt a policy statement on transgender issues/gender identity issues that emphasized its ban on discrimination based on gender identity issues, social work has generally lagged behind other helping professions in putting resources behind its commitment. A more recent publication (NASW, 2003) does, however, do a better job of addressing transgender and gender identity issues.

Although the Council on Social Work Education (1992) revised its accreditation standards to require schools of social work to include foundation content related to lesbian and gay service needs and practice in the core course curriculum (see Humphreys, 1983; Newman, 1989), there has been no such movement toward the integration of transgender or gender identity issues materials into the curriculum. Such reticence signals a reluctance on the part of the profession from allowing transgender persons full and equal access to being included in the curriculum.

Despite inclusive policies and accreditation mandates that call for non-discriminatory professional practice, an inherent difficulty in separating personal attitudes from professional prerogatives with respect to transgender identity issues appears to have made service provision to this population a complex process. While gay and lesbian identity has historically been, and continues to be, a taboo subject for discussion even within most professional climates (Burdge, 2007; Gochros, 1985, 1995; Mallon, 1992a), transgender identity seems to be even more taboo.

Professional literature

Although many authors of articles that focus on lesbian, gay, and bisexual clients add the term "transgender" to these titles, few genuinely focus on the unique needs of this population. Indeed, a very limited assemblage of professional literature has been published in the professional social work literature that specifically focuses on the social service needs of transgender persons. A *PsychLit* and *Social Work Abstracts* computer search using the words "transgender youth" yielded no articles. Those articles that do exist concerning the broader transgender population center almost exclusively on transsexuals or on sexual reassignment surgery (Braunthal, 1981; Chong, 1990; Oles, 1977; Williams, 1997). Around the time of the publication of the first edition of this volume, the *Journal of Gay and Lesbian Social Services* was the first social work journal to initiate a dialogue about the experiences of transgender youth (Mallon, 1999). A recent issue of the *International Journal of Transgenderism* edited by Walter O. Bockting and Joshua M. Goldberg (2006) focused primarily on clinical issues with transgender youth.

Mainstream social work publications (*Social Work*, *Social Services Review*, and *Families in Society*) have lagged behind several of the other professional disciplines' journals, most notably those in psychology and sociology, in recognizing the legitimacy of transgender identity in the professional literature. Burdge (2007, p. 248) sums up this point best when she notes: "There is also a need for more articles related to transgender issues in mainstream social work journals. Currently, such articles seem relegated to specialty journals, where they risk being read by the 'choir'."

If one were to look exclusively within the social work professional literature to develop a knowledge base of practice, one would find a very circumscribed discussion of transgender practice issues in the mainstream social work literature. Although it appears that the major social work journals have been slow to respond to and to publish articles that address the wide and diverse needs of transgender persons, in fairness it is not possible to know how many articles have been submitted and rejected, or how many in total have been submitted on this population. For a fuller understanding of practice with transgender persons, particularly with transgender youth, practitioners would be wise to look outside of social work for guidance. For professionals who work with individuals with gender identity issues, Arlene Lev's (2004) book *Transgender Emergence* is encyclopedic in its approach, and is required reading for any social worker interested in developing her or his knowledge in practicing with trans persons. Israel and Tarver's (1997) excellent sourcebook also provides practitioners with a wide breadth of information and resources about transgender persons. Its focus on recommended guidelines, practical information, and personal narratives addresses issues of cultural diversity, sexual orientation, and trans life that had been previously been ignored in the clinical literature. Our colleagues in Canada, at the Transgender Health Program in Vancouver, British Columbia, have provided four resources that are extraordinary in their scope and depth. They are: "Clinical management of gender dysphoria in adolescents" (de Vries *et al.*, 2006); "Ethical, legal, and psychosocial issues in care of transgender adolescents" (White Holman and Goldberg, 2006a); "Social and medical transgender case advocacy" (White Holman and Goldberg, 2006b); and "Counseling and mental health care for transgender adults and loved ones" (Bockting *et al.*, 2006). All four should be required reading for all social workers and can be obtained online at www.vch.ca/transhealth.

In *True Selves: Understanding Transsexualism—for Families, Friends, Coworkers, and Helping Professionals*, authors Brown and Rounsley (2003) review many aspects of the reality of living as a trans person. These authors also detail the process of transition and include sample "coming-out" letters to employers, coworkers, friends, and family members. First-person accounts from trans people augment general readability and put human faces on the issues discussed. Brill and Pepper's (2008) wonderful text *The Transgender Child: A Handbook for Families and Professionals*, is the only guide which is specifically written about raising transgender children. This comprehensive first of its kind guidebook explores the unique challenges that thousands of families face in raising a trans or gender variant child. Through extensive research and interviews, as well as years of experience working in the field, the authors cover gender variance from birth through college. This book is required reading for any profession interested in raising their level of competence in working with trans children and their families.

First-person perspectives can be found in Bornstein's (1994, 1998) books, which provide practitioners with additional insight into the trans world from a transgender person's perspective. Feinberg's (1993) deservedly honored classic *Stone Butch Blues*, and her more scholarly work *Transgender Warriors: Making History from Joan of Arc to Dennis*

Rodman provide social work practitioners with valuable knowledge-building insights.

Transgender activists Daphne Scholinski (1997) and Phyllis Burke (1997) have from personal experiences documented the brutal adversion therapies to which gender variant youth with gender identity disordered (GID) diagnoses have been subjected to coerce them into conformity. Riki Anne Wilchins (1997) raises many provocative questions about the oppressive nature of gender classification. Her final chapter, documenting hate crimes against transsexuals, underscores the urgency with which Wilchins questions language and gender exclusion. Volcano and Halberstam (1999) introduce readers to the experiences and culture of the drag kings community.

Randi Ettner's (1996) book *Confessions of a Gender Defender* provides first-hand insights into a psychologist's reflections on life among transgender persons. Ettner's book helps clinicians examine their own gaps in training and helps them to assess their own counter-transference issues surrounding treatment of transgender persons. Ettner's (1999) latest work is a comprehensive guide to understanding and treating individuals with gender issues. The book provides an overview of the field, including the history, etiology, diagnosis, research, and treatment of gender variant persons.

Research

If the research on gay and lesbian persons is slim, the research on transgender persons is almost non-existent. Again, the research that does exist focuses almost exclusively on sexual reassignment surgery for transsexual persons. In cases where little quantitative empirical evidence is found, naturalistic research methods have increasingly been seen as a particularly effective means of informing social work practice. The use of these naturalistic means, particularly narrative approaches, may prove to be useful for social work practitioners. McPhail (2004) suggests that when social workers are questioning gender and sexuality binaries, queer theory, transgender individuals, and sex researchers can assist them in developing their knowledge.

Theoretical and conceptual analyses

Theories to guide practice or theoretical constructs, which also help one to better understand and practice with a client system, offer explanations to guide practice. Understanding the process of transgender identity formation will undoubtedly enable the practitioner to carry out informed and sensitive intervention with clients and families struggling with issues of gender identity. However, practitioners must also be aware of the fact that it is not possible for them to utilize the traditional developmental models taught in most human behavior and the social environment sequences

(Blos, 1974; Erikson, 1950; Marcia, 1980; Offer, 1980; Offer *et al.*, 1981), which posit concepts of sex-role identifications that are concerned only with heterosexual development and presume heterosexual identity as an eventual outcome. Utilizing these traditional approaches, which view transgender identity from a developmentally pejorative perspective, does not assist or prepare the practitioner to practice competently with transgender persons.

Unlike their counterparts in the heterosexual majority, those individuals on the transgender spectrum experience a social condition that is attributable to their transgender orientation: oppression, stigmatization, and marginalization. Different forms of oppression, notes Pharr (1988, p. 53), cannot be viewed in isolation because they are interconnected: sexism, racism, homophobia, classism, anti-Semitism, and ableism are linked by a common origin – economic power and control. Backed by institutional power, economic power, and both institutional and individual violence, this trinity of elements acts as the "standard of rightness and often righteousness wherein all others are judged in relation to it."

There are many ways in which norms are enforced by both individuals and institutions. One way to view persons who fall outside the "norm" is to label such individuals as "*the other.*" It is easy to discriminate against, viewing as deviant, marginal, or inferior, such groups that are not part of the mainstream. Those who are classified as such become part of an invisible minority, a group whose achievements are kept hidden and unknown from those in the dominant culture. Stereotyping, blaming the victim, distortion of reality, can even lead the person to feel as though they deserve the oppression that they experience. This process is called internalized transgenderphobia (Norton, 1997; Park, 1998). Other elements of oppression include isolation, self-hatred, underachievement or overachievement, substance abuse, problems with relationships, and a variety of other mental health matters.

Violence, as suggested by Lombardi *et al.* (1998) as well as Herek (1990) and Pharr (1988), is also seen as a theoretical construct in the lives of transgender persons. The threat of violence toward transgender persons, particularly transgender youth who must attend community schools, who step out of line is made all the more powerful by the fact that they do not have to do anything to trigger the violence. It is their lives alone that precipitate such action. Therefore, trans persons always have a sense of safety that is fragile and tenuous, and they may never feel completely secure. Social workers who are unfamiliar with trans persons may view such conditions as a pathology in need of treatment, but for the transgender person such insecurity is an adaptive strategy for living within in a hostile environment (Gitterman and Germain, 1996).

Self-awareness

Many students entering the world of social work think that they are open-minded, and while many may have a genuine desire to help others, some have not delved inside of themselves to assess the role that power, privilege, and influence have played in their own lives.

As social work is a values-based profession, we are ethically obligated to address these issues and to work toward increasing the levels of competence and awareness within both students entering the professional and colleagues who continue to make contributions. Although the professional literature has begun to address these areas, as professionals we also must focus on the issue of self-awareness.

The consequence of not considering theoretical analyses and concepts which are transphobic is that many heterosexual social workers believe that if they avoid society's fear and loathing of transgender persons, then that is all that they will need to do to work effectively with trangendered clients. While most social workers have "politically correct" ideas about gay men and lesbians, many professionals have not always had the opportunity to deal with the deeper prejudices and heterosexual privileges that they possess. Since most professionals continue to have an inadequate knowledge base about the real lives of transgender persons, this in many cases causes them to be more trans-ignorant than transphobic.

Many transgender persons believe that heterosexually oriented social workers still harbor the heterocentric assumption that it is less than normal or less preferable to be transgender. Some social workers, particularly those from a more psychoanalytically oriented perspective, believe that somewhere in the transgender person's system you can find the roots or the cause of transgender identity, and that it secretly has something to do with family dysfunction or childhood sexual abuse.

The desire for abolition of Gender Identity Disorder (GID) from the next edition of the *DSM* (for the current edition, see American Psychiatric Association, 1994, pp. 537–538) is another important issue for social workers to consider. What most workers do not realize, according to Park (1998, p. 16), is that

> GID, as defined in the *DSM-IV*, also represents an effort by the medico-psychiatric establishment to "cure" homosexuality, 25 years after the APA [American Psychiatric Association] removed homosexuality from its catalogue of mental illnesses. Although GID is ostensibly only about gender identity and not sexual orientation, it is striking that the *DSM-IV* advises that psychiatrists note "specifiers" based on the individual's sexual orientation... if GID were exclusively concerned with gender identity, why would the APA feel compelled to advise clinicians to note orientation?

Although this has been a serious issue of contention, the good news is that the APA has appointed a working group on GID to reexamine the GID diagnosis in preparation for the revision that will produce the *DSM*-V.

These are complex issues that need to be addressed within the overall context of diversity and yet, at the same time, from a specific transgender perspective. Moral, religious, and cultural biases still run deep in many students preparing for practice and in professionals who currently practice. Although there are no simple solutions to helping individuals overcome their biases, beginning an honest dialogue and providing students with accurate and appropriate information about gay men and lesbians is an important place to start.

Knowledge derived from the individual case

Information provided by the case itself is the final means toward the generation of knowledge about transgender persons that will be discussed in this chapter. The client within the individual, couple, or family system and the environmental context within which they live provides a great deal of information that is specific to the case and that can guide practice. Listening to what clients say, and observing what they do from initial engagement through assessment, intervention and termination, can provide crucial information.

Although some transgender persons present concerns that relate specifically to issues of gender orientation, many of which are discussed in Chapters 1, 5, and 6, these individuals usually seek help for a range of issues that have little to do with their sexual orientation per se, or are related to it in an indirect way. Like their heterosexual counterparts, transgender persons seek help from social work practitioners to deal with a wide array of problems in living.

A critical aspect of intervening with a client who identifies as transgender is for practitioners to have a firm understanding of the client's identity formation (see Chapter 3).

The practitioner who is sensitive and affirming in his or her work with transgender persons needs to have a complete understanding of the psychological, behavioral, affectional, and attitudinal features of each of the stages of coming out, as well as an internal sense of the "goodness of fit" to a particular stage, and direct their interventions accordingly. A lack of familiarity with this process will cause the practitioner to misinterpret the client's reactions and miss opportunities to assist the client in moving forward in the process of developing comfort with their own identity.

Practitioners need to be aware that certain conditions may be intensified, if not caused, by oppression and stigmatization to which transgender youth may have been exposed in their development and which they may continue to experience as adults. For example, although the coming out process has been conceptualized as a positive developmental step toward healthfulness, the societal or familial response to an individual's disclosure may be less than constructive.

Social work practitioners need to be sensitive to the particular needs and concerns of the transgender person and must also appreciate that the client's membership in a stigmatized and oppressed group (Goffman, 1963) has shaped their identity and may play a role in the presenting problem which they may or may not bring to their initial session. Whether or not the presenting problem is related to the client's sexual orientation, the practitioner who intervenes with the client must be well acquainted with the issues and features of transgender life, develop an expertise in working with the population, and acquire a knowledge of the community resources that exist to help this client. It is also important to recognize that there is as much diversity in the transgender community as in any other community, and therefore there is no one type of transgender individual.

Although Western society has made some positive steps toward altering negative attitudes toward gay men and lesbians, practitioners, in working with individuals, must be aware of the presence of the phenomenon of transgenderphobia (Park, 1998) and a client's own internalized transgenderphobia. Social workers must help clients refrain from reinforcing it through their own bias and stereotypes. Isolation is another problem that frequently arises as a result of the stigma associated with a transgender identity. As has already been mentioned, practitioners need to be knowledgeable about resources that exist in the community and if necessary to support the client by going with them to visit these resources. The development of social support networks through involvement in such programs can be an important task for the client and practitioner to work on together.

Subsequent chapters in this collection will focus on exploring social work practice with transgender persons from the perspectives of several client systems: individuals, groups, families, and organizations.

Conclusions

The social work profession recognizes that a person's gender identity does not always conform to that person's gender at birth. Transgender persons should be afforded the same respect and rights as those whose gender identity is the same as their biologically given gender. Discrimination, oppression, and prejudice directed against any group are damaging to the social, emotional, and economic well-being of the affected group, as well as to society as a whole. All social workers are ethically bound to fight to eliminate such discrimination inside and outside the profession, in both the public and the private sectors.

Adopting non-judgmental attitudes toward gender identity enables social workers to provide maximum support and services to those who are part of the transgender community. Social workers and the profession can support and empower transgender persons through all phases of their coming out process. Utilizing ecological approaches that assist persons in developing adaptation to their environments, social workers should also be aware that they may need to assist in developing supportive practice environments for those struggling with gender identity, both clients and colleagues.

Cultivating a knowledge base of practice to prepare students and practitioners to work more competently and effectively with transgender persons, especially with transgender youth, is an essential element of good practice and needs to be integrated into a foundation-level curriculum in meaningful and conscientious ways. The Council on Social Work Education should require course content on transgender issues, offer research opportunities for investigating issues of relevance to this population, develop and provide training for instructors and students, and seek out field opportunities for students interested in working with transgender persons.

On a societal level, we must work to eliminate the psychological and physical harm directed at transgender persons and to work toward portraying them accurately and compassionately. Programs that address the health and mental health needs of clients must work toward developing sensitive and respectful practice with transgender persons and their families.

From a legal and political action perspective, social workers need to join together with other professional associations and progressive organizations to lobby on behalf of the civil rights of transgender persons. An increase in funding for education, treatment services, and research on behalf of transgender persons is essential. Finally, the repeal of laws that impede individuals from identifying with the gender of their choice and insuring that individuals will not suffer discrimination against them in inheritance, insurance, child custody, and property is part of the proud tradition of social work's mission to fight for social justice for all people.

References

American Psychiatric Association (1994). *Diagnostic and Statistical Manual of Mental Disorders* (4th ed.) Washington, DC: APA.

Blos, P. (1974). *The Young Adolescent*. NY: Free Press.

Bockting, W. O. and Goldberg, J. M. (2006). *International Journal of Transgenderism 9*(3/4).

Bockting, W. O., Knudsen, G., and Goldberg, J. M. (2006). Counseling and mental health care for transgender adults and loved ones. *International Journal of Transgenderism 9*(3/4), 35–82.

Bornstein, K. (1994). *Gender Outlaw: On Men, Women, and the Rest of Us*. New York: Routledge.

Bornstein, K. (1998). *My Gender Workbook*. New York: Routledge.

Braunthal, H. (1981). Working with transsexuals. *International Journal of Social Psychiatry 27*(1), 3–11.

Brill, S. and Pepper, R. (2008). *The Transgender Child: A Handbook for Families and Professionals*. San Francisco, CA: Cleis Press.

Brown, M. L. and Rounsley, C .A. (2003). *True Selves: Understanding Transsexualism—for Families, Friends, Coworkers, and Helping Professionals*. New York: Jossey-Bass.

Burdge, B. J. (2007). Bending gender, ending gender: Theoretical foundations for social work practice with the transgender community. *Social Work, 52*, (8), 243–250.

Burke, P. (1997). *Gender Shock: Exploding the Myths of Male and Female*. New York: Anchor.

Chong, J. M. L. (1990). Social assessments of transsexuals who apply for sex reassignment therapy. *Social Work in Health Care, 14*(3), 87–105.

Council on Social Work Education (1992). *Curriculum Policy Statement for Master's Degree Programs in Social Work Education*. Alexandria, VA: Council on Social Work Education.

de Vries, A. L. C., Cohen-Kettenis, P. T., and Delemarre-Van de Waal, H. (2006). Clinical management of gender dysphoria. *International Journal of Transgenderism 9*(3/4), 83–94.

Erikson, E. (1950). *Childhood and Society*. New York: W. W. Norton.

Ettner, R. (1996). *Confessions of a Gender Defender: A Psychologist's Reflections on Life Among the Transgender*. Chicago: Evanston.

Ettner, R. (1999). *Gender Loving Care: A Guide to Counseling Gender-variant Clients*. New York: W.W. Norton.

Feinberg, L. (1993). *Stone Butch Blues*. Ithaca, NY: Firebrand Books.

Feinberg, L. (1996). *Transgender Warriors: Making History from Joan of Arc to Dennis Rodman*. Boston: Beacon Press.

Gartrell, N. K. (1994). Boundaries in lesbian therapist–client relationships. In B. Greene and G. M. Herek (Eds.) *Lesbian and Gay Psychology: Theory, Research, and Clinical Applications*. Thousand Oaks, CA: Sage.

Gitterman, A. and Germain, C. B. (1996). *The Life Model of Social Work Practice* (2nd ed.). New York: Columbia University Press.

Gochros, H. L. (1985). Teaching social workers to meet the needs of the homosexually oriented. In Schoenberg, R. Goldberg, and D. Shore (Eds.) *With Compassion Towards Some: Homosexuality and Social Work in America*. New York: Harrington Park Press.

Gochros, H. (1995). Sex, AIDS, social work and me. *Reflections, 1*(2), 37–43.

Goffman, E. (1963). *Stigma: Notes of the Management of a Spoiled Identity*. Englewood Cliffs, NJ: Prentice Hall.

Goldberg, C. (1999). Issues of gender, from pronouns to murder. *The New York Times*, June 11, p. B2.

Greene, B. (1994). Lesbian and gay sexual orientations: Implications for clinical training, practice and research. In B. Greene and G. M. Herek (Eds.) *Lesbian and Gay Psychology: Theory, Research, and Clinical Applications*. Thousand Oaks, CA: Sage.

Herek, G. M. (1990). The context of anti-gay violence: Notes on cultural psychological heterosexism. *Journal of Interpersonal Violence* 5(3), 316–333.

Humphreys, G. E. (1983). Inclusion of content on homosexuality in the social work curriculum. *Journal of Social Work Education* 19(1), 55–60.

Israel, G. E., and Tarver, D. E. (1997). *Transgender Care: Recommended Guidelines, Practical Information, and Personal Accounts*. Philadelphia: Temple University Press.

Lev, A. I. (2004). *Transgender Emergence: Therapeutic Guidelines for wWorking with Gender Variant People and their Families*. New York: Haworth Press.

Lombardi, E. L., Wilchins, R. A., Priesing, D., and Malouf, D. (1998). Gender violence: Transgender experiences with violence and discrimination. *American Sociological Association* paper.

McPhail, B. A. (2004). Questioning gender and sexuality binaries: What queer theory, transgender individuals, and sex researchers can teach social work. *Journal of Gay and Lesbian Social Services* 17(1), 3–21.

Mallon, G. P. (1992a). Gay and no place to go: Serving the needs of gay and lesbian youth in out-of-home care settings. *Child Welfare* 71(6), 547–557.

Mallon, G. P. (Ed.). (1999). *Social Services for Transgendered Youth*. New York: Haworth Press.

Mallon, G. P. (Ed.) (2008). *Social Work Practice with Lesbian, Gay, Bisexual, and Transgender Persons*. New York: Haworth Press.

Marcia, J. E. (1980). Identity in adolescence. In J. Adelson (Ed.) *Handbook of Adolescent Psychiatry*. New York: John Wiley.

Mason-Schrock, D. (1996). Transsexuals' narrative construction of the "true self." *Social Psychology Quarterly* 59(3), 176–192.

Mattaini, M. (1995). Knowledge for practice. In C. Meyer and M. Mattaini (Eds.) *Foundations of Social Work Practice*. Washington, DC: National Association of Social Workers.

Meyer, C. (1982). Issues in clinical social work: In search of a consensus. In P. Carloff (Ed.) *Treatment Formulations and Clinical Social Work*. Silver Spring, MD: National Association of Social Workers.

Moore, B. (1999). Proposed public and professional policies: Transgender issues/Gender identity issues. *NASW News*, March, pp. 12–13.

National Association of Social Workers (2000). *Code of Ethics of the National Association of Social Workers*. Washington, DC: NASW.

National Association of Social Workers (2003). Transgender and gender identity issues. In *Social Work Speaks: National Association of Social Workers, Policy Statements 2003–2006* (6th ed.). Washington, DC: NASW.

Newman, B. S. (1989). Including curriculum content on lesbian and gay issues. *Journal of Social Work Education* 25(3), 202–211.

Norton, J. (1997). "Brin says you're a girl, but I think you're a sissy boy": Cultural origins of transphobia. *Journal of Gay, Lesbian, and Bisexual Identity* 2(2), 139–164.

Offer, D. (1980). Adolescent development: A normative perspective. In S. I. Greenspan and G. H. Pollock (Eds.) *The Course of Life*, vol. 2: *Latency, Adolescence, and Youth*. US Department of Health and Human Services Publication No. (ADM) 80–999. Washington, DC.

Offer, D., Ostrov, E., and Howard, K. (1981). *The Adolescent: A Psychological Self-portrait*. New York: Basic Books.

Oles, M. N. (1977). The transsexual client: A discussion of transsexualism and issues in psychotherapy. *American Journal of Orthopsychiatry* 47(1), 66–74.

Park, P. (1998). Are you a gender psychopath? Finding common cause in the battles against homophobia and transgenderphobia. *Lesbian and Gay New York*, November 5, p. 16.

Parlee, M. B. (1996). Situated knowledges of personal embodiment: Transgender activists' and psychological perspectives on "sex" and "gender." *Theory and Psychology* 6(4), 625–645.

Pharr, S. (1988). *Homophobia: A Weapon of Sexism*. Little Rock, AR: Chardon Press.

Scholinski, D. (1997). *The Last Time I Wore a Dress*. New York: Riverhead.

Volcano, D. L. and Halberstam, J. (1999). *The Drag King Book*. London: Serpent's Tail.

White Holman, N. and Goldberg, J. (2006a). Ethical, legal, and psychosocial issues in care of transgender adolescents. *International Journal of Transgenderism* 9(3/4), 95–110.

White Holman, N. and Goldberg, J. (2006b). Social and medical transgender case advocacy. *International Journal of Transgenderism* 9(3/4), 197–217.

Wilchins, R. A. (1997). *Read My Lips: Sexual Subversion and the End of Gender*. New York: Firebrand Books.

Williams, W. (1997). The transgender phenomenon: An overview from the Australian perspective. *Venereology* 10(3), 147–149.

Chapter 2

Ethical issues in the mental health treatment of trans adolescents

Stephanie K. Swann and Sarah E. Herbert

Introduction

With few exceptions (Mallon, 1999; Mallon and DeCrescenzo, 2006), there has been far less attention paid to transgender adolescents than to transgender adults. Yet these adolescents may be suffering from isolation, shame, rejection, school refusal, depression, and suicidality (Rubin, 2003). They may feel desperate enough to take hormones obtained on the street without prescription and without medical follow-up, or engage in self-mutilation in attempts to further their trans identification. These emotions and behaviors may bring them to the attention of mental health professionals and social service workers in a variety of settings. Significant issues may arise for the therapists if trans adolescents wish to cross-dress, use pronouns of the gender with which they feel most comfortable, and participate in activities as their desired gender rather than their biological sex. This engenders difficult ethical discussions among mental health professionals, and requires thoughtful interventions.

This chapter focuses on ethical dilemmas that arise in the treatment of adolescents with transgender orientation. We begin with a discussion of ethical and legal issues pertinent to the treatment of any adolescent, and then proceed to the trans adolescent, since there is a great deal of overlap between the two areas. This discussion reviews legal decisions (Weithorn, 1985), the existing data on adolescent decision making, and ethical principles that may help the clinician in resolving some very complex situations. Three different theoretical approaches to treatment are examined, with attention being paid to the guiding principles behind each approach. Case vignettes of three trans adolescents will provide a pragmatic illustration of the ethical dilemmas involved in evaluation and treatment of these individuals. It is our belief that treatment interventions should be based in respect for the adolescent's autonomy and confidentiality where he or she is deemed competent to make decisions.

Ethical issues and legal decisions involving minors

Issues of autonomy, confidentiality, and competence arise in the treatment of adolescent clients (Gustafson and McNamara, 1987). The clinician faced with complex questions involving adolescents may seek clarification through the law or professional codes of ethics. Legally, under most circumstances it is parents who must give consent for their minor child, even if the child is an adolescent, to receive medical care. Children have been traditionally seen as the property of their parents or guardians, as these individuals are responsible for protecting them and providing for their care (Enzer, 1985; Grisso and Vierling, 1978).

Despite this, legal decisions in the past 30 years have given increasing recognition to the independence of adolescents, enabling them to consent to their own medical treatment (Grisso and Vierling, 1978). Statutory laws in many US states have defined specific conditions, including venereal disease, pregnancy, and substance abuse, that define adolescents as emancipated minors and thus allow them to consent to their own medical treatment (Holder, 1996). Common law uses a "mature minor" exception to the requirement for parental consent for treatment. Under this principle in common law, young people may be judged to be mature enough to make medical decisions for themselves if they are old enough, understand the nature of a proposed treatment and its risks, can give the same degree of informed consent as an adult client, and if the treatment does not involve very serious risks (Holder, 1996). However, legal decisions and statutes that have been enacted may vary from state to state, and at times be contradictory.

Research on adolescent decision-making processes suggests that the abilities of adolescents in their mid to late teenage years are relatively close to those of adults, even though they lack some of adults' life experiences (Mann et al., 1989). The ability to make a reasonable decision is one of the hallmarks of a mature adolescent. Tancredi (1982) defined competence as the "capacity to make rational or intelligent judgment." Embedded in competence is the ability to survey a wide range of alternative solutions, evaluate the positives and negatives of each possible consequence stemming from the options identified, incorporate new information from reliable sources even when it is offensive, and effectively implement the determined choice of action. It is assumed that the more adequately each of these steps is implemented, the more competent the decision maker is (Mann et al., 1989). Patterns of impulsivity, rigidity, defensive avoidance, and complacent adherence or complacent change have been described as incompetent decision making by Janis and Mann (1977).

Ethical codes for various professional organizations are quite general and do not always address the specific issue that is of concern to the clinician. The Code of Ethics of the American Academy of Child Psychiatry states: "The formal responsibility for decisions regarding such participation (in evaluation, treatment or prevention involving a minor) usually resides with the parents or legal guardians" (1980, p. 4) The American Psychological Association Code of Ethics states that psychologists "working with minors or other persons who are unable to give voluntary, informed consent... [are obliged to] take special care to protect these persons' best interests" (Sobocinski, 1990, p. 242). Both codes of ethics would suggest that minors are unable to give voluntary, informed consent. There are no references to the treatment of children and adolescents in the National Association of Social Workers Code of Ethics (NASW, 1996).

There are, as we will discuss next, complex therapeutic situations for which the clinician may not find a clear answer from the law or professional codes of ethics. In these circumstances, it may be helpful to refer to the more fundamental, abstract level of ethical decision making using the ethical principles that are the foundation of the professional codes of ethics (Sobicinski, 1990). The ethical principles of respect for autonomy, beneficence, non-maleficence, and confidentiality are relevant to decision making in these situations.

Respect for autonomy is the ethical principle that involves acknowledging an individual's "right to hold views, to make choices, and to take actions based on personal values and beliefs" (Beauchamp and Childress, 1994, p. 125). Respecting autonomy involves not just an attitude of respect, but respectful action. It involves treating persons to enable them to act autonomously, and not engaging in actions that ignore, insult, or demean them. It is based on recognition of the unconditional worth of all individuals, and their ability to determine their own destiny (Beauchamp and Childress, 1994).

The ethical principle of beneficence "refers to a moral obligation to act for the benefit of others" (Beauchamp and Childress, 1994, p. 260). Beneficence has been defined as promoting good and removing harm, often translated into the best interests concept. It may be invoked when it is felt that an individual's autonomy should not be respected, owing to that individual's to impairment in decision-making capacity. The individual's age, immaturity, cognitive impairment, and inability to reason rationally are all reasons given for not respecting the person's autonomy.

Non-maleficence is an ethical principle that "asserts an obligation not to inflict harm intentionally" (Beauchamp and Childress, 1994, p. 189). This principle is often invoked in discussions that focus on intending, causing, or permitting death to occur. However, it can also include harms involving the person's psychological or physical health in issues other than death.

Confidentiality is a concept involving the relationship between a professional and his or her client. It involves safeguarding and holding in trust disclosed information. Confidentiality "is present when the person to whom the information is disclosed pledges not to divulge that information to a third party without the confider's permission" (Beauchamp and Childress, 1994, p. 420). Implementation of this concept is limited by constraints of the law and by situations where there is significant concern about danger to the individual or others. Clearly, confidentiality is an issue that comes up frequently in treating adolescents.

Ethical issues in treating trans adolescents

These same issues of confidentiality, competence to make decisions, and conflict between the ethical principles of respect for autonomy and beneficence arise in the treatment of adolescents who identify as transgender (Koetting, 2004). As clinicians, we may be confronted with what the limits of confidentiality are with respect to issues around gender identity. If a particular adolescent has significant concerns about his or her gender identity, discloses this in the therapy session, and wants assurance from the clinician that his or her parents will not be told, the clinician will be faced with the question of what his or her responsibility is in this matter. Issues of autonomy arise when parental or psychiatric definitions of healthy gender identity development come into direct conflict with the identity and goals of the trans adolescent. Should parents and/or mental health clinicians dictate what the adolescent's gender identity should be, and set the goals of treatment to achieve this? If parents feel the most beneficent course of action is to involve the adolescent in psychiatric treatment and not permit any expression of cross-gender behavior, should their decision be respected? Should the adolescent be able to participate in determining the goals of treatment – and if so, when? Can the trans adolescent be treated as a competent individual whose autonomy is respected? For example, if a particular adolescent wishes to express his or her cross-gender identification at school or in a residential treatment center, should this wish be honored? Finally, questions arise concerning the adolescent's competence to consent to the significant decisions regarding hormone therapy, or surgical procedures such as breast implants or genital reconstruction.

Theoretical approaches to the treatment of a transgender adolescent

There are several different theoretical approaches to the treatment of trans adolescents. The first is therapeutic intervention that is geared toward altering the adolescent's gender identity to be congruent with the biological sex. The second approach is supportive psychotherapy, an intervention that strives to alleviate intrapsychic distress while allowing the adolescent to continue to mature into adulthood. The third and final approach discussed is an intervention that not only provides ego support, but also recognizes the role of social and cultural values. It addresses the manner in which society polarizes gender, and draws attention to the ways in which gender dysphoric adolescents are marginalized and pathologized for not conforming to norms of Westen culture. This approach is centered on the belief that the desired gender identification is a viable one. Therapeutic interventions may include facilitating the cross-gender transition, as well as assuming an active role in determining appropriateness for hormone therapy, and eventually sex reassignment surgery.

Historically, psychoanalytic psychotherapy and behavior therapy have both utilized the first approach of trying to alter the adolescent's cross-gender identification to be congruent with his or her biological sex. The focus of psychoanalytically oriented treatment is the intrapsychic conflict that is assumed to be responsible for the gender dysphoria. The goal in behavioral interventions is the modification or elimination of specific characteristics and behaviors. However, efforts to change an adolescent's gender identity have not been proven to be effective, with a few exceptions (Zucker and Bradley, 1995). There has been one case report of an adolescent successfully relinquishing his cross-gender identification using behavioral techniques such as fading, voice training, and aversion therapy (Barlow et al., 1973). No long-term follow-up data were provided to determine whether the changes were sustained.

The second theoretical approach, supportive psychotherapy, uses several therapeutic interventions, including individual psychotherapy, family therapy, and case management in an attempt to alleviate psychological distress and strengthen ego functioning. Primary to this approach is the belief that decisions regarding core gender should be made when the adolescent reaches adulthood. The clinician attempts to facilitate the adolescent's exploration of his or her conflict between biological sex and gender identity while assessing sexual orientation and the possible confusion between gender and sexual orientation.

Transgender adolescents are often reported to present with co-morbid personality disorders as well as other psychiatric difficulties such as poor frustration tolerance, increased anxiety, depression, substance abuse, and suicidality. Their cross-dressing behaviors have traditionally been viewed as a defensive solution to the anxiety that is experienced as intolerable (Coates et al., 1991; Person and Ovesey, 1974; Zucker and Bradley, 1995). Supportive psychotherapy therefore places less emphasis on exploration as an aspect of facilitating the gender transition and instead attends to the management of the psychopathology in order for the adolescent to exist in his or her environment with the least amount of dysfunction. Resolution of the cross-gender identification with either a heterosexual or a homosexual orientation is seen as the most successful outcome of therapy in this approach (Bradley and Zucker, 1997).

In a third treatment approach, the ultimate success is not thought of as a heterosexual or lesbian or gay orientation. Instead, the adolescent's transgender identification is viewed as a viable outcome. The therapist acknowledges the constraints and demands of society with regard to gender identity, and the impact this has on the complete development of the gender dysphoric adolescent. This approach is often best suited for the patient who has a childhood history of cross-gender identification that has persisted into the adolescent years. The parents or guardians are often in need of support and education as they come to terms with their adolescent's desired gender identity and the fact that the cross-gender identification does not appear to be a transient phenomenon (Lesser, 1999). The parents may have conflicted feelings about what it means to support their child in this process, and the possible consequences if they do so. If the adolescent has not begun to cross-dress in his or her daily life, the therapist may be needed for guidance as the adolescent confronts the difficult consequences of beginning to live as the desired gender in the same community where he or she has previously lived. Often the adolescent has already begun to express visibly his or her cross-gender identification. If this is so, he or she may already be facing ostracism, harassment, and violence. In this case, it may be necessary for the clinician to advocate for the student within the school system, or assist in transfer to a new school. If appropriate, referral for further evaluation for hormone therapy may be undertaken.

Regardless of the theoretical approach to treatment, it is critical that we as clinicians working with gender dysphoric adolescents remain aware of our countertransference, and the ways in which our own biases may have an impact on the treatment. Ethical issues arise when the belief systems of the clinician, parents, and adolescent come into conflict. Belief systems incorporate not only professional knowledge, but also personal values, religious beliefs, and moral attitudes. Historically, our society has had explicit and implicit rules governing gender and gender role expression. An adolescent whose presentation is out of the realm of what has been defined as acceptable is likely to induce negative feelings for many clinicians, thereby triggering messages from our individual belief systems (Schope and Eliason, 2004). Even if this is not the case, awareness of society's expectations has an impact on our formulation of the problem, the intervention, and the desired solution. This awareness coupled with our own belief systems will contribute to the choice of ethical principles that guide our practice, and help us treat the trans adolescent in the most therapeutic manner.

Next, case vignettes of three transgender adolescents will be utilized to illustrate the difficult ethical dilemmas faced by clinicians attempting to treat these individuals and their families.

Case examples

Case 1

Issues of confidentiality were posed by Faheed, a 15-year-old boy brought for evaluation because of what his mother called "sexual identity concerns." His chief complaint was "I never felt attracted to girls before." He had made two suicide attempts prior to being seen, and when questioned by his mother for the reason, he disclosed that he was very depressed because he was only attracted to same-sex individuals. However, when interviewed separately from his mother at the initial evaluation session, he also stated, "I think of myself as a woman, not as gay." He reported that he disliked his body, giving as an example how he never wanted to go without a shirt in the summer the way other boys did. He hated dressing out for gym and refused to shower around other the boys. Sexually he acknowledged responsiveness to same-sex individuals, but said he didn't touch his genitals, nor did he allow others to touch them. He had had one previous sexual experience in which he had performed oral sex on a man he had casually met in another city when his family was there for vacation. His mother did not report any history of early cross-dressing or other evidence of cross-gender identification, but did describe him as a very sensitive and caring child.

The family was from an East Asian country, and their religion was Muslim. The patient was well aware that homosexuality was absolutely forbidden by his religion, and his parents had told him the penalty for being caught could be death. He said he would like to consider sex reassignment Surgery if it were not for his religion, which forbade any surgical intervention to alter the body.

Faheed was very concerned about the effect of his disclosure about his sexual orientation on his family, and did not want his parents to be told that he had any concerns about his gender identity. This posed an ethical dilemma for the treating psychiatrist. Should she respect this patient's request for confidentiality, and not disclose information regarding his gender identity concerns to his parents? Codes of ethics, when they comment on minors, generally suggest respecting a minor's confidentiality unless a situation of dangerousness to self or others exists. It was not felt that this individual's concerns regarding his gender identity were putting him or others in danger. He was not reporting suicidality, nor was he engaged in any behaviors at that time, sexual or otherwise, that could have put him at risk. What he appeared to need was a place where he could be free to discuss his emerging sexuality. Not respecting his desire for confidentiality would likely have disrupted this process. Since the cross-gender identification reported by Faheed followed his initial description of being attracted to same-sex peers, one consideration was that his internal conflict regarding a gay identification was leading him to consider being transsexual.

Faheed felt alone and isolated in the peer group at his school, and expressed a strong desire to meet other youth with concerns similar to his own. This presented another dilemma for the clinician. Awareness of the dearth of peer support in his current environment coupled with an understanding of the crucial role that a peer group plays in an adolescent's identity formation and consolidation led the psychiatrist to consider referral to a community support group and a helpline for gay, lesbian, and bisexual youth in addition to his individual therapy. The question was whether to inform both Faheed and his parents of these resources. If the parents were informed, it was felt that their strong religious beliefs would interfere with his attending the group, or even being allowed to continue in therapy.

A decision was made to inform Faheed of the possible community resources, and let him decide about informing his parents. The treating clinician felt that this young man was mature enough for his autonomy to be respected, and that he could be allowed to make the decision about whether to inform his parents about these resources. The principle of beneficence, however, guided the psychiatrist to discuss with Faheed the possible consequences of being rejected or further alienated from his family if he were to be more overt about socializing with his gay and lesbian peers, given his continued need to depend on his family.

Case 2

In the next case, issues of confidentiality, beneficence, and autonomy, including criteria for competent decision making, are explored in greater depth. David was a 15-year-old African-American biological male who was referred for outpatient psychotherapy following a brief inpatient psychiatric admission due to a suicidal gesture in which he ingested a mixture of household cleaning solutions. He immediately reported the incident to his high school counselor, at which time he was hospitalized. He began weekly therapy with complaints that included discomfort with his gender identity, depression, and a history of school refusal due to the violence and harassment he had experienced in that setting (see Lombardi, 2001). This was the only treatment David had ever received, with the exception of several sessions with a psychotherapist at age

10 for an inability to make friends, and withdrawn behaviors in the classroom. His biological mother, with whom he was living, began her own individual therapy as well. Shortly after the initial assessment, David turned 16 and subsequently dropped out of school and began cross-dressing daily. David's depressive symptoms resolved and he no longer reported suicidal ideation after he began cross-dressing, dropped out of school, and established a peer group through a local gay and lesbian youth organization.

David reported that he had wanted to be a girl for as long as he could remember, but his mother denied any knowledge of this. She did, however, admit that David had frequently been mistaken for a girl since the age of 2 years. She confirmed that David had experienced a great deal of harassment and subsequent alienation from his peers due to his persistent feminine mannerisms and behaviors. David acknowledged attraction to same-sex peers from the age of 13, but did not consider himself a gay male.

Ambivalence in his gender identity was observed as David displayed incongruence between his cross-dressing behavior and his continued use of his male name. Although David was able to pass, this incongruence between name and appearance was resulting in life problems, such as an inability to acquire a job and harassment from strangers to whom he frequently introduced himself and with whom he attempted to interact as he traveled the city via public transportation.

Over the course of treatment, David's cross-dressing became more seductive and more provocative. He discussed being frustrated by not having a job, but he denied any form of solicitation or prostitution. He did, however, report incidents of being propositioned and harassed while walking alone in an area of the city known for prostitution during late-night hours. When he was confronted with the risks of his behavior and the danger he was placing himself in, David minimized the severity of the situation and rationalized his behavior. He stated that he had to spend time with his friends, he could do so only late at night, and that there was no public transportation after 11 p.m., leaving him with no alternative but to walk home. His therapist suspected that David was not telling the truth, and in fact was possibly engaging in prostitution.

Because of David's inability to effectively generate alternatives that would provide him with greater safety, and his unwillingness to discontinue the behavior, it became necessary at that point to elicit the support of his mother. David informed the therapist that he did not want his mother to know how late he was staying out, or that he had encountered any danger in doing so. He feared that if his mother were aware of his behaviors, she would ground him, and refuse to allow him to hang out with his new friends. He was insistent that he have the freedom to choose his own way of living. He threatened that if his mother attempted to stop him from cross-dressing or seeing his friends, he felt he would have no alternative but to run away from home. David had a history of running away, but had not done so for approximately one year, a time period coinciding with the beginning of his therapy. Was David competent to make his own decisions regarding treatment at this point?

At first glance, David at age 16 and of average intelligence might be an adolescent who would be thought of as a competent decision maker. However, his poor judgment, lack of insight, and impulsivity made it necessary for the therapist to place the ethical principle of beneficence above the principle of respect for his autonomy and self-determination. This was accomplished by requesting that David's mother enter the treatment process, thereby usurping his right to formulate his own treatment plan. It also became necessary to violate his confidentiality to the extent that was needed to provide him with the safety that he was unable to provide for himself.

The ethical conflicts involved in the decision to override David's autonomous decision making and violate his confidentiality were further complicated by the therapist's hesitance to disrupt the therapeutic alliance with her client. Involving his mother and violating his confidentiality diminished the trust, and threatened the continuation of his therapy. The therapy provided a place where he could explore his cross-gender identification in a safer setting than that afforded to him on the streets. The therapist was concerned that he might resume his runaway behaviors, thus placing himself at further risk of being harmed. This was particularly worrisome given the improvement in his psychiatric symptoms and the stability of his living situation that had taken place in the year he had been in therapy. The life-threatening consequences of respecting his autonomous decision making in this case forced the clinician to take a more paternalistic stance despite the risk of negatively impacting the therapeutic relationship.

Case 3

Questions regarding respect for patient autonomy and competence to consent for treatment were handled differently by the clinician treating Daniel, an 18-year-old Caucasian biological male who was initially seen for evaluation when he was 16-and-a-half years old. His mother, Mrs. M., requested a consultation to clarify his diagnosis. The psychologist who had been seeing Daniel felt that he was gay, yet Daniel did not agree with this, and Mrs. M. wanted another opinion to know if Daniel was transsexual. A month and a half prior to being seen, he had dropped out of school because of persistent taunting by peers about his femininity, and had begun cross-dressing full time. He had attended a support group for gay, lesbian, and bisexual adolescents on one occasion at his mother's urging, but did not feel this group reflected how he saw himself. At the initial interview he commented, "I think I'm transsexual; I feel so much more natural dressing like this."

Mrs. M. had been seeking help regarding Daniel's cross-gender identification since he was 3 years old. Daniel's mother acknowledged wanting a girl for her second child, but did not feel she had treated Daniel any differently than his brother. As early as age two-and-a-half, Daniel would try to wear high heels, and would put dish towels on his head to simulate long hair. At age 4, he told his girlfriend to call him by a female name, and told people that he wanted to be a girl. Toy interests were for feminine ones such as "My Little Pony," where he could spend time combing the pony's long mane and tail, and Mrs. M. described how he took the role of mother when playing house. Mrs. M. reported that until fifth grade his feminine gender role behaviors were more overt, but that they diminished after this point. Daniel said the gender issues were present, but he learned by fifth grade not to talk about his desire to be female.

Since the age of 10, Daniel has been aware of an attraction to same-sex peers. In an effort to explore his sexuality, he became involved in some telephone sex in early adolescence, and then in mid-adolescence met men and performed oral sex when cross-dressed several times, apparently in both situations passing as a woman. In his first sexual interaction at age 13, and in all subsequent ones, he has never allowed a partner to touch his penis through masturbation or oral sex. He has performed oral sex, and been penetrated himself in anal intercourse. At the time of the initial assessment, Daniel had a 16-year-old boyfriend who apparently had not known he was a biological male until he disclosed this after they had been seeing each other a short time. Daniel said his only friends were straight girls at the school he had attended. He remarked that there were few guys who were willing to be seen around him.

Mrs. M. had initially sought consultation about her son's atypical gender role behaviors when he was 3 years old. Family counseling had been recommended at that time, but the family did not follow through on this recommendation. However, Daniel was in therapy from ages four-and-a-half to six-and-a-half years with another psychologist, apparently to help him in coping with the parents' divorce, but also with gender identity issues. Mrs. M. sought consultation with the chief of child psychiatry at a local medical school around this same time. He said he could give no final opinion, that it would take time to determine what the outcome would be, and his recommendation was for Daniel to continue in therapy. During this time, Mrs. M. reported doing as much as possible to offer more stereotypically masculine toys, to reinforce more masculine gender role behaviors, and to find activities in which he could participate with other boys. Daniel remembers being offered a Mickey Mouse watch he desperately wanted if he would act in less feminine ways; he reports doing so just long enough to get the watch, but he then reverted to his previous ways of behaving. In fifth grade, he began weekly therapy with the psychologist he had been seeing for six years at the time he came for evaluation.

It was clear that Daniel had had a long-standing gender identity disorder that had not abated with time, despite multiple attempts at psychotherapy and behavioral intervention, and that a transsexual resolution was becoming obvious. Prior to the consultation, he had decided on his own that he could no longer tolerate going to school and living as a male, and began cross-dressing full time. Daniel understood the consequences of this, but did not feel he could continue to handle the harassment he had been experiencing in the school setting. At the time of the consultation, Daniel expressed a desire to begin hormone therapy as soon as possible. He knew that the longer he waited to begin, the more his body would show the masculinization that caused him so much distress. Mrs. M. made it clear that she and Daniel's father were willing to consider this. The risks and the benefits of hormone therapy were discussed with Daniel both on his own and with his mother present. He was able to grasp this information, and understood that some of the changes, such as the development of breast tissue, might not be reversible should he want to change his mind. Daniel understood that the professionals treating him might worry that he would change his mind, but articulated a strong belief that this was what was right for him. Daniel was referred for consultation to a local endocrinologist, who began hormone therapy shortly after this evaluation, when Daniel was 16-and-a-half years of age.

Since the time of the initial evaluation, Daniel has asked family, friends, and treating clinicians to use female pronouns and the female name selected in the legal name change. At this point in the case, the female pronoun will now be used, and Daniel referred to as Danielle. Danielle has consistently taken the hormone therapy prescribed by her endocrinologist, she has lived as a female, had a legal name change, and had a series of jobs where she has successfully passed as female. She continues to ruminate about what she sees as "boy features" when she looks in the mirror, but overall is making a positive adaptation. She has difficulty maintaining a job, not because of having trouble passing but because of conflicts that arise with her supervisors. After recently turning 18, she received breast implants and has continued to work toward her goal of sex reassignment surgery. The psychiatrist in this case has provided referral information and consultation with the other physicians treating Danielle during this time of gender transition.

Respect for autonomy is an ethical principle that acknowledges an individual's right to hold views, make choices, and take actions based on that individual's values and beliefs (Beauchamp and Childress, 1994). Choices made by an autonomous individual rest on the assumption that the person is competent. The dilemma in adolescence is that one cannot assume that adolescents are fully competent in all areas of their lives. To deny that they have any competence to make decisions, however, is likewise unjustified (Sobicinski, 1990). A review of articles that are pertinent to the subject of minors and informed consent suggests that older adolescents do have decision-making capacity that is comparable to that of adults. In fact, some authors have suggested there are no psychological grounds on which to deny adolescents of 15 years and older the option of giving informed consent for their medical treatment and the decisions that entails. Piaget's theory of cognitive development would suggest that once an adolescent has achieved formal operations, he or she has a better ability to conceptualize future consequences of decisions made.

In order for someone to give informed consent, the following criteria must be met: the consent is truly voluntary, there is adequate disclosure of information, there is comprehension of this information, and the person is competent to decide. Danielle's psychiatrist felt that she was able to understand the risks and benefits of pursuing her goal of sex reassignment surgery. She was able to articulate the risks and benefits of hormone therapy, and was also able to discuss the risks and benefits of not getting treatment until age 18. There was no one pressuring Danielle to go ahead, and thus her consent was voluntary. Her decision-making capacity was felt to be adequate for giving informed consent for hormone therapy. Danielle's autonomy was respected by her mother and treating physicians, as it was felt that she was competent to make these decisions, and give informed consent.

Conclusions

In conclusion, ethical dilemmas arise in the treatment of adolescents of transgender experience. As social workers and mental health professionals, we may face situations in which we are asked to answer complex questions for which there is no obviously correct or easy answer. What we can know is that these adolescents are individuals whose struggles with cross-gender identification need to be listened and responded to with respect and sensitivity. No longer is it acceptable to equate transgender identification with severe psychopathology. This affects not only the way we formulate our understanding of the gender dysphoric adolescent, but also the theoretical approach to treatment and the way in which we resolve ethical dilemmas.

References

American Academy of Child and Adolescent Psychiatry (1980). *Code of Ethics*. Washington, DC: AACAP.

Barlow, D. H., Reynolds, E. J., and Agras, W. S. (1973). Gender identity change in a transsexual. *Archives of General Psychiatry*, 28: 569–579.

Beauchamp, T. L. and Childress, J. F. (1994). *Principles of Biomedical Ethics* (4th ed.). New York: Oxford University Press.

Bradley, S. J. and Zucker, K. J.(1997). Gender identity disorder: A review of the past ten years. *Journal of the American Academy of Child and Adolescent Psychiatry* 36, 872–880.

Coates, S. W., Friedman, R. C., Wolfe, S. (1991). The etiology of boyhood gender identity disorder: A model for Integrating temperament, development, and psychodynamics. *Psychoanalytic Dialogue*, 1:481–523.

Enzer, N. B.(1985). Ethics in child psychiatry: an overview. In D. H. Schetky and E. P. Benedek (Eds.) *Emerging Issues in Child Psychiatry and the Law*. New York: Brunner/Mazel.

Grisso, T. and Vierling, L. (1978). Minors' consent to treatment: A developmental perspective. *Professional Psychology 9*, 412–427.

Gustafson, K. E. and McNamara, J. R. (1987). Confidentiality with minor clients: Issues and guidelines for therapists. *Professional Psychology: Research and Practice 18*, 503–508.

Holder, A. R. (1996). Legal issues in professional liability. In M. Lewis (Ed.) *Child and Adolescent Psychiatry: A Comprehensive Textbook* (2nd ed.). Baltimore, MD: Williams and Wilkins.

Janis, I. L. and Mann, L. (1977) *Decision Making: A Psychological Analysis of Conflict, Choice and Commitment*. Collier Macmillan, New York.

Koetting, M. E. (2004). Beginning practice with preoperative male-to-female transgender clients. *Journal of Gay and Lesbian Social Services 16*(2), 99–104.

Lesser, J. G. (1999). When your son becomes your daughter: Counseling the mother of a transsexual. *Families in Society 80*(2), 182–189.

Lombardi, E. (2001). Gender violence: Transgender experiences with violence and discrimination. *Journal of Homosexuality 42*(1), 89–101.

Mallon, G. P. (Ed.) (1999). *Social Services for Transgendered Youth*. New York: Haworth Press.

Mallon, G. P. and De Crescenzo, T. (2006). Transgender children and youth: A child welfare practice perspective. *Child Welfare 85*(2), 215–241.

Mann, L., Harmoni, R., and Power, C. (1989). Adolescent decision-making: The development of competence. *Journal of Adolescence 12*, 265–278.

National Association of Social Workers (1996). *Code of Ethics*. Washington, DC: NASW Press.

Person, E, and Ovesey, L. (1974). The transsexual syndrome in males. I: Primary transsexualism. *American Journal of Psychotherapy, 28*, 4–20.

Rubin, H. (2003). *Self-made Men: Identity and Embodiment Among Transsexual men*. Nashville, TN: Vanderbilt University Press.

Schope, R. D. and Eliason, M. J. (2004). Sissies and tomboys: Gender role behaviors and homophobia. *Journal of Gay and Lesbian Social Services 16*(2), 73–97.

Sobocinski, M. R. (1990). Ethical principles in the counseling of gay and lesbian adolescents: Issues of autonomy, competence, and confidentiality. *Professional Psychology: Research and Practice 21*, 240–247.

Tancredi, L. (1982) Competency for informed consent: Conceptual limits of empirical data, *International Journal of Law and Psychiatry, 5*. 51–63.

Weithorn, L. A. (1985). Children's capacities for participation in treatment decision-making. In D. H. Schetky and E. P. Benedek (Eds.) *Emerging Issues in Child Psychiatry and the Law*. New York: Brunner/Mazel.

Zucker, K. J. and Bradley, S. J. (1995). *Gender Identity Disorder and Psychosexual Problems in Children and Adolescents*. New York: Guilford Press.

Chapter 3

Internal and external stress factors associated with the identity development of transgender and gender variant youth

W. Christian Burgess

Introduction

Transgender youth are among the most neglected and misunderstood groups in our society today. In addition to undergoing the regular perils of adolescence, these young people face an extraordinary degree of additional internal and external pressures associated with their identity development, centered around a society that is overwhelmingly uncomfortable with gender non-conformity. When left unchecked, these pressures amount to extreme isolation and confusion, which can lead to an array of biopsychosocial problems, from substance abuse to self-mutilation.

No exact numbers are known regarding the prevalence of self-identified trans individuals in the United States or other countries. This is perhaps due to the broad scope that the label "transgender" encompasses. In the early 1990s, different communities of gender-variant individuals began to unite politically and socially to demand the rights and respect they deserve. These communities include cross-dressers, drag kings and queens, transsexuals, transgenderists, gender-benders, masculine women, feminine men, androgynes, etc. The word "transgender" then emerged to unite these groups under an umbrella term that includes all of those who challenge the boundaries of sex and gender. In recent years, some persons of transgender experience have also adopted the term "trans" to identify their experience (Carranante, 1999; Feinberg, 1996).

Given these definitions, it is appropriate to make the assumption that the transgender community, while small compared to the overall population, is still large, diverse, and significant. In fact some might argue (Davis, 2008) that there is no such thing as a single "trans community," but rather there are multiple trans communities, as the communities are far too diverse to be united by a single variable. This diversity is reflected within the overall population of adolescents as well. As the transgender communities gain more visibility within societal institutions, especially the media, more and more young people are becoming comfortable in asserting their gender nonconforming characteristics.

Concurrently, with increased visibility can come an increase in backlash. Families, schools, peer groups, places of employment, and other institutions are often ignorant or ill-equipped with accurate knowledge of this population, and as a result isolate these young people or ignore them altogether. To help stem this problem, it is incumbent upon social service agencies and human service professionals to work with transgender youth in easing the isolation and confusion, and in bridging the gaps between themselves and their families, schools, peers, and other social systems.

The goal of this chapter is to present an alternative to a traditionally held view that transgender youth suffer from some sort of disorder, and instead shed light on the external factors that may lead the young person to seek help. Social service professionals need to be aware of such factors in order to make a full assessment of what a potential transgender adolescent client's issues are, and in order to work at changing some of these external pressures societally so that more transgender youth can attain peaceful identity integration.

Review of the literature

There are, even after ten years, just a few published books specifically on transgender youth (Beam, 2007; Mallon, 1999a, Brill and Pepper, 2008). However, increasingly there has been a proliferation of popular literature on the general topic of transgender issues. Leslie Feinberg (1996), Helen Boyd (2007), Kate Bornstein (1994), Michael Brinkle (2006), Ricki Ann Wilchins (1997) and others have written extensively on the subject of transgender theory, culture, and politics, but have by and large neglected to mention issues specifically affecting transgender youth in their works. Despite the inclusion of transgender youth in agencies serving lesbian, gay, and bisexual young people, the books focusing on these populations have failed to include transgender youth in their titles or in their content, with an occasional two to three pages on gender identity included but no more.

There is a similar paucity of information on the subject among academic and formal research. A search for literature using the keywords "transgender youth" within the *Social Work Abstracts*, *Sociofile*, and *PsycLit* research systems yielded very limited results except for one special issue of the *Journal of Gay and Lesbian Social Services* (Mallon, 1999b). Even when one uses more clinical and outdated terms such as transsexual or Gender Identity Disorder when describing this community, results are minimal and, owing to the clinical nature of the literature, limited in scope.

Much of the literature written about this community is punitive in nature, or contains language that pathologizes the group as a whole.

Words such as "miserable" or "troubled," and reference to an individual's transgender identity as a "problem," are common, do not include differentiation between one's gender identity and other psychosocial issues that may be present (substance abuse, depression, etc.), and generally fail to mention society's role in creating the distress within the individual (Lothstein, 1983; Steiner, 1985; Wicks, 1977). These attitudes and thoughts may be due to the popular thought of the time in which they were written, but nonetheless point to the need to revise and add to the current crop of academic literature, so that such negative references can be counterbalanced with accurate and unbiased reflections of this community.

The greater part of the literature regarding trans youth specifically focuses on treatment of those within this community who identify or who are labeled as transsexuals, or who are diagnosed with gender identity disorder. Suggested treatment approaches run from forced behavioral modification during childhood and adolescence (Riseley, 1986; Zucker, 1985) to cognitive therapy emphasizing self-exploration and identity integration (Kahn, 1990; Levine, 1978).

Limited literature (Glenn, 1999; Pazos, 1999) was found that simply paints an objective, descriptive account of the developmental aspects of transgender youth outside the clinical setting. This is significant because while information obtained from youth who seek treatment is valuable, it may be skewed if such accounts are taken to be representative of an entire population. The distinction between one's gender identity and mental health issues becomes blurred, and the result is often that the individual's gender identity is seen as the "problem" – the source of the adolescent's pain and confusion.

Fortunately, more literature is being written today (Valentine, 2007) that shifts the focus from the gender identity as the "problem" to the external factors that lead to internal distress. For transgender youth, the external factors are manifested most often through social pressures to conform to traditional gender expectations. These social pressures emanate from popular culture, families, schools, peer groups, social service agencies, and other institutions that define society's culture. When an adolescent defies these expectations – to varying degrees and through a variety of means – confusion and isolation settle in and then lead to intrapsychic problems and symptoms and behaviors such as depression, low self-esteem, substance abuse or hormonal abuse, and self-mutilation, compounded by additional factors such as running away from or being kicked out of his or her home, homelessness, prostitution, increased risk of exposure to sexually transmitted diseases (STDs), dropping out of school, and unemployment (Cohen, 1991; Denny, 1995; Galambos et al., 1990; Kahn, 1990; Rodgers, 1997; Ryan and Futterman, 1998).

Within the clinical community of psychiatrists, psychologists, and therapists, much of the dominant thought regarding transgenderists rests on the "condition" known as gender identity disorder (GID). To gain an understanding of where these clinicians are coming from, and thus gain an understanding of the preponderance of literature on the subject, it is important to review this issue.

Gender identity disorder is a classification of the *Diagnostic and Statistical Manual of Mental Disorders*, fourth edition (American Psychiatric Association, 1994). The diagnostic criteria for GID are as follows:

A. A strong and persistent cross-gender identification (not merely a desire for any perceived cultural advantages of being the other sex).

In children, the disturbance is manifested by four (or more) of the following:

1 repeatedly stated desire to be, or insistence that he or she is, the other sex;
2 in boys, preference for cross-dressing or simulating female attire; in girls, insistence on wearing only stereotypically masculine clothing;
3 strong and persistent preferences for cross-sex roles in make believe play or persistent fantasies of being the other sex;
4 intense desire to participate in the stereotypical games and pastimes of the other sex;
5 strong preference for playmates of the other sex

In adolescents and adults, the disturbance is manifested by symptoms such as a stated desire to be the other sex, frequent passing as the other sex, desire to live or be treated as the other sex, or the conviction that he or she has the typical feelings and reactions of the other sex.

B. Persistent discomfort with his or her sex or sense of inappropriateness in the gender role of that sex.

In children, the disturbance is manifested by any of the following: in boys, assertion that his penis or testes are disgusting or will disappear or aversion toward rough-and-tumble play and rejection of male stereotypical toys, games, and activities; in girls, rejection of urinating in a sitting position, assertion that she does not want to grow breasts or menstruate, or marked aversion toward normative feminine clothing.

In adolescents and adults, the disturbance is manifested by symptoms such as preoccupation with getting rid of primary and secondary sex characteristics (e.g., request for hormones, surgery, or other procedures to physically alter sexual characteristics to simulate the other sex) or belief that he or she was born the wrong sex.

C. The disturbance is not concurrent with a physical intersex condition.

D. The disturbance causes clinically significant distress or impairment in social, occupational, or other important areas of functioning.

(American Psychiatric Association, 1994)

There are many arguments against the GID classification: it is used as a subliminal means to diagnose homosexuality (and subsequently try to "cure" it); and it stigmatizes children, adolescents, and adults who fail to conform to traditional gender norms, even those who fail only very slightly. In essence, opponents of the classification charge that it results in the diagnosis of a disorder that is in reality not present; it creates a stigma around the identity of those receiving the diagnosis that leads to internalized shame; and in some cases, especially for children and adolescents, it leads to forced treatments involving the imposition of gender norms (Osborne, 1997; Wilson, 1997).

Proponents of maintaining the classification argue that a GID diagnosis is necessary to satisfy requirements of the Harry Benjamin *Standards of Care*, a list of guidelines that candidates for sex reassignment surgery (SRS) must follow. Further, those in favor of keeping the classification say that it validates the experiences of those who are transgender (often called "gender dysphoric" in clinical circles) by giving practitioners a framework from which to operate (Osborne, 1997; Steiner, 1985).

Kathy Wilson (1997) from the Gender Identity Center of Colorado offers a solution to the debate: "It is possible to retain a diagnosis that specifically addresses the needs of the pre-operative transsexuals, requiring medical sex reassignment, with criteria that clearly and unambiguously exclude others for whom the diagnosis serves no therapeutic purpose." Wilson and others encourage clinicians to make a diagnosis on the basis of other psychosocial factors that may be present, such as depression or multiple personality disorder.

Physical and psychological changes

Adolescence is a time for great social, biological, and psychological changes. For almost all young people, this is a confusing time fraught with unexpected twists and turns. Perhaps the most intense changes come during puberty, when the body undergoes physical growth and sexual maturation. While many adolescents find solace in these changes through standard health curricula that teach them what to expect and in peer groups where they can share stories of their physical trials and tribulations, transgender youth seldom have such support systems.

Puberty is often the time when transgender adolescents become the most confused and isolated. Where gender non-conformity in childhood may not have been taken as seriously by external systems, and the child may have been content with the idea that they would soon become the opposite sex, in adolescence those premonitions are shattered.

Physically, transgender youth may become repelled or ashamed of their developing sexual characteristics. They may begin to wear bulky clothing year-round to mask physical changes, or to use tight undergarments or bandages to bind breasts or genitals. In extreme cases, young people may also make attempts at removing unwanted sex organs through auto-castration or constant repeated pounding of breasts. Hormonal abuse may occur as well, with young people self-administering estrogen or testosterone supplements.

Other ways of attempting to alter physical appearance include, in male-to-female transgendered youth, injecting silicone in their lips, chest, buttocks, or thighs. For female-to-male youth, steroid abuse or the excessive use of powders meant for bodybuilding may be tried (Brown and Rounsley, 1996; Denny, 1995; Rodgers, 1997; Ryan and Futterman, 1998).

Psychological changes are also heightened for transgender youth. The mood swings and "testing of limits" through increased risk taking, typical in adolescence, may signify deeper trouble for these youth. Because of the internalization of negative attitudes toward gender non-conformity, transgender youth are at increased risk for low self-esteem, which may manifest itself through depression, substance abuse, self-mutilation, and/or suicide.

External pressures

The biological and psychological distress of transgender youth is often symptomatic of pressures created from the macro and mezzo systems surrounding these young people. Pressures to conform to traditional gender norms intensify during adolescence, and the degree of those expectations greatly shapes how the individual copes with the physical and psychological changes. Zastrow and Kirst-Ashman (1995, p. 144) summarize the importance of these systems:

> Family and peer group mezzo systems are dynamically involved in childhood growth, development, and behavior. Social interaction with other people in childhood provides the foundation for building an adult social personality. Macro systems within the environment, including communities, government units, and agencies, can provide necessary resources to help families address issues and solve problems typically experienced with children. Impinging macro systems within the social environment can act either to help or hinder family members fulfill their potential.

Family

The family is the system with perhaps the greatest influence on one's development. From birth through young adulthood, this unit has as one of its primary tasks the "physical, mental, emotional, and social development of each of its members" (Duvall, 1971, cited in Schriver, 1995). No matter what the makeup of the family, no matter what the cultural background, gender expectations are often strong and unswerving. Families often intervene during childhood if a child does not meet these expectations, through discipline or therapy, or they let the child push the boundaries with the presumption that the behavior is a phase.

If the child continues to express her- or himself outside of gender expectations into adolescence, however, the interventions become swifter and more severe. The expression of identity becomes an act of rebellion in the parent or guardian's eyes, one that must be punished more severely or with more intense therapy. Parents or guardians take out their own discomfort with gender nonconformity on their child, resulting in strained relations and further isolation of the adolescent.

Of course, the degree of negative reaction usually corresponds with the degree of gender nonconformity. For instance, a parent's reaction to a male-to-female youth wearing black nail polish and having his ears pierced may not be the same as their reaction to a female-to-male youth wearing a tuxedo to the prom. These behaviors may still be viewed by the family as testing the limits and identity formation, and they may think the adolescent will still grow out of it, but as the adolescent gets older and/or as the behaviors and expressions of gender identity become more gender nonconforming, the parent or guardian may view the situation more seriously.

In the event of extreme and/or persistent gender nonconformity, or if the youth discloses to her or his parents that they are transgender, the family may react with extreme behaviors in turn. Physical, emotional, and verbal abuse may occur, or the youth might be thrown out of the home. Also, the youth may become so isolated in the home as a result of the family's discomfort and shame that she or he runs away. Lesser's (1999) first-person account of her experience as the mother of a trans youth is one exception in the literature.

Parents, Family and Friends of Lesbians and Gays (PFLAG), a national US organization comprising a network of local support and advocacy groups, has recently fostered initiatives to assist families with transgendered children in acquiring the knowledge and skills necessary to create a healthy environment in the home. In addition, more sensitive clinicians are encouraging families to allow adolescents to express their own gender identity, albeit with compromises (until the child is older), such as cross-dressing at home but not in public. Still, many families are unaware of such organizations or therapeutic techniques, and even if they are, are so entrenched with rigid gender roles that for transgender youth the family is a system that more often than not fails to fulfill its roles as nurturer and caretaker.

Schools

Next to families, schools have the second most significant impact on one's development during adolescence. Schools are the testing ground for social skills, and through this testing, identity formation takes place. Fortunately, there are cliques where transgender youth may be accepted, and in some schools, cliques of lesbian, gay, bisexual, and transgender youth are forming on their own, through clubs and informal friendship networks. Transgender youth are "coming out" in schools in increasing numbers, asserting their identity and demanding attention.

Despite these positive strides, school communities still have a long way to go. Curricula still fail to mention transgender issues, from historical figures to reading assignments to sexuality education. It is also rare that sensitivity training occurs among faculty and staff on the unique needs of transgender youth. Further, many rites of passage that occur within the context of schools are traumatic for transgender youth. Physical education, pressures to date, classes that track the specific sexes (shop for boys and home economics for girls, for instance), and the prom are all examples of middle and secondary school rituals that adhere to strict traditional gender norms. Teasing and harassment are also something that most transgender youth must endure, and can take the form of violence. As with family, pressures at school lead to further isolation of transgender youth.

Other systems

In addition to the family and school systems, other institutions also exert pressure on transgender youth to conform and suppress their identity. Healthcare professionals, employers, and places of worship are too often dead ends for these youth, offering no solace and more isolation. The social service agencies that transgender youth then turn to for help or to which they are referred through no choice of their own often continue the path of ignorance and neglect. Foster care and group homes, youth homeless shelters, juvenile detention centers and jails, community centers, after-school programs, and other institutions are commonly just as ill-equipped at welcoming transgender youth as the institutions the youth are attempting to escape from (I. Robledo and D. Nish, personal interview, April 8, 1999).

Safe space

Exceptions do abound, though, and must be mentioned. Across the country, youth-service agencies that serve all youth and/or lesbian, gay, and bisexual youth are becoming better equipped to address the unique needs of transgender youth, offering safe havens where they can "be themselves" free from persecution.

Streetwork is one such program. Located in New York City, Streetwork is a program of Safe Horizon, an agency that provides assistance to victims and survivors of crime and abuse. The mission of the program includes "reaching out to the homeless and disenfranchised youth of New York City, offering them respite from hunger, cold, loneliness and fear, and the opportunity to reclaim for themselves a sense of dignity and self-worth." In essence, the program fills the void left by the families of many of these youth, many of who identify as transgender.

Ines Robledo, the drop-in center coordinator for Streetwork, and David Nish, Vice President of Youth Programs for Safe Horizon, state that Streetwork strives to provide alternatives for the youth to counteract the negative experiences they often encounter when accessing mainstream services. Healthcare and legal services are provided on-site; support and discussion groups are available, as well as safe and confidential counseling, social alternatives, and access to showers and food. A team of outreach workers also goes to the streets to provide services directly.

Implications for practice

It is in the interest of human service professionals to duplicate the efforts of agencies such as Streetwork. Social workers are in a unique position to address the isolation and persecution of transgender youth from many angles.

A multisystems approach needs to be utilized so that interventions can be developed that will address all of the institutions that affect the identity development of transgender youth. The American Psychiatric Association should be targeted to reevaluate its current classification of gender identity disorder. The lesbian, gay, and bisexual community should continue to strengthen its effort to include transgender individuals in its organizing efforts and agency services, and the transgender community should be pushed to be more aware of and inclusive of transgender youth. The organizing work of transgender youth themselves needs to gain more recognition and support from the above communities and the youth services community, as these young people create their own groups, publications, and websites.

At the therapeutic level, clinicians must truly embrace the philosophy of "meeting the client where they are," by providing a safe space where transgender youth can express themselves and discuss their identity formation free from bias. Accurate information regarding the transgender community and issues affecting the transgender community such as sex reassignment surgery (SRS), hormones, etc. should be available to youth. Such access to information may instill hope in frustrated transgender adolescents and deter them from misusing hormones or altering their bodies using unsafe, harmful techniques. Support and discussion groups, the creation of social alternatives such as drop-in centers, and access to positive role models are needed. All of these methods are vital steps in assisting with the formation of an integrated identity for transgender youth.

Above all else, the very core of what social service professionals can do is provide acceptance and positive affirmation for these youth. Just a simple validation of who the individual is, including his or her gender identity, can make all the difference in the world for that person. Acceptance will lead to a willingness to learn, the willingness to learn will lead to understanding, and understanding will lead to the eventual cessation of oppression and isolation of transgender youth.

Areas for further study

Because this is such an understudied field, any additional research on the issues affecting transgender youth would be beneficial. Numerous topics would benefit from further scrutiny, such as transgender youth in the foster-care system, on the streets, female-to-male transgender youth, etc. Comprehensive interviews and questionnaires administered to transgender youth would be an especially useful research tool, as no major studies have been undertaken to survey the needs and experiences of this population. The varied experience of transgender youth according to race and ethnicity is also an important area of study, as these variations are often overlooked in all subjects of research. Finally, studies that look at the long-term effects of various treatments would be useful to the debate over gender identity disorder, and would help shape intervention approaches in general.

Conclusions

Transgender youth deserve the attention of the social services community, for they have been neglected for far too long. This neglect has resulted in a group that is one of the most marginalized in US society, compounded by the extreme isolation and violence suffered within their families, schools, and other social institutions. Some say that oppression based on sex and gender is at the root of all of our society's evils. If this is true, then it is surely our youth that are suffering the most, for it is often too difficult for them to speak for themselves. Social service professionals can help them find their voices and become the wonderful transgendered individuals they are meant to be.

References

American Psychiatric Association (1994). *Diagnostic and Statistic Manual of Mental Disorders* (4th ed.). Washington, DC: APA.

Beam, C. (2007). *Transparent: Love, Family, and Living the T with Transgender Teens.* New York: Harcourt.

Bornstein, K. (1994). *Gender Outlaws: On Men, Women, and the Rest of Us.* New York: Routledge.

Boyd, H. (2007). *She's Not the Man I Married: My Life with a Transgender Husband.* Emeryville, CA: Seal Press.

Brill, S. and Pepper, R. (2008). *The Transgender Child: A Handbook for Families and Professionals.* San Francisco, CA: Cleis Press.

Brinkle, M. (2006). *Returning to Michael: A Transgender Story.* LA: iUniverse.

Brown, M. L. and Rounsley, C. A. (1996). *True Selves: Understanding Transsexualism.* San Francisco: Jossey-Bass.

Carranante, T. (1999). Glossary of gender/transgender terms. Unpublished document.

Cohen, Y. (1991). Gender identity conflicts in adolescents as motivation for suicide. *Adolescence* 26(101), 19–29.

Davis, C. (2008). Social work with transgender and gender non-conforming persons. In G. P. Mallon (Ed.) *Social Work Practice with Lesbian, Gay, Bisexual, and Transgender People.* New York: Haworth Press.

Denny, D. (1995). Transgendered youth at risk for exploitation, HIV, hate crimes. Unpublished manuscript, American Educational Gender Information Services, Inc.

Feinberg, L. (1996). *Transgender Warriors: Making History from Joan of Arc to Dennis Rodman.* Boston: Beacon Press.

Galambos, N. L., Almeida, D. M., and Petersen, A. C. (1990). Masculinity, femininity, and sex role attitudes in early adolescence: Exploring gender intensification. *Child Development* 61, 1905–1914.

Glenn, W. (1999). For colored girls: Reflections on an MTF trans identity. *Journal of Gay and Lesbian Social Services* 10(3/4), 83–94.

Kahn, T. J. (1990). The adolescent transsexual in a juvenile corrections institution: A case study. *Child and Youth Care Quarterly* 19(1), 21–29.

Lesser, J. G. (1999). When your son becomes your daughter: Counseling the mother of a transsexual. *Families in Society* 80(2), 182–189.

Levine, C. O. (1978). Social work with transsexuals. *Social Casework* 59(3), 167–174.

Lothstein, L. M. (1983). *Female-to-male Transsexualism.* Boston: Routledge and Kegan Paul.

Mallon, G. (Ed.) (1999a). *Social Services with Transgendered Youth.* New York: Haworth Press.

Mallon, G. (Ed.) (1999b). Social services with transgendered youth. Special issue of the *Journal of Gay and Lesbian Social Services* 10(3/4).

Osborne, D. (1997). An attack on our most vulnerable: The use and abuse of gender identity disorder. *Lesbian and Gay New York*, October 28.

Pazos, S. (1999). Practice with female-to-male transgendered youth. *Journal of Gay and Lesbian Social Services* 10(3/4), 65–82.

Riseley, D. (1986). Gender identity disorder of childhood: Diagnostic and treatment issues. In W. A. W. Walters and M. W. Ross (Eds.) *Transsexualism and Sex Reassignment*. New York: Oxford University Press.

Rodgers, L. L. (1997). Transgendered youth fact sheet. Transgender protocol: Treatment services guidelines for substance abuse treatment providers (2nd ed.). Unpublished report, Transgender Protocol Team of the San Francisco Lesbian, Gay, Bisexual, Transgender Substance Abuse Advisory Committee.

Ryan, C. and Futterman, D. (1998). *Lesbian and Gay Youth: Care and Counseling*. New York: Columbia University Press.

Schriver, J. M. (1995). *Human Behavior in the Social Environment: Shifting Paradigms in Essential Knowledge for Social Work Practice*. Boston: Allyn and Bacon.

Steiner, B. W. (Ed.) (1985). *Gender Dysphoria: Development, Research, Management*. New York: Plenum Press.

Valentine, D. (2007). *Imagining Transgender: An Ethnography of a Category*. Durham, NC: Duke University Press.

Wicks, L. K. (1977). Transsexualism: A social work approach. *Health and Social Work 2*(1), 180–193.

Wilchins, R. A. (1997). *Read My Lips: Sexual Subversion and the End of Gender*. Ithaca, NY: Firebrand Books.

Wilson, K. (1997). *Do Cross-gender Expression and Identity Constitute Mental Illness?* Retrieved on May 25, 2008 from the World Wide Web: http://www.transgender.org/tg/gic/awptext.html#intro.

Zastrow, C. and Kirst-Ashman, K. K. (1995). *Understanding Human Behavior and the Social Environment* (3rd ed.). Chicago: Nelson-Hall.

Zucker, K. J. (1985). Cross-gender identified children. In B. W. Steiner (Ed.) *Gender Dysphoria: Development, Research and Management*. New York: Plenum Press.

Chapter 4

Social work practice with transgender and gender variant children and youth

Gerald P. Mallon and Teresa DeCrescenzo

Introduction

The film *Ma Vie en Rose* (My Life in Pink) (Berliner and Scotta, 1997) is a story about the innocence of childhood as told through the experiences of a 7-year-old boy, Ludovic. Ludovic desperately wants to be a girl, and everything about him says that he already is one. He has it all figured out: God messed up his chromosomes, simple as that – no judgment, no morality. Ludovic is a representative example of a child with a female brain in a male body, and he is putting up a valiant struggle not to be erased as a person. It's all very honest and natural to him. He is only a small boy and is much more in tune with his needs and desires than is his family.

Ludovic, born to a middle-class, suburban family, is very much like other children except in one key way: he is sure that he was meant to be a little girl, not a little boy – and he waits for a miracle to "correct" this mistake. Whenever able, he dresses in typical girl outfits, grows long hair, and is certain of his gender identity despite the fact that others are less sure. His parents, while tolerant of his gender nonconforming behaviors, are embarrassed by his insistence that he is a girl rather than a boy. His siblings, although loving their "brother" in their home, are tired of having to fight for him in school, where he is teased and harassed. Even though everyone else is unsure, Ludovic muddles along, praying for the miracle that will change him into the girl he knows he is. Everything falls apart, however, when he falls in love with a boy who happens to be the son of his father's boss, a man who is uncomfortable in his own skin.

When Ludo's father is fired from his job because his boss cannot abide Ludovic's crush on his son, Ludovic's mother increasingly blames his gender nonconforming dress and behavior for the family's estrangement from their community. The gender variant behavior that was once tolerated is now unsupportable: Ludovic's hair is cut into a typical boy's style, he is forced to wear traditional boy's clothing, he is brought to therapy, and he is encouraged to play sports and to be more like his brothers – all "corrective" actions designed to make him to be more like a boy, to make him "fit in," by force if necessary.

Ostracized by his schoolmates, misunderstood by his family, and eventually run out of town by bigoted neighbors, Ludovic accepts that he cannot be the boy his family want him to be. In a desperate attempt to break away from his life, Ludo tries to commit suicide, at which point his family realize that in spite of what their community thinks, Ludovic should be accepted for who he really is. The final lines in the film are "Do whatever feels best. Whatever happens, you'll always be my child. Our child." These are words that every transgender child longs to hear from his or her parent.

Ah, if life could just be as simple as it is in the movies... Although *Ma Vie en Rose* is a powerful story of a gender variant child who struggles to be accepted by his family, and finally is, contemporary real-life childhood remains a very difficult period for gender variant children or youth and their parents, as well as other family members. Virtually no social supports exist in any US child welfare or educational institutions for children or youth who are gender variant. Parents who attempt to negotiate a fair accommodation for the gender variant child can expect to be met with misunderstanding, incredulity, and resistance, even hostility, from almost everyone they encounter. "Help that child be more like a boy, get him into sports!" and "Don't let that girl be too much of a tomboy" are among the kinder things that families and gender variant young people are likely to hear.

In such a hostile environment, blaming the child for their failure to adapt to traditional gender norms is easy. Often the gender variant child will respond to such a poor fit with symptoms of depression, anxiety, fear, anger, low self-esteem, self-mutilation, and suicidal ideation. Unfortunately, these at-risk behaviors are often taken as further evidence that something is wrong with the child, rather than that they are normal responses to attempts to accommodate oneself to a hostile environment.

Instead of putting the focus on the systems that will not allow gender variant children to develop in their own natural way, "treatment" approaches usually focus on the child's "maladaptive" gender identity, and attempts are frequently targeted on "corrective" actions.

Using an ecological frame to discuss the cases in this chapter (Germain, 1973, 1978, 1981), the existing literature, available research, and the authors' own combined 60 years of clinical practice with children, youth, and families, this chapter examines gender variant childhood development from a holistic perspective, where children and youth and their environments are understood as a unit, in the context of their relationship to one another (Germain, 1991). As such, the authors' goal is to examine the primary reciprocal exchanges and transactions transgender young people face as they confront the unique person, and the environmental tasks involved in being a gender variant or atypical child or youth in a society that assumes (and expects) all of its members to fit within certain pro-scribed behavioral parameters – in other words, to be gender typical. The focus of this chapter is limited to a discussion of the recognition of gender identity; an examination of the adaptation process that gender variant children and youth go through to deal with the stress of an environment where there is not a "goodness of fit," and consideration of the overall developmental tasks of a transgender childhood or adolescence. Recommendations for competent child welfare practice with gender variant children and youth are presented in the conclusion to the chapter.

Gender identity development in children

As of this writing, most demographic information about transgender children and adolescents is derived from research conducted by specialized clinics in Toronto, England, and The Netherlands (Bradley and Zucker, 1990; Cohen, de Ruiter, Ringelberg, and Cohen-Kettenis, 1997; Zucker, 2004). As there is no empirical data to support generalizations about gender-variant children or adolescents, we will focus our discussion on clinical issues in this client population, that we believe have implications for clinical assessment, care planning, and treatment.

Although it is a commonly accepted fact that gender identity develops in children by the age of 3, when most identify themselves as either boys or girls (Bailey and Zucker, 1995; Cohen-Kettenis and Pfafflin, 2003; Fausto-Sterling, 1999: Fast, 1993; Green, 1971, 1974; Kohlberg, 1966; Langer and Martin, 2004; Meyer-Bahlburg, 1985; Money, 1973; Stoller, 1965, 1968), American society steadfastly refuses to believe that children have sexuality. Because people widely assume that a "natural" relationship exists between sex and gender, children who question their birth-assigned gender are pathologized and labeled "gender dysphoric." Children who deviate from the socially prescribed behavioral norms for boy or girl children are quickly corrected, pushed back in line by parental figures, and urged to conform to gender-typical behaviors. Behaviors, mannerisms, and play that appear to be gender nonconforming to a parent may feel perfectly normal to the child. Although gender nonconforming behavior alone does not necessarily indicate that a child is transgender, Western society continues to reward parents who socialize their children to gender-bound roles. The male child who wants a Barbie, the female child who plays baseball "like a boy," the boy child who carries his books "like a girl," the girl who states that she feels uncomfortable in a dress are examples of children who express gender variant mannerisms and behaviors that are natural for them.

Like the child Ludo in *Ma Vie en Rose,* the gender variant child might wonder what is so "bad" about their behavior, what it is that upsets parental figures. Because most children desire to please parental figures, many gender variant children unsurprisingly go to great extremes to alter their "gender nonconforming" behaviors once they are pointed out. Other children – those who cannot change or refuse to change – are treated and judged much more harshly by a society that insists on adherence to strict gender behavioral norms. Children who are forced to comply with social stereotypes may develop behavioral problems that can lead to depression and other serious mental health issues, caused not by their gender variant nature, but by society's (and often their own parents') non-acceptance of them. For an excellent discussion of one trans child's experience in a family see Rosin's (2008) article. In fact, as Israel and Tarver (1997) point out, as a result of being prevented from exploring their gender identity as a child, these children frequently, and ironically, become examples of the very stereotype the parent had hoped to prevent – a gender-conflicted adult.

Incidence of gender variant children and youth

Transgender youths may identify their sexual orientation – that is, to whom they are romantically and sexually attracted – as gay, lesbian, bisexual, questioning, straight, or by some other label; one's sexual orientation is different from, and not determined by, one's gender identity. Transgender youths are highly diverse in terms of sexual orientation as well as in terms of gender identification and presentation, race, age, religion, disability, nationality, language, and class background.

The term "gender identity disorder" (GID) first appeared in the American Psychological Association's *DSM*-III in 1980. GID is described as "incongruence between assigned sex [that is, the sex recorded on the birth certificate] and gender identity." *DSM*-III went on to describe a broad range of gender variant behaviors that may be observed in individuals, and resolutely indicated that "in the vast majority of cases the onset of the disorder can be traced back to childhood." Somewhat incongruously, GID is considered to be a disorder even though "some of these children, particularly girls, show no other signs of psychopathology" (APA, 1980).

The introduction of GID in children in the *DSM* came as the result of federally funded experiments on gender variant boys that took place in the 1970s. These studies found that very few "feminine" boys went on to become transsexuals, but that a high percentage of them (one-half to two-thirds) became gay (Burke, 1996). GID was added to the *DSM*-III following the removal of homosexuality as an illness from that volume (Bern, 1993). Treatment, which was justified in the name of preventing transsexualism, focuses instead on modifying gender variant behavior and may be easily used covertly to "treat", perhaps even prevent, emergent lesbian or gay identity.

Children are particularly vulnerable to medical and mental health injustices in the name of treating GID. As minors, children have no legal standing to make an informed choice to refuse "treatment." The criteria for a diagnosis of GID in children may be overly broad, taking into account all cross-gender behavior. In boys, GID is manifest by a marked preoccupation with traditionally feminine activities: playing house, drawing pictures of beautiful girls and princesses, playing with dolls such as Barbie, playing dress-up, and having girls as playmates. Girls diagnosed with GID display intense negative reactions to parental attempts to have them wear dresses or other feminine attire. By addressing this issue from an ecosystems perspective, social workers can provide parents with a broader focus and expertise than might be provided by other helping professionals.

Given the extent of medical, cultural, and social misunderstanding that gender variant children endure, many, unsurprisingly, will become socially isolated and depressed, and suffer from self-esteem problems. Children who are diagnosed with GID often are treated with brutal aversion therapies intended to adjust or "correct" their gender orientation (Burke, 1996; Langer and Martin, 2004; Scholinski, 1997).

Boys and girls diagnosed with gender identity disorder, as described by Zucker and Bradley (1995), display an array of sex-typed behavior signaling a strong psychological identification with the opposite gender. These behaviors include identity statements, dress-up play, toy play, role play, peer relations, motoric and speech characteristics, statements about sexual anatomy, and involvement in rough-and-tumble play. Signs of distress and discomfort about their status as male or female also occur. These behaviors, note Zucker and Bradley (1995), occur in concert, not in isolation. The following case examples are illustrative of the behaviors that Zucker and Bradley discuss:

The case of Brian

Brian is an 8-year-old African-American boy of average intelligence who was referred by his counselor at an after-school program. Brian lived with his parents, who had a middle-class socioeconomic background, and his younger brother. His parents had noted cross-gender behavior since Brian was aged 2. He presents as a small, slightly built child with longish dark hair.

Brian preferred girls as playmates, and since the age of 2 has enjoyed cross-dressing both at home and in school. He had stereotypical girl toy preferences, including a purse, a Barbie, and jewelry. He sometimes spoke in a high-pitched voice and talked of wanting to marry a boy when he grew up. Brian avoided rough play and sometimes verbally stated that he wished that he did not have a penis because he was a girl, not a boy, and girls did not have penises.

The case of Betsy

Betsy is a 9-year-old girl with an IQ of 105 who was referred at her mother's request. Her parents are of working-class socioeconomic background. Betsy's father was concerned about his daughter's gender nonconforming behavior; her mother was less concerned, but agreed to have her evaluated to appease her husband.

Betsy wore jeans and a white T-shirt with a hooded sweatshirt, which she hid behind for the first half of the interview. When she became more comfortable, she allowed the hood to fall and the interviewer noted that her hair was short and styled in a fashion more characteristic of a boy's haircut. She said people frequently mistook her for a boy, particularly if she was in the girl's rest room.

When Betsy was 3, her mother reported that she steadfastly refused to wear a dress, and in fact would throw a temper tantrum when asked to do so. Betsy reported that she hated dresses and preferred to be free to dress as she pleased.

Betsy preferred boys as play partners, engaged in baseball, hockey, and other outdoor sports, and spoke openly about wishing that she were a boy, not a girl. In fact, Betsy spoke openly about having "the operation" to become a boy when she was older. When asked to draw a picture of herself, she drew a boy with bulging muscles, which she indicated looked like her hero, "The Rock," of professional wrestling fame.

Although some may view the conditions of Betsy and Brian through a lens of pathology, others who approach practice from a trans-affirming perspective might ask, "Why can't Betsy construct her identity to be male as she sees it, and how can it be so terrible if Brian envisions himself as a girl?" The larger question is: Why are gender variant children so disturbing to people, especially to parents and frequently to counselors, psychologists, and child welfare professionals?

Transgender development for youth

The issues of gender dysphoria for trans adolescents are different from those of trans children. Over time, the pervasive societal stigmatization and pathologization of trans youth allows the low self-esteem of these young people to incubate, eventually growing into the internalized self-hatred of many transgender adults.

Family issues

Coming out as transgender may be challenging for everyone. Some male or female teenagers who cross-dress (which may have nothing to do with being transgender) may do so in secret, never telling their families and friends about it. As adults, some may continue to keep their cross-dressing private, sometimes seeking approval through transgender support groups (see Rosenberg, 2002) and, most likely, in Internet communities. Those who disclose their trans identity to their families may experience a variety of reactions ranging from loving acceptance to complete rejection.

If an adolescent's cross-dressing is discovered by his or her parents, it is likely to precipitate an emotional crisis for the entire family. A female-to-male's "cross-dressing" may be disguised as a "tomboy" phase that a daughter stubbornly refuses to grow out of, causing friction within the family only later. If a youth is intent on gender transition, however, major changes are ahead for the entire family. Being "out" about one's sexual orientation is usually a matter of choice for some gay sons and lesbian daughters, but rarely so for those who are entering a gender transition, because gender and gender presentation are so visible. Moreover, the changes arising from gender transition will be much more profound than just physical appearances, including changes in physical appearance, as well as emotional and hormonal changes.

While an increasing number of parents are acknowledging their child's gender struggle, most trans youth may try to keep their gender issues secret until they cannot hold them back any longer. For this cohort, their revelation takes most parents by surprise. Mothers and fathers of these kids then must deal not only with shock, denial, anger, grief, misplaced guilt, and shame, but also with many real concerns about the safety, health, surgery, employment, and potential future love relationships of their child. In addition, the family system must learn to call their family member by a new name, and, even more difficult, begin to use new pronouns.

Psychological issues and risks

When a trans youth comes out, the ability to pass in their new gender is usually limited; development of a sense of "realness" is a very important issue for most trans youth. Realness is not only about passing (being perceived as real), but also about feeling real inside. Hormonal therapy, a very controversial area, especially in child welfare systems, can take years to produce a passable appearance and may have some health risks as well.

Trans youth often feel that their true gender identity is crucial to the survival of self. If their parents refuse to permit their gender transition, or if their families and friends withhold support, these youths may encounter the same risks as those faced by gay and lesbian youth with non-accepting families (Burgess, 1998). Some may run away from home and live on the streets, or they may seek to escape the pain of their lives through abusing substances. Like gay and lesbian youth, trans youth also are at significantly higher risk for suicide than the average American teen.

Because of severe employment discrimination, transgender youth who are homeless, runaways, or throwaways may need to find work in the sex industry in order to survive and pay for their hormones, electrolysis, cosmetic surgery, and gender reassignment surgery. These youth, therefore, are at increased risk for HIV/AIDS and other sexually transmitted diseases, and they should be referred to understanding, compassionate, trans-friendly healthcare providers for evaluation and treatment. Female-to-male youth may resort to con games or other marginal means to support themselves (Klein, 1998).

Ingesting or injecting street hormones or high-dose hormones without medical supervision also is commonplace and may result in lethal complications. Hormonal sex reassignment can be safely done only under the supervision of an experienced endocrinologist following the Harry Benjamin *Standards of Care* (Harry Benjamin International Gender Dysphoria Association, 2001). Some trans youth who are impatient with the slow pace of hormonal sex reassignment may seek silicone injections to improve their body shape immediately and may experiment with androgen blockers or other substances, which may prove to have some health risks later in life (Wren, 2000). Often, trans youth in the child welfare system, frustrated with that system's slowness and reluctance to arrange for hormonal treatments, buy "street hormones" as a group, and have "pump parties" where they inject large amounts of hormones and/or whatever else is in the syringes they buy. This behavior is often labeled by law enforcement and child protective workers as "acting out," when it is actually adaptive behavior on the part of youth who desperately want to be, and feel, "real."

Referral for hormonal and surgical sex reassignment

Trans youth may go to extraordinary lengths to obtain relief from their gender dysphoria (see Dreifus, 2005, for a thorough discussion of this topic). The compelling need to modify the body to conform to one's gender identity cannot be adequately explained by someone who is transgender, nor can it be fully understood by someone who is not (see Israel and Tarver, 1997, for a complete discussion of this area). This self-perceived need becomes a determined drive, a desperate search for relief and release from one's own body. The urgency itself cannot be easily understood (see Pazos, 1998, for a discussion of female-to-male transition, and Glenn, 1998, for a discussion of the male-to-female transition). Trans youth face an urgent need to match their external appearance with their internal feelings, in order to achieve harmony of spirit and shape, of body and soul.

Although parents and child welfare professionals may be alarmed by a young person's desire for physical transition, it is important that they recognize the intensity fueling that desire. Referral to a psychotherapist or social worker experienced in trans issues who can conduct a proper assessment and arrive at a correct diagnosis is the key first step.

Is GID in childhood or adolescence really a disorder?

From a strictly diagnostic perspective, if the young person meets the criteria as established for GID in childhood in *DSM*-IV (APA, 1994), it is not difficult to make a diagnosis. Based on the sketchy history of this diagnostic category, however, one must also consider whether or not GID is really a disorder. One of the criteria for a disorder is whether or not the person diagnosed is distressed by their condition. Are gender variant young people distressed by their condition, and, if so, what is the source of their distress? Or do they become distressed when they are told that they cannot be what they are sure they are? Or are they distressed because of the social ostracism they must endure?

In our own clinical experiences with transgender children and adolescents, young people have been more harmed than helped by clinicians who insist on "correcting" the gender variant child by attempting to make them more gender conforming. One needs only to read the superb memoir of Scholinski (1997), the powerful work of Feinberg (1993), or the compelling story by Colapinto (2001) to see that these attempts to "correct" for gender variance fail miserably. Professionals are directed to the work of Bartlett *et al.* (2000) and Langer and Martin (2004) as well, for a thorough discussion of this debate. With true transgender young people (and yes, for some young people, this is not a genuine gender identity issue but a phase of development), no treatment program, no residential program, no child welfare program, no group therapy, no aversion treatment plan can change who they are.

More often than not, the authors have seen parents who are greatly distressed by their gender variant child. Even mild, typical gender nonconformity sends terror into the hearts of most parents. One student who was a mother panicked when her 6-year-old son asked for an "Easy-Bake Oven." "What's so scary," the professor (Gerald P. Mallon) asked? "It's a girl toy, what do you think I should do?" "Buy the oven, if you can afford it," answered Mallon, "and then in a couple weeks your child will either enjoy it as his favorite toy, or cast it aside when the next new toy arrives."

Such advice provides no solace for other parents. They are embarrassed, guilty, ashamed, and fearful that somehow their parenting is to blame for what "went wrong," as the following case illustrates:

The case of Jon

Jon was a 13-year-old American-born Trinidadian child referred by his great-grandmother's Medicaid social worker. Jon was of average intelligence. His family background was working class socioeconomically; the family lived in a housing project in Manhattan. On the day of the interview, Jon arrived for the interview dressed in boy's clothing, but with a very clear "girl" hairstyle. His great-grandmother, who was his primary caretaker and 85 years old, accompanied Jon. An obvious warm and affectionate relationship existed between the two, although some negative feelings also existed because of Jon's insistence that he was a girl. Jon's great-grandmother explained that it was causing her great distress that Jon was insisting that he was a girl. She feared losing her standing in the community because neighbors were beginning to ask her what she had done to make the child "that way." She was embarrassed by Jon's cross-dressing, by his insistence on being called by his preferred name "Simone," and by other gender nonconforming mannerisms and behaviors. Jon simply said, "I can't be what I am not, and I am not a boy." Jon's great-grandmother said to the interviewer, "Mister, I have one question for you. Can you change him back?" When I replied, "No," she responded, "Then you can keep him."

As she got up to leave, the interviewer stopped her and explained that she could not leave her great-grandson with him. Then they explored the possibility of family supports for her and her great-grandson and discussed the possibility of out-of-home placement options. Both of these prospects were quite dismal; transgender children and youth are not accepted easily in child welfare agencies, nor are there many competent practitioners in the field. After some discussion, the great-grandmother agreed that he could stay at home with her, but they settled on a treatment plan that included some compromises for both her and her grandson. It was not an ideal plan, but it was a better scheme than an out-of-home placement.

Transgender children and their families

Although some transgender children and youth are healthy and resilient, many gender variant children are at great risk within their family system and within institutional structures (Cooper, 1998). Gender variant children and youth, because they are told that they do not fit in, are in a constant search for an affirming environment where they can be themselves. In the search for this situation, many transgender youth are at risk for the associated symptomology of depression, anxiety, self-abuse, substance abuse, suicide, and family violence. In their desperate search for affirmation, they often place themselves in risky environments, such as public venues where adults congregate seeking sexual contacts.

Parents seeking to find answers may seek to have their transgender child "cured" through punishment, physical violence, or endless mental health assessments. Transgender young people may be locked in their rooms, forced to wear their hair in gender-typical styles or dress in gender-typical clothing, and denied opportunities to socialize. Transgender young people, as in the filmic story of Ludovic, are viewed as the "problem" in the family. Such classification leads the family to scapegoat them, such that they become the reason for everything that goes wrong. Families may begin to project their anxieties about other family conflicts on the transgender child as a way of avoiding confronting the real issues.

Some transgender children and youth are shipped away to behavioral camps, psychiatric hospitals, or residential treatment facilities, where rigidly enforced gender conformity further represses their needs and does more harm than good. In the authors' combined 60 years of experience in child welfare, we rarely have come across a mental health professional or social worker who is knowledgeable and proficient about working with a transgender child in an affirming manner. Most do not understand the condition, and few have ever had training to prepare them for competent practice with transgender children and youth. At present, very few gender-specialized services exist in mental health and child welfare systems across the country, with Green Chimneys in New York and GLASS (Gay and Lesbian Adolescent Social Services) in Los Angeles as two exceptions.

Regrettably, most schools of social work are not preparing practitioners to respond to the needs of this population. In his recent research, Brooks (2005) makes some important suggestions for integrating content on trans youth into existing social work curricula. Utilizing trans persons in case examples in human behavior and clinical casework classes, and utilizing social work literature that addresses trans issues in classes, are two ways in which social work educators can assist students in deepening their knowledge of this population. As with other populations, contemporary social work interventions focus on empowerment and resiliency, and approach treatment assessment and planning from a strengths-based perspective.

Israel and Tarver (1997, pp. 134–135) observe:

> As there are no treatment models for curing transgender feelings, needs and behaviors, one is left to wonder what types of treatment transgender children and youth endure at the hands of parents and professionals. Such treatment approaches are little more than abuse, professional victimization, and profiteering under the guise of support for a parent's goals.

Minter (1999) and Haldeman (2000), however, offer trans-affirming perspectives of diagnosis and treatment, as well as providing a thorough examination of the clinical and social issues affecting trans youth. Such guidance is welcome where affirming literature on this topic is scarce.

Many parents are surprised initially when they hear a trans-affirming professional state that compromise is the best approach to supporting young people who have strong transgender feelings and need. After all, don't parents always know what is best for their children? To judge by the high incidence of familial abuse (both verbal and physical) toward transgender children that we, the authors, have witnessed, we would have to answer "no"; parents do not have the training or preparation for dealing with a transgender child. Recommendations for parents are presented in the conclusion to this chapter.

Transgender young people in educational settings

Educational settings, unfortunately, are among the least affirming environments for gender variant young people. School officials who perceive children and adolescents as gender variant target them as individuals to be closely monitored for "acting out" behaviors. In their riveting film *Out in the Cold*, Criswell and Bedogne (2002) document the extent to which gender-atypical youth are rejected by families and the institutions they were raised to believe in, especially school.

Gender variant boys will likely be mercilessly teased for not being rough-and-tumble. It might be assumed that they are gay by ill-informed adults, and some such boys are moved toward what the authors term "the sports corrective." They are pushed into organized sports teams, as if participation in such activities will correct their gender nonconformity. During the 1970s and beyond, the National Institutes for Mental Health funded programs in New York and in Los Angeles, aimed at "curing" GID, also often called "pre-homosexuality." At UCLA, the government-supported, federally funded Feminine Boy Project used behavioral techniques to get "sissy boys" to engage in more "appropriate" masculine behaviors. Parents were involved and trained by staff in techniques to reinforce and "cue" gender-appropriate behaviors. A close review of the case histories is chilling.

Gender variant girls are also verbally harassed for being too much like a boy and not enough like a girl. Although many girls seldom wear dresses nowadays, gender variant girls are almost always confronted by both peers and adults who try to enroll them in what the authors term "the etiquette corrective." Turn them from tomboys into ladies and everything will be all right. It seldom, if ever, works for them, and only adds to the pain and the self-blame, as this vignette from Scholinski (1997, p. 6) illustrates:

Pinning me to the ground, the girls at school forced red lipstick onto my mouth... the social worker with the pointy high heels said I was wrecking the family and that if I kept things up the way they were going, with my bad behavior getting all of the attention, my parents were going to lose my sister too. I knew I was bad, I wasn't crazy though.

Confusing gender variant young people with gay or lesbian young people

Gender variant young people frequently have been confused with youth who are gay or lesbian. In fact, many of the same diagnostic criteria used to justify a diagnosis of GID are also supposed "cues" to a gay or lesbian identity. In some contexts, GID is specifically referred to as "pre-homosexuality." Some gay boys play with girls, enjoy girl toys, have effeminate mannerisms, and avoid rough-and-tumble play. Some young lesbians enjoy playing with the boys, play sports and games associated with boys, possess mannerisms and speech associated with boys, and dress in typical boy clothing. The biggest difference, and a critical one, is that gay boys and lesbian girls generally do not express dissatisfaction with their gender – that is, their sense of maleness or femaleness. In some cases, children with limited information about their emerging gay or lesbian identity may speak about *wishing* that they were a boy or a girl, but seldom do they state that they *are* a boy or a girl. The following case illustration represents an example of this misperception:

The case of Damond

Damond is a 10-year-old Latino child who was referred because his therapist felt inadequate in treating what he described as a transgender child. Damond lives with his mother, her second husband, a younger sister, and an older brother in a two-bedroom, middle-income housing project in Brooklyn, New York. An MSW therapist at a community mental health clinic sees both Damond and his mother. Damond is bright, very verbal, and precocious.

The interview, which consisted of Damond, his therapist, his mother, and me [the interviewer], began with a series of questions initiated by Damond. Who was I? Was I a doctor? Why was I interested in seeing him? I answered directly and honestly and then proceeded with my own questions. First, given that he was a bright child, what were his career ambitions? He asked whether he could draw his answer and on his own pad of paper that he had with him. He drew a naked boy.

When I asked what his drawing represented, he informed me that he wanted to be the first nude male dancer. He suggested that if he were a naked dancer, then boys would like him. He then went on to explain that first he would need "the operation" because the only way he could get boys to like him was if he was a girl.

He then asked if he could share a secret with me, and when I agreed, he wrote on another piece of paper, "I AM GAY." He also inquired as to whether or not I was gay, and then whether or not his therapist was gay. We all answered. He also was clear, when probed, that he did not see himself as a girl, but felt that to get boys to like him, he needed to become a girl and for that he would have to have "the operation."

On the basis of this interview, this child did not seem to be transgender, but rather a child who may be gay and in need of some accurate information about sexual identity development. I also sensed that there might be some issues of sexual abuse occurring in the household, such as when I inquired about his older brother and his stepfather. He replied with responses that required further exploration, but that was not the purpose of the interview, so I passed that insight along to the child's therapist. We do not mean to imply, nor do we infer in any way, that gender identity development or sexual identity development are influenced by sexual abuse; these are separate treatment issues and should be treated as such.

In this case, Damond most likely was not transgender, because he seemed comfortable in his gender identity and self-identified as gay in his sexual identity. Other cases may not be always so clear. It is just as important that transgender children and youth are not mislabeled as gay or lesbian, although they frequently self-label as such prior to coming to a full understanding of their transgendered nature. Similarly, gay and lesbian young people must not be mislabeled as transgender. Coming to understand the childhood experiences of transgender persons is a complex phenomenon that requires specialized training and supervision from a trained and skilled transaffirming social worker. Practitioners who listen carefully to the narratives of their young clients and who do not permit their own negative judgments about transgender persons to misguide them are the most effective, and appropriately neutral. The following section provides further recommendations for child welfare practice with transgender children, youth, and their parents.

Implications for practice

Professional workers who are unfamiliar with transgender young people's issues need guidance about how to proceed. The following recommendations provide a foundation for practitioners interested in enhancing their practice with transgender children, youth, and their parents.

1   Social work professionals should begin by educating themselves about transgender children and youth. Practitioners should not wait until they have a transgender young person in their office to seek out information. Books, especially those written by transgender persons (several of which have been identified in this chapter), are extremely useful ways of gathering information about transgender persons. Films that portray transgender persons through a non-pathological lens, most specifically *Ma Vie en Rose,* the brutal but true story of Brandon Teena in *Boys Don't Cry*, and the 2005 release *TransAmerica* – all of which are available in video stores – can be extremely informative and enlightening. Professional articles in print journals also can be educative. The plethora of Internet resources provides a rich array of resources and information. One should be cautious in exploring Internet resources, as some may be misinformed, misguided, or even exploitative in nature. As bibliotherapy has been proven to be useful with clients, many of these materials – print, video, and virtual – also can be shared with clients to increase their information and knowledge.

2   Social work professionals must assist parents in resisting outright electroshock, reparative, or aversion-type treatments. There is never a justification for using these approaches to "treat" gender variance or gender identity disorder. These are unethical and dangerous practices, and inappropriate interventions to use. Residential programs that offer to turn trans children into "normal" children should be avoided because they do more harm than good. Most of them have been disavowed by major professional organizations, including but not limited to the American Psychiatric and Psychology Associations, the National Association of Social Workers, and the American Association of Marriage and Family Therapists.

3   Treatments for depression and associated conditions should not attempt to enforce gender-stereotypical behavior and should focus on practice from a trans-affirming perspective. Rather, they should focus on helping the clients to get at, and eliminate, the depression or other condition. In these situations, it is always important to assess what part systemic reactions – those of parents, schools, churches, peer groups, etc. – play in contributing to the presenting depression. Often, when the systems change, the depression lessens.

4   Child welfare professionals should assist parents in developing mutually acceptable compromise strategies, which can include asking the gender variant child to dress in original-gender clothing for formal events such as weddings, but permitting the child to dress androgynously for school and peer activities. Young people who insist on using opposite-gendered names can be encouraged to adopt an androgynous name until they are old enough to be certain what name they want to take on a permanent basis.

5   Parents and young people must work with practitioners to keep communication open (Crawford, 2004). All young people, irrespective of gender issues, need love, acceptance, and compassion from their families. These are among the things they fear losing the most. Children and youth need to be reminded that their parents' love for them is unconditional.

6   Practitioners need to be able to identify resources for trans children, youth, and families in the community, or be willing to take the risks necessary to create them (Minter, 2002).

7   Transgender children and youth should be assisted with developing strategies for dealing with societal stigmatization, name calling, and discrimination.

In completing an assessment of a transgender child, child welfare professionals should be familiar with the criteria in *DSM*-IV for GID; be comfortable with discerning the differences between a gay, lesbian, bisexual, or questioning child, and a transgender child; and use a modified version of Israel and Tarver's (1997) Gender Identity Profile. The Transgender Health Program in Vancouver, British Columbia, has also provided a very comprehensive and well-written set of guidelines for the clinical management of gender dysphasia in adolescents (de Vries *et al.*, 2006). A companion publication from this same organization entitled "Ethical, legal, and psychosocial issues in care of transgender adolescents" (White Holman and Goldberg, 2006) should be very useful reading for all social workers. The authors of this chapter however wish to acknowledge a new and wonderful resource by Brill and Pepper (2008). The Transgender child: A handbook for families and professionals is a groundbreaking work which uses a combination of available research and practice wisdom to guide and educate both professionals and families. Although Brill and Pepper's (2008) resource is a great addition to the available literature on this topic, further work is needed to gain a complete picture of the clinical concerns of gender-variant children and adolescents throughout the US particularly in rural and remote settings.

8   Although Pleak (1999) and Raj (2002) provide more current models, professionals also may find relevance in reading the works of Rekers (1977, 1988) and Rekers *et al.* (1977) on this topic.

9 The decision-making process for any gender procedure must include consideration of the critical factors of age, maturity, and physical development. Hormone administration and gender reassignment surgery, which should always be conducted under the supervision of a qualified medical doctor who specializes in gender reassignment procedures, are not advised during childhood or adolescence. The recommended standard is for the transgender person to wait five years beyond achieving age 18 before submitting to complete surgical gender reassignment surgery.

10 Practitioners should be aware that transgender young people are part of every culture, race, religion, class, and experience. Transgender young people of color and their families face compounded stressors resulting from transgenderphobia and racism, and may need additional emotional and social support, as well as legal redress of discrimination.

11 Practitioners should make sure that all individual, self-help, family, and group treatment approaches are appropriate for intervening with a transgender child and his or her family (Benestad, 2001; Swann and Herbert, 1998).

12 Practitioners must be aware of the possibility that violence both within and outside of the child's family might be directed toward the transgender child. Sexual violence, including rape, is also prevalent, and the practitioner should closely monitor the safety of the youth.

13 Practitioners must be ready to respond and reach out to siblings, grandparents, and other relatives of the transgender child to provide education, information, and support.

14 Practitioners should help parents understand that the gender variant child's behaviors and mannerisms are natural to that child.

15 Practitioners should help parents to develop a strategy and sometimes a script for addressing the questions neighbors and members of the community may have about their transgender child.

16 Schools, social service, child welfare systems, mental health systems, religious institutions all are likely to encounter gender variant youth. These organizations and the individuals who work within them need to identify consultants to act as trans-affirming professional guides and provide in-service training to assist them with the process of becoming trans-affirming systems. These systems must set about trans-forming their organizational cultures to include sensitive and welcoming services for all children, youth, and families (Mallon, 1998a). Child welfare systems that are residential in nature and may have unique issues will need specialized training to care for transgender children, youth, and their families.

17 Child welfare organizations and state-level policy makers must develop clear, written policies about hormone use for trans youth in

their care. In most states, if a person is over 18 he or she may consent to his or her own medical or mental health treatment. In the absence of clearly stated policies, however, trans youth may use a variety of approaches, including injectable hormones, usually obtained illegally on the street and used without medical supervision: androgen blockers to stop the development of secondary sexual characteristics (see Cohen-Kettenis and Van Goozen, 1998); in some cases even Wesson Oil has been injected to create feminine-looking hips; and, in other cases, irreversible surgical procedures to alter their appearance (see Smith *et al.*, 2002). Child welfare policy makers, with consultation from professionals in their field, must struggle to develop these guidelines in-house (see DeCrescenzo and Mallon, 2002). Failure to do so will result in youth developing their own very individualistic policies and, most likely, may cause litigation for the state.

18 Gay, lesbian, bisexual, and questioning youth providers must also work to respond to the unique needs of transgender young people (Lev, 2004; Mallon, 1998b). Most lesbian, gay, and bisexual organizations solely meet the needs of lesbian, gay and bisexual teens and young adults; services for trans youth and younger trans youth should also be explored.

19 Practitioners must accept the reality that not everyone can provide validation for a transgender child or teen. Some will simply not be able to understand the turmoil and pain transgender children and youth experience (see Brooks, 2000). In these instances, practitioners must be prepared to advocate vigorously on behalf of these youths.

Conclusions

The authors cannot imagine a better way to conclude this chapter than to pay homage to the powerful words of Leslie Feinberg (1993, p. 116), transgendered activist, who knows firsthand the pain that accompanies the life of a transgender child:

> I didn't want to be different. I longed to be everything grownups wanted, so they would love me. I followed their rules, tried my best to please. But there was something about me that made them knit their eyebrows and frown. No one ever offered me a name for what was wrong with me. That's what made me afraid it was really bad. I only came to recognize its melody through its constant refrain: "Is it a boy or a girl?"
>
> "I'm sick of people asking me if she's a boy or a girl," I overheard my mother complain to my father. "Everywhere I take her, people ask me."

I was ten years old. I was no longer a little kid and I didn't have a sliver of cuteness to hide behind. The world's patience with me was fraying, and it panicked me. When I was really small I thought I would do anything to change whatever was wrong with me. Now I didn't want to change, I just wanted people to stop being mad at me all the time.

References

American Psychological Association (1980). *Diagnostic and Statistical Manual of Mental Disorders* (3rd ed.) (*DSM*-III). Washington, DC: APA.

American Psychological Association (1994). *Diagnostic and Statistical Manual of Mental Disorders* (4th ed.) (*DSM*-IV). Washington, DC: APA.

Bailey, J. M. and Zucker, K. J. (1995). Childhood sex-typed behavior and sexual orientation: A conceptual analysis and quantitative review. *Developmental Psychology 31*(1), 43–55.

Bartlett, N. H., Vasey, P. L., and Bukowski, W. M. (2000). Is gender identity disorder in children a mental disorder? *Sex Roles 43*(11/12), 753–785.

Benestad, E. E. P. (2001). Gender belonging: Children, adolescents, adults, and the role of the therapist. *Gecko 1*(2), 58–80.

Berliner, A. (director, cowriter) and Scotta, C. (producer) (1997). *Ma Vie en Rose* [film]. Available from Sony Classics, Los Angeles.

Bern, S. L. (1993). *The Lenses of Gender*. New Haven, CT: Yale University Press.

Bradley, S. J. and Zucker, K. J. (1990). Gender identity disorder and psychosexual problems in children and adolescents. *Canadian Journal of Psychiatry*. 35:477–86.

Brill, S. and Pepper, R. (2008). *The Transgender Child: A Handbook for Families and Professionals*. San Francisco, CA: Cleis Press.

Brooks, F. (2000). Beneath contempt: The mistreatment of non-traditional/gender atypical boys. *Journal of Lesbian and Gay Social Services 12*(1/2), 107–115.

Brooks, F. (2005). Transgender behavior in boys: The social work response. Unpublished doctoral dissertation. Boston: Simmons School of Social Work.

Burgess, C. (1998). Internal and external stress factors associated with the identity development of transgender youth. In G. P. Mallon (Ed.) *Social Services for Transgendered Youth*. New York: Haworth Press.

Burke, P. (1996). *Gender Shock: Exploding the Myths of Male and Female*. New York: Bantam Books.

Cohen-Kettenis, P. T. and Pfafflin, F. (2003). *Transgenderism and Intersexuality in Childhood and Adolescence: Making Choices*. Thousand Oaks, CA: Sage Publications.

Cohen-Kettenis, P. T. and Van Goozen, S. H. M. (1998). Pubertal delay as an aid in diagnosis and treatment of a transsexual adolescent. *European Child and Adolescent Psychiatry 7*(2), 246–248.

Colapinto, J. (2001). *As Nature Made Him: The Boy who was Raised as a Girl*. New York: HarperCollins.

Cooper, K. (1998). Practice with families of transgendered youth. In G. P. Mallon (Ed.) *Social Services for Transgendered Youth*. New York: Haworth Press.

Crawford, N. (2004). Understanding children's atypical gender behavior: A model support group helps parents learn to accept and affirm their gender variant children. *Monitor on Psychology 34*(8). Accessed December 6, 2005, at www.apa.org/monitor/sep03/children.html.

Criswell, E. and Bedogne, M. (2002). *Out in the Cold* (documentary film). Denver, CO: Matthew Shepard Foundation.

DeCrescenzo, T. and Mallon, G. P. (2002). *Serving Transgendered Youth: The Role of Child Welfare Systems*. Washington, DC: Child Welfare League of America.

de Vries, A. L. C., Cohen-Kettenis, P. T., and Delemarre-Van de Waal, H. (2006). Clinical Management of Gender Dysphoria. *International Journal of Transgenderism 9*(3/4), 83–94.

Dreifus, C. (2005). Declaring with clarity, when gender is ambiguous. *New York Times*, May 31, p. D2.

Fast, I. (1993). Aspects of early gender development: A psychodynamic perspective. In A. E. Beall and R. J. Sternberg (Eds.) *The Psychology of Gender*. New York: Guilford Press.

Fausto-Sterling, A. (1999). Is gender essential? In M. Rottnek, (Ed.) *Sissies and Tomboys: Gender Nonconformity and Homosexual Childhood*. New York: New York University Press.

Feinberg, L. (1993). *Stone Butch Blues*. Ithaca, NY: Firebrand Books.

Germain, C. B. (1973). The ecological perspective in casework practice. *Social Casework: The Journal of Contemporary Social Work 54*, 323–330.

Germain, C. B. (1978). General-systems theory and ego psychology: An ecological perspective. *Social Service Review 35*, 535–550.

Germain, C. B. (1981). The ecological approach to people–environment transactions. *Social Casework: The Journal of Contemporary Social Work 62*, 323–331.

Germain, C. B. (1991). *Human Behavior and the Social Environment*. New York: Columbia University Press.

Glenn, W. (1998). Reflections of an emerging male to female transgendered consciousness. In G. P. Mallon (Ed.) *Social Services for Transgendered Youth*. New York: Haworth Press.

Green, R. (1971). Diagnosis and treatment of gender identity disorders during childhood. *Archives of Sexual Behavior 1*, 167–174.

Green, R. (1974). *Sexual Identity Conflict in Children and Adults*. New York: Basic Books.

Haldeman, D. C. (2000). Gender atypical youth: Clinical and social issues. *School Psychology Review 29*(2), 192–200.

Harry Benjamin International Gender Dysphoria Association (2001). *The HBIGDA Standards of Care for Gender Identity Disorders* (6th version). Minneapolis, MN: The Harry Benjamin International Gender Dysphoria Association. Accessed April 5, 2006, from www.hbigda.org.

Israel, G. and Tarver, D. (1997). *Transgender Care: Recommended Guidelines, Practical Information, and Personal Accounts*. Philadelphia: Temple University Press.

Klein, B. (1998). Group work practice with transgendered male to female sex workers. In G. P. Mallon (Ed.) *Social Services for Transgendered Youth*. New York: Haworth Press.

Kohlberg, L. (1966). A cognitive-developmental analysis of children's sex-role concepts and attitudes. In E. E. Maccoby (Ed.) *The Development of Sex Differences.* Stanford, CA: Stanford University Press.

Langer, S. J. and Martin, J. I. (2004). How dresses can make you mentally ill: Examining gender identity disorder in children. *Child and Adolescent Social Work Journal* 21(1), 5–23.

Lev, A. I. (2004). *Transgender Emergence: Therapeutic Guidelines for Working with Gender Variant People and their Families.* New York: Haworth Press.

Mallon, G. P. (1998a). A call for organizational trans-formation. In G. P. Mallon (Ed.) *Social Services for Transgendered Youth.* New York: Haworth Press.

Mallon, G. P. (Ed.) (1998b). *Social Services for Transgendered Youth.* New York: Haworth Press.

Meyer-Bahlburg, H. F. L. (1985). Gender identity disorder of childhood: Introduction. *Journal of the American Academy of Child Psychiatry* 24, 681–683.

Minter, S. (1999). Diagnosis and treatment of gender identity disorder in children. In M. Rottnek (Ed.), *Sissies and Tomboys: Gender Nonconformity and Homosexual Childhood.* New York: New York University Press.

Minter, S. (2002). *Listening to Gender Variant Children: A Humanistic Strategy for Advocates.* San Francisco: NCLR. Accessed December 6, 2005, at www.nclrights.org/publications/gvchildren.htm.

Money, J. (1973). Gender role, gender identity, core gender identity: Usage and definition of terms. *Journal of the American Academy of Psychoanalysis 1,* 397–403.

Pazos, S. (1998). Practice with female–male transgendered youth. In G. P. Mallon (Ed.), *Social Services for Transgendered Youth.* New York: Haworth Press.

Pleak, R. (1999). Ethical issues in diagnosing and treating gender-dysphoric children and adolescents. In M. Rottnek (Ed.) *Sissies and Tomboys: Gender Nonconformity and Homosexual Childhood.* New York: New York University Press.

Raj, R. (2002). Towards a transpositive therapeutic model: Developing clinical sensitivity and cultural competence is the effective support of transsexual and transgendered clients. *International Journal of Transgenderism* 6(2). Accessed March 15, 2004, at www.symposion.com/ijt/ijtvo06no02_04.htm.

Rekers, G. A. (1977). Assessment and treatment of childhood gender problems. In B. B. Lahey and A. E. Kazdin (Eds.) *Advances in Child Clinical Psychology.* New York: Plenum.

Rekers, G. A. (1988). Psychosocial assessment of gender identity disorders. *Advances in Behavioral Assessment of Children and Families 4,* 33–71.

Rekers, G. A., Bentler, B. M., and Lovaas, O. I. (1977). Child gender disturbance: A clinical rationale for intervention. *Psychotherapy: Theory, Research, and Practice* 14(1), 2–11.

Rosen, H. (2008, November). A boy's life. *The Atlantic,* pp. 56–71.

Rosenberg, M. (2002). Children with gender identity issues and their parents in individual and group treatment. *Journal of the American Academy of Child and Adolescent Psychiatry* 41(2), 619–621.

Scholinski, D. (1997). *The Last Time I Wore a Dress.* New York: Riverhead Books.

Smith, Y. L. S., Cohen, L., and Cohen-Kettenis, P. (2002). Postoperative psychological functioning of adolescent transsexuals: A Rorschach study. *Archives of Sexual Behavior* 31(2), 255–261.

Stoller, R. J. (1965). The sense of maleness. *Psychoanalytic Quarterly 34*, 207–218.

Stoller, R. J. (1968). The sense of femaleness. *Psychoanalytic Quarterly 37*, 42–55.

Swann, S. K. and Herbert, S. E. (1998). Ethical issues in the mental health treatment of adolescents. In G. P. Mallon (Ed.) *Social Services for Transgendered Youth.* New York: Haworth Press.

White Holman, N. and Goldberg, J. (2006). Ethical, legal, and psychosocial issues for transgender adolescents. *International Journal of Transgenderism 9*(3/4), 95–110.

Wren, B. (2000). Early physical intervention for young people with atypical gender identity development. *Clinical Child Psychology and Psychiatry 5*(2), 220–231.

Zucker, K. J. and Bradley, S. J. (1995). *Gender Identity Disorder in Children and Psychosexual Problems in Children and Adolescents.* New York: Guilford Press.

Zucker, K. J. (2004). Gender identity development and issues. *Child and Adolescent Psychiatric Clinics of North America, 13*(3), 551–568.

Chapter 5

Social work practice with female-to-male transgender and gender variant youth

Sofia Pazos

Introduction

Adolescence is a period of development focused on discovering one's role and identity in the world. It is a time of exploration, self-discovery, and testing new independence. Such challenges and changes provoke anxiety and stress for all adolescents, but especially those who cannot conform to the social norms expected from their peer group, family, and/or community. Adolescents who are lesbian, gay, bisexual, or transgender feel their difference more deeply. One person I interviewed described it as "living alone with a chasm between me and the rest of the world."

While there is increasingly ample literature that documents the challenges of gay and lesbian adolescents (Hunter and Mallon, 1999; Mallon, 2001), there are very few works that speak about adolescents of transgender experience (Mallon, 1999; Pazos, 1999). Many helping professionals erroneously perceive gender difference (termed by many as gender dysphoria) as an indicator of a lesbian or gay identity or as an inherent pathology. Some social workers and mental health practitioners act upon these feelings, treating transgender youth as though they are dysfunctional. The early literature concentrated on the intrapsychic characteristics of transgender identity, ignoring how the various systems in the environment contribute to the person's overall health and mental health. In addition, much of the literature is based on research with male-to-female transsexuals (Koetting, 2004), which is a significant population to be studied, but a very different experience from female-to-male transgender persons.

This chapter examines the multiple experiences of female-to-male transgender-identified adolescents, sometimes known as FTMs. The information utilized in this chapter is based on the available literature on FTMs and the result of over ten years of listening to the narratives of FTM transgender adolescents with whom I have worked and from professional counseling experiences with several FTMs ranging in age from their mid to late teens to their early forties.

For the most part, individuals who are active in the transgender community are persons who have been able to afford treatment and surgery (even though not all transgender persons opt for surgery) and keep in contact via the Internet. Hence, the majority of the individuals with whom I have worked with are white, and socioeconomically from middle- and upper-class backgrounds. However, several with whom I worked were African-Americans and one was Native American. Literature reflecting the experiences of transgender people of color and transgender individuals living in poverty and isolation from a larger community is scarce.

Gender history and theory

It is easy to presume that gender is always seen from two absolute perspectives, male and female, blue and pink. Feinberg (1996) documents several instances in the history of Western Europe where gender variance existed in prominence. Joan of Arc, Amelia Earhart, and "Rebecca's Daughters" – cross-dressing Welsh resistance fighters – are all examples of women who defied the traditional female assigned roles that society prescribed for them. Although their communities may have initially looked on these women with scorn, they were ultimately esteemed by the people in the communities where they lived. Gender diversity also had its place in non-Western societies. Various Native American cultures performed rituals in which a child chose what gender roles they preferred to live in. These "not-men" and "not-women" were often revered and given high status (Brown, 1997; Jacobs *et al.*, 1997).

Society's aversion to gender ambiguity is another area that has not been justified by science (Fausto-Sterling, 1993). In reality, there are naturally occurring genetic mutations that result in gender ambiguity. Medical professionals argue that there are several criteria for determining sex: secondary sex characteristics, genetic makeup, hormone levels, and genitalia. Yet most people are assigned at birth a gender identity according to the observation of their external genitalia. Kessler and McKenna's (1978) study implied that this observation had more to do with a person's subjective experiences than with objective scientific criteria.

Gender theory is evolving rapidly in different fields of academic discourse. Bornstein (1994), for example, argues that gender is essentially a binary class system in which one class will always try to oppress the other. Bornstein's perspective further posits that there will never be any true freedom and equality until all gender is done away with and relegated to nothing more than conscious choice. Others (Garber, 1992; Paglia, 1991; Steiner, 1981) discuss gender in terms of feminism, politics, and spirituality. With few exceptions (Davis, 2008; Mallon, 1999), the social work profession unfortunately has been slow to join in this debate.

Trends experienced by FTMs[1] during childhood

As early as 5 years of age, many FTMs have already reported that they had an awareness that something was "different" about them (Scholinski, 1997). Many reported feelings of shock when they realized their bodies were different than those of biological males, as this young person reported: "The first time I saw my brother naked, I couldn't understand how I felt so much like him but he had totally different body parts." As a means of coping with the daily stress of living in a hostile environment, many FTMs reported engaging in magical thinking and daydreaming about being a boy. Such adaptive strategies continued well into their pre-teen years. Some even verbalize their wishes to others: "When I was little, I would go whine to my mother: 'I'm tired of being a girl, can I be a boy now?'"

In attempting to "make the change," some FTMs tried to adopt male external genitalia, creating penises for themselves with toys or socks and attempting to urinate while standing up. Many females who experienced their lives as male reported that they refused to wear shirts or bathing suits during the summer, preferring to wear bathing trunks like boys. Although not all FTMs recall feeling this way, nearly all of the FTMs I spoke with reported that they enjoyed traditionally male-oriented activities such as baseball, soccer, and basketball as children. Most young people I met with recalled that they preferred pants over skirts, wanted their hair cut short, and preferred socializing with boys rather than girls as friends. When these children played with girls, many preferred to assume the male role in play; in a game of house they were the father or they were assigned by the other children to be in the male role, as if the other children tacitly understood their female friend to be male. In her brilliant memoir *The Last Time I Wore a Dress*, author Daphne (now Dylan) Scholinski, a person of transgender experience, corroborates this suggestion:

> I wore Toughskin jeans with double-thick knees so I could wrestle with Jean and the neighborhood boys. My mother cut my hair short so father wouldn't brush my long-hair snarls with No More Tangles spray. I took off my shirt in the summer when the heat in Illinois smothered me in the yard and I got on my bike and glided down the hill no-handed. The wind on my chest felt like freedom until three boys in the neighborhood saw me and said, "Daphne, let me see your titties", which was ridiculous since my chest was as flat as theirs but they held me on the ground. My ride was ruined and I put on a shirt, but not before I punched one of them hard in the stomach and they all backed off.
>
> (Scholinski, 1997, p. 46)

In some cases it seemed as though professionals also tacitly understood gender issues in some children, as this quotation, also from Scholinski, suggests:

> They send me to the school counselor... her favorite game was The Career Game. She held up cards with pictures of a policeman, a farmer, a construction worker, a secretary, a nurse, and I said which ones I'd like to be: police officer and construction worker. She looked at me with a curious face... she was one of the first ones who said I had a problem with my gender. I didn't know what that meant, but later I found out she thought I wanted to be a boy.

Family reaction to the "tomboyishness" of their female youth varied. Younger FTMs reared during the 1970s and 1980s reported that gender difference was, for the most part, ignored or tolerated by their families. They attributed this to the fact that gender roles for men and women had changed, owing to the feminist movements of the 1960s and 1970s. One woman recalled: "I think my mom thought my 'tomboy phase' was my way of empowering myself. She never tried to change the way I looked or acted. She just bought me tailored slacks for special occasions." FTMs raised 15 years earlier remembered daily battles with their parents, who demanded that they dress and act in a more "ladylike" way, as this woman remembered:

> When I was six, seven years old it was still rare to see girls in pants so I had to wear a skirt every day to school. Needless to say I hated waking up in the morning, because I knew that I would have to wear a skirt.

Scholinski had a comparable memory:

> When I was little my mother dressed me in a frilly dress and combed my hair back tight along my scalp. ...My dress was immaculate and stiff. I couldn't wait to take off my dress and be myself again. When I wore a dress I'd be flooded with remarks – "Oooh, you look so pretty today" – which were meant to inspire me but it didn't. I wasn't interested with being pretty. I wanted to be free to run. ...I hated that I couldn't wear what I wanted and be left alone about it.
>
> (1997, pp. 30, 59)

When families were required to attend social obligations, such as clubs or church, or when they occupied a more elevated socioeconomic status, most tended to place more emphasis on their tomboy daughter's need to act in a more feminine way. Some families attempted to persuade their "gender-different" children to conform by enrolling them in "socially corrective" situations such as etiquette classes, charm school, and the Girl Scouts. One FTM remembers his disappointment at joining the Girl Scouts where instead of camping they learned how to make silver polish. Scholinski (1997, p. 97) self-defined this phenomenon as "trying to make me into a girly-girl."

In some cases with the older group, there was verbal abuse that was clearly associated with their perceived "gender deviance."

If acceptance was found at home, at school many FTMs were often the target of verbal harassment by both male and female peers. Among the most frequent insults hurled at them were "lezzie," "dyke," "freak," "tranny," or "tomboy." Many FTMs responded to such verbal attacks in one of two ways: either by engaging in physical confrontations with peers or by withdrawing altogether from social activities. Solinski recalled:

> I was having trouble with friends. The boys who teased me about not wearing a shirt in the summer came after me, called out "tomboy, tomboy" and knocked my books out of my arms, so other kids stayed away from me.
>
> (1997, p. 69)

Some young people involved themselves into solitary activities such as academic work, reading, or writing. As they entered their pre-teen years, some FTMs became involved in any activity that would allow them to engage in fantasy. A large proportion of FTMs I spoke to had interests in drama, science fiction, and role-playing games. A majority of FTMs in their twenties and thirties were self-described computer "geeks" and remember first immersing themselves in computers as a means of escape from reality.

Adolescence

Brown and Rownsley (1996) describe puberty for transsexuals as "nature's cruel trick". Puberty brings about the end of the fantasizing and magical thinking FTMs have previously used to cope. As their bodies develop secondary sexual characteristics – breasts grow, hips widen, and menarche begins – their world of fantasy, which permits them to envision themselves as male, crumbles. Reactions in the individuals I interviewed ranged from shock to betrayal and disgust. One individual understood the experience of change this way:

> I saw all these changes going on with my body and all I could think of was NO.
> All my praying didn't work. I hated God for a long time. Not only was I born with a female body but He had to go and give me large breasts as well.

> I didn't want to believe it was happening. I had to be forced to wear a bra and I ruined some underwear before I realized I couldn't deny my period.

Wearing men's clothes, binding breasts and pants stuffing became even more imperative in order for these individuals to feel comfortable in their body. When these options were not possible, FTMs used disassociation as a coping mechanism. The FTMs I have worked with went "through the motions of living," detaching emotionally from their bodies. Others acted out against their bodies on a more subconscious level by developing eating disorders or becoming accident-prone. In more extreme cases, some FTMs engaged in self-mutilating behaviors, usually slashing or pounding on their chests until they were badly bruised (Brown and Rownsley, 1996).

Some FTMs currently in their twenties and thirties did not have the language to express the emotions they felt. Transgender identity was not part of everyday conversation. Except for some references to male-to-female cross-dressers, FTMs did not see themselves represented in the larger world; they were an invisible and marginalized population. The refusal to allow this invisibility to continue into the next generation has been the primary motivation for many transgender persons to take on some sort of public role to prevent other gender-different teens from suffering the same traumas.

There are fewer incidents of negative body images among the younger FTMs than with the older FTMs whom I spoke with. Many credited this variation to their early awareness of transgenderism and FTM transsexuality, in some cases spurred forward by the popularity and use of the Internet, which they credit with creating a psychological and physical affirming support system. The Internet has opened the closet door for many transgender persons. The ability to gather information about one's identity, to communicate with others who share your experience yet at the same time to remain anonymous, has liberated thousands from the gloom and pain of the closet. This young person's recollection confirmed this occurrence:

> I saw Nico's MySpace web page with his diary about his transition and everything made sense. Through Nico I am now connected with other FTMs my age. It's made looking in the mirror a little less difficult.

Social support was identified as a huge factor in how FTMs survived in the most hostile system affecting their lives: the high school.

FTMs and high school

Although many FTMs were the target for verbal taunts by their peers, many also found their niche in the social hierarchy of high school. Some excelled in academic work or athletics. Others continued with their interests in drama, role-playing, and computers. Being involved in various activities was a way of keeping busy and not thinking about their inner turmoil (Brown and Rownsley, 1996). A positive result of these prominent social activities was being able to identify one or two close friends who accepted their "quirky" behaviors. One young man suggested that the presence of these significant friendships made a difference to how FTMs functioned emotionally:

> I made friends with some of the guys from a club who related to me as a guy, which was a lifesaver for me.
> My best friend was a girl from the soccer team who didn't seem to care that I wasn't interested in girl things and liked that I acted like a brother.

Although these social friendships were rewarding, dating was usually a frustrating experience. Dating patterns with FTMs usually fell into two extreme categories.

- FTMs who identified as heterosexual saw teenage boys as friends and were shocked and disappointed when male friends had a romantic interest in them, but many believed that dating girls was not an option. Gender and sexual orientation once again played a very complex role in this process. Because of their female-appearing body, FTMs would be perceived as lesbian, when in their minds they were dating the opposite sex. FTMs who identified as gay wanted to date boys but did not want to relate to them sexually in a female body. Stuck in this Catch-22, many FTMs chose not to date either gender or dated very rarely.
- Some FTMs became involved in several sexual and romantic encounters as a means of proving that they were normal. If they dated several boys, rumors of their being lesbian would usually subside. Some FTMs also dated boys as a way of living vicariously through their boyfriends, as this young man recalled: "I loved dating guys because then I had an excuse to go to the department store and buy men's clothes and colognes 'for my boyfriend.'"

While many older FTMs reported mixed experiences in high school, recent findings by the Gay, Lesbian, and Straight Education Network (GLSEN) clearly indicate that the educational system still falls short of providing a safe, supportive environment to all LGBT youth. In its 2005 National School

Climate Survey, GLSEN found that 26.1 percent of students surveyed reported harassment in school, and another 11.8 percent reported physical assaults. GLSEN reports that LGBT students who are harassed repeatedly are more likely to skip school and not enter college, and on average have lower academic success than non-harassed peers (www.glsen.org).

Some FTMs felt that they were in fact lesbians. In a society that equates gender difference with homosexuality, this was a natural assumption. Depending on their own feelings about lesbians and gays, this either brought comfort or added to the stress. Depending on where they lived and the resources which were or were not available for lesbian and gay youth, some FTMs came out and lived as lesbians first before identifying as transgender later. Thus, utilizing a lesbian identity as a bridge to a transgender identity is similar to the way some gay or lesbian youth will initially identify as bisexual before identifying as lesbian or gay.

Jason Cromwell (1999) chronicles what he describes as "border wars" between individuals who identify as FTMs and those who identify as butch, a traditional identity within the lesbian community. Both groups have similar experiences and exhibit similar masculine traits but disagree on how they view themselves and each other along the gender, sex, and sexual orientations spectrums.

On the whole, high school evoked painful memories for most of the young people whom I interviewed. Undressing in locker rooms and using bathrooms represented moments of extreme anxiety. Scholinski has vivid narratives about bathroom use:

> "This is the line for the women's room." "I know." I looked at her if she was the fool, but inside I was sweating. She reminded me again. "I am a woman." I hated saying that: I have never quite fit in that box. She said, "You don't look like a woman. You don't sound like a woman." What was I supposed to do with that? I was like, "What do you want to see my i.d.?" I pulled my i.d. out of my wallet and showed her. I knew I didn't have to do it, but I thought it would end it. I avoid public bathrooms. I'll never be a girly-girl.
>
> (1997, p. 194)

Despite having friends, some FTMs still felt they were living lives of deception and invested a great deal of energy into trying to conform to the social norms assigned to their biological gender. Such attempts at finding transactional fits that were positive and nurturing were an emotionally exhausting process. When we consider this, combined with the guilt and shame at being perceived as a freak, anger at not being able to be who they are, as well as the normal amount of angst associated with adolescent development, it is not surprising to report that many FTMs suffer from extremely low self-esteem.

Without friends or support, many FTMs fell into deep depression. Feelings of despair and isolation often led to self-medication with prescription and street drugs, alcohol, and other substances. While there are no verifiable statistics that speak to issues of drug abuse among FTMs, more than half of the individuals whom I interviewed are currently in recovery programs. All of those interviewed traced part of their addiction to their emotions regarding their gender difference. Several reported that they had contemplated and/or attempted suicide. The comments of this young man confirm that there may be more transgender youth that hold these feelings: "Since I first came out in 1995, I've lost two friends and had at least five others try suicide. There are probably lots more that the research shows since FTMs and other transgender teens are still invisible."

FTMs and the family

Families of FTMs that I interviewed may not have been accepting of their gender variant child, but at the very least they were described as tolerant of a "tomboy girl." When the tomboy phase lasted longer than anticipated, however, most FTMs reported that their family's reaction changed. In these cases, parents exerted more pressure on their teens to conform to societal prescribed gender roles. These efforts, while often well intentioned, if misguided, were reflected in this comment by the parent of a transgender person with whom I worked:

> I wanted my child to be accepted by the high school. I had dreams of homecoming queen, college, and marriage. To see my daughter act so masculine and so angry... I thought I was doing the right thing to force her to act like a lady.

Devor (1997) interviewed several FTMs on a variety of topics including their relationships with their families during adolescence. In her work, Devor (1997) found that FTMs had close relationships with female relatives when they were able to take on protective "male head of the household" roles within the family. Relationships with female relatives were reported to remain indifferent or unusually tense if they did not take on the protective male role. There was a tendency noted in Devor's (1997) work which suggests that female relatives exerted more pressure on FTMs to conform to gender roles.

Devor found that relationships FTMs had with male relatives did not fare any better. FTMs who reported close relationships with their brothers during childhood found that adolescence caused a shift. Their brothers grew into the bodies they silently desired and gained the privileges of being male. FTMs, on the other hand, saw their bodies as having betrayed them and their freedom to "act masculine" curtailed. FTMs also resented how adolescence changed the way fathers treated them. FTMs found their fathers to be poor role models, partly because they could not form the father–son bond they wanted.

Increased pressure to act like a girl, coupled with an adolescent's struggle for independence, resulted in extreme tension within the family. There were frequent arguments affecting all family members. Siblings were often caught in the middle: "I hated the fights and I loved my 'sister' but it just seemed that my parents had a point. We all thought all 'she' had to do was stop acting so different and everything would be all right."

When FTMs began to act out their pain, in some cases by becoming more involved with substance abuse, such behavior gave families impetus to force their children into therapy. Many times, just the gender difference was enough to push their children into therapy. If therapy failed to fix the problem, some FTM teens were psychiatrically hospitalized for treatment of gender identity disorder. The thoughts of one individual with whom I worked spoke of that horrifying experience:

> They kept me drugged at all times. They forced me to wear dresses. I'll admit I was depressed and suicidal but what did wearing dresses have to do with making me feel better? Others I knew received electric shock treatments.

When tensions reached a breaking point, some parents threw their children out of their homes. Some parents forbade their children from taking part in any family events; other children were denied access to extended family, as this narrative suggests:

> My parents sort of accept me but they'd rather I not attend any family functions. I'm not allowed to speak to my grandparents or other relatives. I wasn't able to see my sister graduate high school.
>
> In the past three years my mother has tried to have me committed, changed the locks on the doors, and tried to prevent me from collecting my grandmother's inheritance. The other day she called saying that her divorce was all my fault.

If parents withdrew financial support, most teens were left poor and homeless. Some went into foster care, where they were frequent targets for abuse (Mallon, 1999). Others became transients, moving from house to house or sofa to sofa. A few joined other teens in street life, creating their own "families" and using whatever means they could to survive, as this young person suggests: "When people think about gay prostitutes they think about the gay boys and male-to-female transsexuals. But there are a lot of FTMs hustling too."

Current theories concerning treatment of transgender and gender variant youth

The *DSM*-IV describes gender difference as gender identity disorder (GID), a "persistent cross-gender identification and a persistent discomfort with [the person's] sex" (American Psychiatric Association, 1994). This description of transsexualism is the basis for the prevalent theory of transsexualism that views it as pathology. Viewing the client as having a pathological condition, many clinicians based their interventions on guiding the patient to accept the gender roles related to their birth sex.

The presence of GID in the *DSM* has enabled many clinicians to use this diagnosis not only to treat transsexuals, but also to apply the same therapies to gay and lesbian youth who exhibit transgender behaviors. By equating gender with sexual orientation, clinicians such as Moberly and Zucker have been able to utilize treatment approaches that are essentially harmful to transgender persons. Many in the psychiatric profession and most in the transgender community reject the current medical model, and an appeal for different, affirmative treatment models is essential.

Toward a strengths-based treatment model

Increasingly, professionals in psychology, psychiatry, and other fields are advocating for more affirming approaches to therapeutic models for treating transsexualism. Ekins and King (1998) argue that psychiatrists have viewed transgender identity from an individual perspective, ignoring the societal factors that affect a person's overall mental health. Many transgender persons do not see themselves as sick but have a lower level of functioning and higher stress due to society's inability to accept gender difference. The quest for "realness" causes them additional unrest.

Schaefer *et al.* (1995) remind us that helping professionals should not make the assumption that the gender difference is the cause of all of a patient's problems. Davis (2008) and Lev (2004) further affirm these points in their work. Stressing the importance of a holistic psychotherapeutic model involving education, individual and family therapy, and improving interpersonal relations rather than the patient's being hampered by "gender guilt," these authors advocate the role of a therapist as a guide to help the patient understand and accept their gender difference and decide on the best way to live with a trans identity. Their approach is clearly a departure from the traditional role of the gender therapist as a gatekeeper or judge of who is and who is not really a person of trans experience.

Hormone therapy

Transsexual youth have not fully benefited from these changes in approach to gender therapy. The current Harry Benjamin *Standards of Care* used as guidelines for treating transgender persons exclude anyone under the age of 18 from receiving hormone therapy or sexual reassignment surgery (Harry Benjamin International Gender Dysphoria Association, 2001). Transsexual adolescents need the full support of their family to enter any kind of gender program. Helping professionals either minimize the issue of gender difference or use interventions meant to discourage it. Even if a therapist may recommend it, very few parents grant that permission.

Claudine Griggs (1998) makes several valid points in her argument that transgender teens should be allowed to "transition." Physically, hormonal therapy at adolescence would retard undesired secondary sex characteristics and enhance desired characteristics, thus eliminating the need for cosmetic surgery in the future. The psychological effect of puberty is devastating for most transsexuals. This suffering is a factor in the high incidence of depression, suicide, and substance abuse among transsexuals. Early diagnosis and treatment of transsexuals may prevent long-term psychological trauma. From a legal standpoint, an adolescent or young adult has less of a bureaucratic history (i.e. driver's license, professional credentials transcripts) that would need to change after transition. Early transition would also give a transsexual a longer period of socialization in the gender role they choose to live in. It might also help family and significant others adjust to a person's new gender identity.

Implications for social work practice

Even in the best scenario, transgender youth face enormous challenges. Very few states and only a handful of cities in the United States have gender identity and expression included in non-discrimination laws and ordinances. Transgender persons without legal protections are left vulnerable to discrimination in housing, employment, and access to education and adequate health services. They are vulnerable, too, to the bias of some family court judges in cases of custody, divorce, family violence, and adoption cases.

In addition, perceived gender difference makes transgender individuals the target of verbal harassment and physical attacks (Minter and Daley 1997). The New York City Gay and Lesbian Anti-Violence Project (2007) reported that during 2006, 20 percent of the victims of reported hate crimes were transgender males. Persons under 18 experienced a 38 percent increase in hate crimes. Hate crimes are routinely underreported or often not classified as hate crimes by law enforcement officials. The transgender community are also reluctant to work with law enforcement service, because they are routinely harassed by law enforcement individuals (www.avp.org).

Social workers first need to educate themselves on transgender issues, especially by familiarizing themselves with works by authors who are themselves transgender (Davis, 2008). Education on transgender issues should be taught in all social work agencies and become part of the curriculum taught at graduate schools of social work. When social workers are counseling gender different youth and their families, a psychoeducational approach may be useful to dispel popular myths associated with trans identity. Gender-questioning youth will also need as much information possible about support, resources, and options available to them, and social workers must know where to access such supports and resources.

Counseling gender different youth from a strengths perspective involves viewing transgender identity as an integral part of the client's identity, not as pathology. Some transgender youth may be resistant to therapy, especially if previous therapists have tried to discourage gender-transgressive behaviors or attempted to "change" them. It is important in forming a therapeutic alliance to respect the client's wishes in being called by their preferred name (as opposed to their birth name) and by using the pronoun that they prefer to be identified by. If possible, clients should also have the safe space to dress in the manner that they feel most comfortable with (Israel and Tarver, 1997; Mallon, 1999).

As the transgender community continues to grow and develop its own theories, language used for identity expression is ever-changing and fluid. FTMs vary in what terms they use to describe themselves and what medical and physiological procedures they choose to implement in order to "transition." Some trans masculine persons are choosing not to use hormones or undergo any surgical alterations of their body, preferring to live in a more "gender-fluid" or "gender-queer" space. Social workers have a responsibility to explore all alternatives with their clients and to keep appraised of current trends in transgender discourse.

To assist families, compromises may need to be negotiated between parents and their teens. Such compromises may include the use of a unisex name and clothing and by refraining from forcing them to dress in biological gender-specific clothing. Families of transgender teens will need support as they will undoubtedly also "transition" along with their child. Many family members will go through emotional stages similar to those making up the grieving process: denial, anger, guilt, shame, and shock. Most parents are concerned about their child's future in regard to health, employment, safety, and the chances for happy love relationships. Furthermore, family members will need to adjust to different names and pronouns. To make this shift successfully will take time.

Because of societal stressors, some transgender youth may engage in at-risk behaviors such as substance abuse, sexual promiscuity or prostitution, and using illegally obtained hormones. Some individuals interviewed reported that their substance abuse was related to their self-hatred for being a transgender person. Until the individual has addressed his or her low self-esteem and is ready to begin recovery, harm reduction methods, rather than complete abstinence, should be attempted. Trans youth involved in sex-work (see Chapter 7) and sexually dangerous behavior also need to bolster their self-esteem and will need support in finding training and educational sites that will be tolerant of a person's gender difference. Social workers will almost assuredly need to be advocates between their transgender clients and the medical profession.

Finally, social workers need to be involved in creating policy and laws supporting the rights of transgender individuals (Currah *et al.*, 2006). The International Bill of Gender Rights outlines the basic guidelines (International Conference on Transgender Law and Employment Policy, n.d.) that would ensure for transgender individuals full freedom and protection under the law. These may provide some clear guidance for social workers:

- the individual's right to define gender identity;
- the right to free expression of gender identity;
- the right to control and change one's own body;
- the right to competent medical and professional care;
- the right to freedom from psychiatric diagnosis and treatment;
- the right to sexual expression;
- the right to form committed loving relationships and enter marital contracts;
- the right to conceive or adopt children; the right to nurture and have custody of children and exercise of parental rights.

Conclusions

The Harry Benjamin International Gender Dysphoria Association (2001) recently included Master's-level social workers among its list of professional qualified to be gender therapists within the Standards of Care (www.transgender.org, 1997). Since social workers are accessible to large populations, they can expect an increase in the number of transgender youth and their families seeking therapy and referrals. With this revision, more transgender youth and their families will undoubtedly seek out social workers for assistance. With increased discussion of transgender issues, agencies targeted to family, children, and youth services may also see an increase of transgender and transsexual youth seeking services. Social work has an opportunity to add systems-based and strengths-based perspective to current theories on treatment and transgender youth. The social worker will have to take on roles such as therapist, advocate, and policy maker in order to provide the best services to this growing population.

FTMs live with the double-edged sword of invisibility and passing. A female with masculine traits is either dismissed, ignored, or feared. While this may provide a mantle of safety for some time, viewing FTMs in this way keeps their service needs from being fully known or addressed. Perhaps it is most appropriate for Scholinski to have the last word:

> These words [those used in *DSM*-IV to describe gender identity disorder] are ludicrous, but not if it's you they're talking about, not if it's you they're locking up. Not ludicrous at all for the ones who continue to be diagnosed as mentally ill. A mouthy girl in cowboy boots or a boy who drapes a scarf on his head to pretend his hair is long like a princess – well, they are targets for the Dr. Madisons of the world... I know I could have done worse, if my father hadn't had his fat insurance policy, if I hadn't been from a middle class, white family, I could have ended up in jail instead of the psych ward. If I had been a young kid of color no one would have thought I was worth fixing.
>
> (1997, pp. 196–197)

As more and more of these unique young people come out into the open, it is a social worker's responsibility to educate, to empower, and, most importantly, to listen.

Note

1 FTM is an identifying term that not all transmasculine persons choose to utilize, but for purposes of simplifying text in this chapter it is utilized throughout.

References

American Psychiatric Association (1994). Diagnostic *and Statistical Manual of Mental Disorders* (4th ed.). Washington, DC: American Psychiatric Association.

Bornstein, K. (1994). *Gender Outlaw: On Men, Women, and the Rest of Us*. New York: Routledge.

Brown, L. B. (1997). Women and men, not-men and not-women, lesbians and gays: American Indian gender style alternatives. *Journal of Gay and Lesbian Social Services* 6(2), 5–20.

Brown, M. and Rownsley, C. A. (1996). *True Selves: Understanding Transsexualism for Family, Friends, Co-workers and Helping Professionals*. San Francisco: Jossey-Bass.

Cromwell, J. (1999). *Transmen and FTMs: Identities, Bodies, Genders and Sexualities*. Chicago: University of Illinois Press.

Currah, P., Juang, R. M., and Minter, S. (2006). *Transgender Rights*. Minneapolis: University of Minnesota Press.

Davis, C. (2008). Social Work Practice with Transgender and Gender Non-Conforming Persons. In G. P. Mallon (Ed.) *Social Work Practice with LGBT People* (pp. 83–111). New York: Routledge.

Devor, H. (1997). *FTM: Female to Male Transsexual in Society*. Bloomington: Indiana University Press.

Ekins, R. and King, D. (1998). Blending genders: Contributions to the emerging field of transgender studies. In D. Denny (Ed.) *Current Concepts in Transgender Identity*. New York: Garland.

Fausto-Sterling, A. (1993). The five sexes: Why male and female are not enough. *The Sciences*, March/April, 20–25.

Feinberg, L. (1996). *Transgender Warriors: Making History from Joan of Arc to Dennis Rodman*. Boston: Beacon Press.

Garber, M. (1992). *Vested Interests*. New York: Routledge, Chapman and Hall.

Griggs, C. (1998). *S/he: Changing Sex and Changing Clothes*. Oxford: Berg.

Harry Benjamin International Gender Dysphoria Association (2001). *The HBIGDA Standards of Care for Gender Identity Disorders* (6th version). Minneapolis, MN: Harry Benjamin International Gender Dysphoria Association.

Hunter, J. and Mallon, G. P. (1999). Gay and lesbian adolescent development: Dancing with your feet tied together. In B. Greene and G. Crooms (Eds.) *Gay and Lesbian Development: Education, Research and Practice*. Thousand Oaks, CA: Sage.

International Conference on Transgender Law and Employment Policy (n.d. [1998]). *International Bill of Gender Rights*. Retrieved on May 25, 2008 from the World Wide Web: [www document]. http://www.abmall.com/ictlep.

Israel, G. and Tarver, D. (1997). *Transgender Care: Recommended Guidelines, Practical Information and Personal Accounts*. Philadelphia: Temple University Press.

Jacobs, S., Thomas, W., and Lang, S. (Eds.) (1997). *Two-spirit People: Native American Gender Identity, Sexuality, and Spirituality*. Chicago: University of Illinois Press.

Kessler, S. and McKenna, W. (1978). *Gender: An Ethnomethodological Approach*. New York: John Wiley.

Koetting, M. E. (2004). Beginning practice with preoperative male-to-female transgender clients. *Journal of Gay and Lesbian Social Services* 16(2), 99–104.

Lev, A. I. (2004). *Transgender Emergence*. New York: Harrington Park Press.

Mallon, G. P. (Ed.) (1999). *Social Services with Transgendered Youth*. New York: Haworth Press.

Mallon, G. P. (2001). *Gay and Lesbian Youth: A Youth Worker's Perspective*. Washington, DC: CWLA.

Minter, S., and Daley, C. (1997) *Trans Realities: A Legal Needs Assessment of San Francisco's Transgender Communities*. San Francisco: NCLR.

New York City Gay and Lesbian Anti-Violence Project (2007). *Anti-lesbian, Gay, Bisexual and Transgender Violence in 2006*. A publication of the National Coalition of Anti-Violence Programs. New York: Anti-Violence Project.

Paglia, C. (1991). *Sexual Persona*. New York: Vintage Books.

Pazos, S. (1999). Practice with female-to-male transgendered youth. *Journal of Gay and Lesbian Social Service 10*(3/4), 65–82.

Schaefer, L. C., Wheeler, C. C., and Futterweit, W. (1995). *Gender Identity Disorders in Treatment of Psychiatric Disorders*, vol. 2. Washington, DC: American Psychiatric Association.

Scholinski, D. (1997). *The Last Time I Wore a Dress*. New York: Riverhead Books.

Steiner, B. W. (1981). From Sappho to Sand: Historical perspectives on cross-dressing and cross gender. *Canadian Journal of Psychiatry 36*, 502–506.

Chapter 6

"For colored girls only"

Reflections of an emerging male-to-female transgender and gender variant youth consciousness

Wendell D. Glenn

Editor's prelude

The use of first-person narrative in helping social workers to understand the experiences of transgender youth has been quite limited. Practitioners solicit the opinions of transgender male-to-female transgender youth only rarely. First-person accounts offer a unique perspective. Each story of a transgender person's life is different, unfolding around the particulars of that person's life. But listening for the themes and the patterns that emerge from the narrative may, if one is an astute listener, helps one to acquire some sharp cues to good practice.

Personal narratives can also offer professionals feedback about how their services are experienced. By creating an open dialogue, these stories allow controversial issues to be addressed more honestly, and harmful practices to be distinguished from helpful ones. The opportunity to tell one's story can be an empowering and healing event. The first-person account also helps shift our attention from pathology to adaptation. When those who literally "live the life" are willing to speak out, they might be better advocates for themselves than professionals, who are usually seen as the experts.

The narratives of those who have emerged wiser or who overcame adversity can be a source of inspiration. The willingness of successful people to discuss their personal experiences publicly is a powerful technique for reducing the stigma attached to the condition of transgenderism.

In acknowledging the pitfalls of first-person narrative, it is also important to keep in mind that the experiences of particular individuals do not necessarily generalize to those of a group as a whole. For narratives to help us understand how to improve services to a population, multiple accounts from varying perspectives, including accounts by transgender persons at different developmental phases and across a spectrum of cultures, are essential. Only then can we hope to discern some universal truths as we design interventions and techniques to help transgender youth.

Professionals involved in designing approaches to working with transgender youth must listen to these individual voices for the valuable information that they can share with us. In the narrative that follows Wendell Glenn provides us with the gift of a first-person account of his own personal experiences as a "plainclothes" transgender person – a term that he has coined to define his own experiences.

Back story: the recognition of a sense of "difference"

"I wonder what kind of dresses we're going to get this time…" That was my thought when I was four years old. Actually, what happened is that my mother did domestic work in South Carolina for a white household that gave her hand-me-down children's dresses after she had cleaned for them all day. Then my sisters (I had seven sisters and five brothers) would rummage through the dresses to select the ones they wanted to wear to school. The dresses left over after my sisters selected what they wanted were usually torn or had some flaw which made them inappropriate for school.

My brothers and I used these discarded dresses as pajamas and we all slept in these newfound pajamas. That is, all but my baby brother, who just cried and cried, and for some reason, unknown to us, he would never wear one of the dresses so… he'd sleep in a T-shirt. As for me, I'd sit and wait until the hand-me-down dresses came my way. My other brothers would resist it; they usually slept naked or found some kind of privacy. All of us would sleep in the bed together anyway or on the floor, or whatever we had at that particular time.

When we got a little older, my brothers would rebel and not wear the dresses, but I couldn't wait to wear one. I had a little blue one that became my favorite thing to sleep in, but eventually I grew out of it – the dress, I mean. I always wondered why I was the one brother that was so interested and happy to wear that dress to bed. Around that time I also began to discover that there was a distinct difference between me and my brothers or other guys that were my age.

In this first-person narrative, I want to talk about my personal experience as an African-American transgender youth growing up in a family that wouldn't even know what a transgender person was. In fact, ironically enough, my life as a "gender-blender" was at first really glorious. I say that because there were so many people who were fascinated with how I appeared or acted in what I call an external sense. For instance, the little boys that were my favorite friends noticed that I wore really tight pants, or ironed the best creases onto them, or that I always had my hair perfectly slicked. I remember how they used to admire how I used to take my time and groom myself. When the little girls sang "snakes and snails and puppy-dog tails," I would sing back "sugar and spice and everything nice," because I really kept up a polished appearance.

I also was the one in class that the boys copied answers from, the one whose paper they habitually peeked at. Or, if something happened in school, then I'd sometimes take the fall for the boys. I think what I really wanted was the affirmation and attention from them. For me there was even more of a reason than just wanting attention at that particular time. I think that I just enjoyed the intimacy of receiving attention from the males I encountered at the time. The females – the little girls – loved me, because in a lot of ways I was like them and they somehow recognized that in me, but they also saw me as their competition with the boys. Because I was their competition, and yet was not a biological girl, I overcompensated – I had to be better than them! I made sure that I jumped rope better, or the hopscotch grid I drew on the ground was neater or I hopped on one leg better than the girls. I was always the one who became their best friend and the one who helped them fight when they got in a mess. The prettiest girls, the cheerleaders especially, used my masculinity for protection, and what I got in return was I gravitated toward them as female role models to emulate.

As a kid coming up in the South, it was fun to go sneak out to the "juke joint" and dance the night away. These places weren't just an "adults-only" environment; children, youths, and families were welcomed as well. It was in these juke joints that bootleg liquor sold (my mother's secret formula) and a live band played all night long into the morning and everybody jived and danced. I remember myself being in the middle of the room – being the center of attention. People looking at me and loving everything I did. I felt great happiness there. My community looked at me as a treasure because I was a performer, a chameleon… the older guys threw quarters or patted me on the butt and the girls always wanted me to dance with them.

I stood out. There was a goodness about me. "Look at the way he walks," people would say. But for me there was always a sense of protection. Part of the external was so celebrated by everybody around me that I didn't really know that I was different, because I was so busy being happy and making everyone else happy.

As I got older, and ventured into other communities outside of the one that protected me, I found myself sticking with my own community – with my own people. I had so much in common with these folks. The poverty that we all lived in, our shared common experiences, made us all stick together. In the cold winters we helped each other and in the spring we worked together or cut wood for the next winter. So I really didn't have time to look at who was different or what made you look different or act different because we were so busy dealing with survival.

This changed once I started to mingle with people from other neighboring areas. I can remember when I was in the first grade in an all-black school, being there with my peer group, but also for the first time I was clustered along with some of these outsiders. That was the first time

I started hearing comments like "Look at him, he walks funny." That's when they start calling me "sissy" and all those hurtful names. They recognized my "difference" and unlike the people in my community – it mattered to them. So it was an amazing feeling to have felt so celebrated by your community and then all of a sudden to be so ridiculed when I came into contact with outsiders. Some of the people from my community began to protect me but others began to align themselves with the outsiders, and for the first time they began to look at my "difference" too. These were the same people I performed for or was celebrated by – and yet now they only saw my "difference" where they once saw a fun member of their community. It was at this juncture that the internal dilemma started to kick in; it was right around the first or second grade.

I realize now, although obviously I didn't at the time, that it's most important that a transgender-oriented person struggling with peer-group identification receives the support and the encouragement of parents, or an aunt or family member that they can count on for a support system. There were days I went home from school crying because I hurt so bad. But remember, once I was back in the community, I was still the performer for everybody. No one expected me to cry and so I had to put on this front. Most of the negative part that I was feeling, most of the stuff that was going on and burning inside of me internally, was now hidden. That same person that performed for you was really a very isolated and lonely boy. Who was I going to tell? Who was I going to go to? There was no one else that I could identify who was like me. And I really couldn't even articulate or communicate what was going on.

This sense of isolation and loneliness is one of the reasons that many transgender people have such a hard time with socialization. It is only when they become healthy adults or healthy-thinking people that they start to build their own support systems. It is at this period of time that parents really need to become that particular force in their child's life, but most parents are clueless, because they expect their children to be heterosexual, not gay or lesbian, and certainly not transgender. What would be so helpful is if the parents could pick up some of that misery that is paining that child. To identify, speak to it, to get help for it. But, unfortunately, most parents are ill-equipped to care for a transgender child. Fortunately, even though she was not armed with the proper information to deal with my transgender identity, I did have a mother who I could go to. It would always be a different story about what I was sad about, but I knew enough to never tell her about the real thing, because again, it was not only that I didn't know how to communicate what the "difference" felt like, but even then I didn't have the words for it. But, nonetheless, I began to hate how I felt and in some ways to hate myself as well.

In my case, I was a typical child of the Deep South growing up in a large family with a single parent, my mother. And even though my mother was one of the most nurturing and loving parents that anyone could ever have, and still is, she wasn't experienced enough with gender issues to assess or look at what I was going through at that time. So I have long since gotten over any blaming behavior or saying, "Why didn't you do this?" or "Why didn't you do that?" My mother did the best she could with 12 children, but she simply was not prepared in any way to deal with her child who was transgender. There were other factors as well – especially in light of the fact that the Church was so important in our everyday life. Not only did everybody know me in the community, but everybody basically went to the same church. During sermons, the preacher was openly condemning – I mean very openly condemning – about women going with women, men going with men, and for me at the time, going to church was the worst time of my life because every time, I left out of there feeling ridiculed and harassed. And what really got to me was that some of these same people who threw quarters at me or patted me on the butt in the jook joint on Saturday night looked at me like I was the worst thing in the world on Sunday in church.

So it was all of these mixed messages, mixed feelings, mixed emotions that I went through that were balled up like a volcano that doesn't erupt. Most of the time I felt incredibly isolated. But I also overcompensated for the inadequacy I felt inside, I overexerted myself. I did this because I was so desperate, so busy trying to fit in – especially trying to fit into the Church. In the church I joined the choir. Or, in school I tried to get on the football team. I tried so hard to be good that when I came home from school, I did extra chores or whatever it took to make sure I compensated for all the loss I felt internally.

Balancing internal and external factors

In looking at the internal facets and external facets, although they run neck and neck, I realized that there has to be some type of balance. There is always a struggle between trying to feel good about yourself internally and have that supported externally. In my own family, I think that my brothers and sisters always knew that there was something different about me. But again, we were in survival mode, a close-knit family but struggling to survive poverty. So it was not something that we really openly discussed. It wasn't that they looked at or saw a "difference," but they did perceive difference. In many ways, they knew, but we never talked about it. I was the son who was beside my mother for hours and hours in the kitchen, who would just look at her cook and then begin to learn to do it myself. I even learned to prepare meals better than some of my sisters. So that was classified as "He's flaunting," or "He's going to be a chef." An extra hand in the kitchen didn't hurt. So... I made lots of compromises. Most of the compromises that I made entailed always being available to lend a hand to someone else being more happy, and so my happiness became derived from someone else's.

Becoming a teenager changed everything for me. Going into the teen stage, when teenagers want to date and be intimate with each other, caused the struggle between internal and external to worsen. It was at this time that I began to bring out some of what was happening to me internally, to the external world. When I look back on the days in high school, there were a couple, two or three others, of the same orientation. There's a comfort in finding others like you, you kind of seek each other out. When you meet another person like you – you know when another person is identifying like you – there's a certain look, it's a feeling. That's why the trans family has become so popular because you really do begin to form a family, to know each other, once you find your people.

This was the time that some of the guys in our community started to wear dresses to school – it was different than pajamas just to wear at night! But to wear the lipstick and wear the dresses to school is when the guys who felt this way started to say internally, "I cannot take it anymore, I need to play this out, I need to express this." I never dressed in women's clothes at school and usually I became alienated from my friends who did this. They caught a lot of heat. But I was different. For me, it wasn't the way I *looked or dressed*, it was the way I *felt*. It's who I *was*, it's how I identified at that particular time inside.

"For colored girls only..."

During the adolescent period of development, some of the transgender psychosocial aspects begin to manifest themselves externally. Some of the same teenagers that were my age and had gender issues began to dress in the clothing of the opposite gender. A few of them were actually accepted and respected, but only on certain occasions. This clear change on their part became a predicament for me. Even at a young age I always believed there were certain limitations to my internal feelings of femaleness. I was a great believer in blending in, being comfortable with who I was but not sticking out like a sore thumb. When I mention the transgender psychosocial aspects, I mean first and foremost the loneliness. And I mean loneliness in a way where your peer group becomes very narrow, very small, and you can almost predict the one or two people who you can secretly talk to. Some of those same guys who, when you were younger, celebrated you, at this point have this straight macho-type image and you become ridiculed by them. I remember thinking to myself at this time – "You're crazy. You're a crazy faggot or even worse." These were some of the same guys who behind closed doors are waiting to have a sexual run-in with you. And after that, when they saw you again in public, they didn't want to be bothered. The girls at this particular time started seriously looking at me as "the competition." Or some of the girls whom I knew I could talk to at this time would use me to talk to my brothers who were active in sports because they liked them. So... they would use me to approach them. Or they would allow me to be friends with them because they knew you could fight and keep jealous girls off of them.

All in all, although I socialized, these relationships were not genuine friendships; I was used by people to get what they wanted. It's a type of loneliness that cut me to the core; the message was clear – stay in the closet! We will take you out when and if we need you for something – to entertain us, to do something for us, or to defend us. Who was I going to go to when I needed something? It was a question I asked myself repeatedly over those years. The reality was – there wasn't any support system. There wasn't anybody there for me. Apart from this loneliness, I felt shame; guilt started setting in because I began to wonder if I had become a failure to myself and my family. I guess if I had a healthy perception myself at this point, I would have begun to build on where I was and set goals and just go further and move on. But I realized that this is what it was, that this is what my life was worth and I had to either sink or swim. Fortunately, I decided to swim – meaning that I made peace with myself and my transgender orientation, and set about beginning to actualize myself professionally. And I'm still swimming.

When I really again began to realize who I was, and whether or not that deviated from everyone else, I realized too that I was no different than who anybody else was. I was a person – a human – with feelings. I wanted love, I wanted to belong, I was an emotional person that had needs, and those needs were not so different from other people's needs. It was society that began to color me crazy – not my transgender nature. I had ridiculed myself for too long hiding my feelings. My feelings were real and could no longer be denied. Not only do *we* look different to *them*, but *they* look different to *us*. So there had to be a sense of give-and-take, compromise if you will, but not just on my part.

For me the "shame game" was a sport I decided I wasn't going to play. I could not be a part of the "shame game." I realized early on that it is the "shame game" that will destroy you. My guilt was an inner guilt, not rooted in whether or not I was successful in the eyes of family and friends, or whether or not I was a failure to them, but whether I was successful to myself. Although this was a time of great personal transformation, it was also a time of great depression, which came mainly from the stress of wanting people to buy into who you are. Wanting people not to look at you as out of the ordinary. And you begin to look for this particular love and acceptance. Sometimes it leads you to all the wrong places – right into substance abuse, manipulating, stealing... behavior that's unacceptable. I've been there, done that. I would have done anything to be loved by someone or accepted by someone, be it family or not.

At this particular time, those of us who feel tortured do not seek out support systems, support groups, or counseling or therapy, but instead opt for "home remedies" – to enable ourselves to get better and move on. Such "remedies" could lead right into some point of suicide, substance abuse, risk taking – all of which makes us a very vulnerable population. There's a saying that "you have to stand for something or you'll fall for anything." At this point, the yearning for meaningful human contact is so strong that we can fall for literally anything.

"Color me crazy"

Trying to find a true, healthy identity of self within the context of a transgender identity is difficult. Most of the confusion and frustration about who I was stemmed from my own peer group – and I mean my transgender peer group! There is a point of view that is guided solely by the physical attributes one has, as compared with what one has from the opposite sex. Transgender people are constantly comparing and criticizing each other in the area of looks. Whether or not you can pass as a woman (or a man in the case of FTMs) becomes the main focus of survival and preoccupation. REALNESS is everything! Your level of acceptance is determined by how well you are able to hide your penis (known as tucking) to make it appear as if it were a vagina. There is also a high outlay of energy placed on the art of putting on makeup, making sure to cover up razor bumps, battling unwanted hair growth, or making sure you are crafty enough to fix your chest to present just the right breast size. This process becomes a preoccupation for some and so much a part of everyday routine for others that it is normal grooming. Day after day, night after night, life becomes an interchangeable transformation, and only when it is time to sleep, and you pull off the mask making sure not to look in a mirror or you could be horrified at the physical reality, does it all come off.

As a young adult MTF, transgender life is most crazy-making. Especially if you are a career-oriented individual with a goal in mind. For example, if you are scheduled to work at 8 a.m., you have to allow enough time to fix yourself up. Fixing yourself up could consist of anything from propping your wig or hair weave correctly, to making sure you are taking the right hormone pill or shot.

It is a rarity – pure luck and a blessing – when a transgender person becomes successful outside of the world that they create for themselves. This world of the MTF transgender involves everybody meeting together at each other's homes. Getting together for house parties, or hanging out in the private homes of others who are part of the trans family, involves the same activities as others are involved in: cooking a dinner, scheming about the latest juicy gossip, sewing clothes, and just plain old having fun.

Another means of socializing, as well as a way of making life meaningful, is hanging out at the local gay bars. Many of "the girls" (the familiar name for MTFs) are able to perform on stage and show off their latest fashions. The bar becomes symbolic of a new created family system – the trans family. With a mixture of gay, lesbian, bi-, and questioning individuals, the transgender person is still the most ridiculed and misunderstood, but at the same time admired for her performance. Again, the performer is revered, the real person rejected. After the performance you become a thing, or the subject of the next joke waiting to be told.

Relational issues are always questionable. There is always the feeling of whether or not the person is relating to me or relating to the person I have created. I have seen friends who are "bent down" (passable as another gender) destroy themselves over the fact that they have fallen in love with a man that does not know the "T" (true gender identity). The stresses of depression and suicidal ideation, hopelessness, despair, low self-esteem, as well as vulnerability to crimes, violence, drugs, and risky health behaviors, are all revisited periodically throughout the lives of transgender people.

"Keeping my craziness within"

A "plainclothes" transgender, the category that fits me, seems to blend into the framework of normalcy in American lifestyles. If you take away the lipstick, the padding, the female clothing, the modulation in voice, the change in name and pronoun use, what is left is the same person. The only difference is that this person becomes more acceptable to others, and, with luck, to themselves. We are acceptable to the larger social world because we "fit in." The "plainclothes" transgender and what I term "the fixed/prepared" transgender both are the same internally. The only thing that keeps us apart and makes us different is the terminology – terminology that is either created by us, or by society. There are, of course, some actual differences also. First and most importantly, "plainclothes" transgender persons are permitted to move in and out – to circulate, if you will, among all of the genders through "acceptable" eyes – again, because we "fit in." We are sometimes erroneously viewed as closeted by both gay and straight society. "Plainclothes" transgenders, because we are invisible to most, are usually more employable and find it easier to have access to membership with groups that have societal approval – the gym, the Church, and fraternities. In the gay bar, the "plainclothes" transgenders are part of the audience, not part of the performance. After the show, the individual really does exist. Although this "plainclothes" individual is even more misunderstood than the average transgender, they are generally healthier internally.

The nurturing support and relationship connections from one's family permit the plainclothes transgender to be more equipped to function in the world, systematically without the physical barriers that many "fixed/prepared" transgenders face. Relational issues are more feasible because what you see is what you get. Like our fixed/prepared MTF counterparts, the plainclothes transgender person is intimately attracted to heterosexual men – men who recognize the women in us, without the additional paraphernalia of female clothing, makeup and other accoutrements. Most plainclothes transgender persons do not date, and are not interested in dating, gay men. The men whom we date are also more comfortable being seen with us in public, as the experiences that intimately bond us are internal, and therefore undetectable to the average person.

Whether plainclothes are fix/prepared, transgender persons are some of the most ambitious people on the face of this earth. Part of our problem is, "How do we get there?" No one has actually developed or devised programs for third-gender populations to advance themselves, socially, economically, or politically. Although there are some very unique needs within this population, most of us want the same things that everyone else wants: respect, a decent living wage, affordable housing, adequate health care, and people around us who really care about us. We have yet to see a legislative body or social program with the mandate and the agenda to adequately serve this population. Optimistic as I am, I do not believe that in my lifetime that we will see that, but we must learn to work to take care of our own people.

Implications for practice with MTF transgender youth

Listed below are some suggestions that social work practitioners can utilize when working with male-to-female transgender youth.

1 In addition to being understanding, empathic, and providing a non-judgmental environment, when working with these young people, professionals need to possess accurate information regarding both plainclothes and fixed/prepared transgender youth.
2 Make sure that you listen more than you talk.
3 Help your clients to understand and clarify their feelings about their trans nature.
4 The social worker should be able to provide accurate and age-appropriate information, which is readable and understandable, to the young person. Currently literature for and about trans youth is limited, but websites such as amazon.com and barnesandnoble.com and transgender.org can help social workers identify books and videos that may be useful.
5 Social workers must seek out resources that offer information which assists the young person in abolishing myths and stereotypes.

If these do not exist, social workers need to help develop them in communities.

6 Help clients to develop appropriate contacts within the transgender and the youth community. Social workers should educate themselves about these resources and be able to refer clients to them. Agencies within the gay, lesbian, and bisexual community frequently offer services to this population.

7 Help clients to develop effective interpersonal coping mechanisms to deal with the negative effects of societal stigmatization. Assist young people in exploring and developing mechanisms to clarify identity confusion and deal with conflict, relationships, depression, safer sex, and peer pressures.

8 Be aware of the signs of suicidal ideation and abuse of alcohol and other substances. Know resources to which clients can be referred to for services. If they don't exist, help to create them.

9 Social workers should assist their client in clarifying gender identity confusion, and whether or not they are appropriate candidates for hormone therapy. Social workers should educate themselves on the appropriate resources available for hormone therapy in accredited healthcare settings with trained healthcare practitioners.

10 Social workers should discuss the young person's feelings and concerns associated with dressing in or not dressing in gender preference clothing. The same is true for makeup use or lack thereof.

11 Social workers should be prepared to advocate for a young person who is having trouble at school, in a group or foster home, on the streets, or in their own families. The protection of these youth is an important task for the social worker.

12 Respect confidentiality at all times. The relationship must be based on trust.

13 Remember to work with trans youth's parents and siblings. They will also need education, opportunities to talk about their transgender family member, and safe places to process their feelings.

Chapter 7

Group-work practice with transgender and gender variant youth

Gus Klein

Introduction

The practice of group work with gender variant and transgender youth represents a complex area for innovation by social service providers. In 2000, the National Association of Social Workers (NASW) adopted a policy to support the transgender and gender variant community, which states:

> A nonjudgmental attitude toward gender diversity enables social workers to provide maximum support and services to those whose gender departs from the expected norm. Social workers must encourage the development of supportive practice environments for those struggling with gender expression and identity issues, including both clients and colleagues.

Transgender youth face multiple risk factors that affect their health, safety, and well-being. Lack of access to housing, education, employment, medical, and mental health services leaves transgender and gender variant youth at increased risk for homelessness, unemployment, depression, suicide, substance misuse, sexually transmitted drseases, HIV/AIDS, hepatitis C infection, and sexual and physical violence.

Working with transgender and gender variant youth requires social service providers to view gender on a continuum and to challenge beliefs about the "nature" of gender. Social service providers must have knowledge of the harms that gender variant and transgender youth face, and risk-reduction strategies to assist them to reduce these potential harms. However, providers must have group-work knowledge and skill in order to take the necessary steps to reduce these risks in the group experience.

This chapter explores the practice of group work with adolescents and its relevance in addressing the needs of gender variant and transgender youth. I will use examples from my experience as a group worker in a residential program where many of the residents were gender variant and transgender youth. My hope is to encourage more social service providers to use group work to create supportive programs that meet the needs this growing population.

Group-work practice

It is important to create a group experience for gender variant and transgender youth that addresses all their needs, not just their gender identity. Providers must bring attention to and address the strengths and abilities that the members bring to the group. These strengths need to be affirmed and given room for expression through the group process. The members need to know that they are more than the sum of their problems, more than the reputation they have gained, and more than some diagnostic label that has been assigned (Malekoff, 1997).

Group work with adolescents requires providers to be eclectic in their approach, taking from several theoretical frameworks rather than adopting a one-size-fits-all approach. The direction of a group is influenced by the needs of the group members, as well as the purpose and goals of the group. Understanding need is a requirement to establishing group purpose and setting individual goals and objectives. The needs of the potential group members encompass the individual desires and areas of concern that are specific to gender variant and transgender youth as well as those that are universal during the period of adolescence.

Assessing need

Need may be determined a variety of ways, through interviewing and testing or more informally by hanging out. Asking group members what their needs are does not often elicit the response that most providers are hoping for. Before creating a group, the provider must take on the role of "participant-observer." By hanging out and listening to what the youth talk about and do among themselves, the worker begins to get a sense of what their interests and concerns are and how they spend their time. Providers must be careful when attempting to base a group solely on a diagnostic or theoretical assessment of how gender variant and transgender youth ought to be. This is an inadequate measure of need and a poor predicator of behavior. The worker must remember that everyone responds and acts differently from situation to situation depending on the conditions set before them.

Case example 1

While working as the group-work coordinator in a foster care group home where many of the residents were gender variant or transgender identified,

I came in thinking that because I identified as queer and had a theoretical understanding of what the needs and experiences of transgender youth were, I would have no problem getting the residents to attend my groups. As I began creating groups and saw that nobody was attending, it didn't take me long to realize that another approach was needed that was based on the needs and interests of the residents. Here is where hanging out came in. As I took a step back and began to observe the flow of the group home, I realized that to get to know the needs of the residents I had to spend time hanging out on the front stoop.

This was the hangout spot, the place where gossip, dance moves, laughter, and sadness were shared among the residents. This was where over time through talking, laughing, and even dancing I learned about the experiences that each resident was having by themselves and with each other.

On one particular afternoon, while I sat in the middle of the group gathered on the steps, two of the girls came down to show the group some of the new clothing they had bought. As they bragged about how much the clothing cost, I asked where they got the money to buy the clothes. Everyone laughed and told me that they got the money working on the pier. It was known by staff that most of the transgender residents in the house would have sex for money at the pier, sometimes being dropped off in the morning by their "dates." However, none of the staff had actually talked about this with them, let alone been told the stories of what went on when they were down at the pier.

I realized that by hanging out and engaging in what was important to them, I was beginning to be trusted and shown what the residents' lives were really like once the staff left. This "in" allowed for open discussion about sex, drug use, relationships, and many other topics to occur.

Establishing the purpose of the group

The purpose signifies where the group is headed. It incorporates the goals and objectives that the group will carry out collectively, as well as the expectations that each group member has for what they will individually gain from participating in the group. The worker develops the purpose and goals of the group from the needs of the potential members. For a group to be successful, the purpose must be stated simply, clearly, and explicitly. Too often the group worker and agency have a different agenda that has not been shared with the members. The purpose of the group must be valid for both the group worker and members.

Case example 2

Now that I had been allowed "in" to the world and experiences that the residents were living, both inside and outside the group home, it was time to develop an overall purpose for the group-work program. Because the majority of the residents fell somewhere along the gender variant spectrum, it was important that I find ways to "invite the whole person" into every group experience. Most of the gender variant and transgender youth living in the group home had been moved from group home to group home because they did not conform to societal or cultural expectations of male or female. Once they arrived at our group home, they had spent so much of their adolescence fighting both the social service system and society that by the time it was safe for them to be themselves, it was apparent that very many of their needs had not been addressed because their gender variance was often seen as the root of the problem.

The purpose of the group-work program was that by "inviting the whole person" and not pathologizing a fluid gender expression, the members could develop the socialization, conflict resolution, and problem-solving skills that were universal to all adolescents while at the same time addressing the issues that are specific to gender variant and transgender youth. This included addressing issues around relationships, sex, family, coming out, hormone therapy, sex reassignment surgery, and educational and employment opportunities, to name but a few.

Strategies for effective intervention

Before entering into group work with gender variant and transgender adolescents, social service providers must look at their own ideologies about gender, with the understanding that if they choose to work within this community, those views and beliefs will be challenged. Hence, providers must assess their own feelings regarding societal expectations of gender and their level of comfort in talking about this sensitive subject matter.

For gender variant youth, a group that is structured to "invite the whole person" provides a safe space that is non-judgmental where exploration of the many layers of one's gender expression is encouraged. However, providers must be aware that this freedom of expression may be overwhelming and uncomfortable for some members. Together with the group members, the worker helps to set guidelines that protect their physical and emotional health. Leaving the members open to express themselves on a gender continuum allows them to feel as if during this group, if at no other time, they can "be the real me."

The responsibility of the group worker is to start the group process and to keep it on task by reminding the members why they are all there. However, the group members also share responsibility for the group's success. Mutual aid refers to the support that group members provide to each other. The group allows members the opportunity to share ideas and experiences, bringing with it a sense of validation and belonging. The realization that others experience and feel the same (or similarly) helps reduce the sense of alienation and loss that transgender and gender variant young people deal with. Brandler and Roman (1991) state that sharing of feelings provides a reality-testing base where members' ideas are accepted, confronted, and challenged by others. This process allows other group members to offer possible alternative responses to various situations. The group is a place for taking "safe risks" in a safe environment and playing out new and different parts of oneself. This process allows for the group to have more than one expert in the room, by placing value on the abilities and experiences that each member brings.

The unique challenge to group work is to facilitate a group process that centers on strengthening the potential for growth, belonging, and health, as group members reach out to each other and to a world that extends beyond the boundaries of the group (Schwartz, 1976). Creating an environment that focuses on empowerment and peer support, group work allows members to identify together activities that will strengthen their functioning within the group and the larger society.

The following example highlights a group that I co-facilitated with a media literacy collective with six of the group home residents. The purpose of the group was to teach the members media literacy and video production skills as a form of self-expression, advocacy, and community activism. Members planned, executed, and edited a video documentary about their lives in the group home. The group process included storyboarding (developing the focus of the video), learning how to use the video equipment, developing interview questions, interviewing staff and residents, videotaping important events such as holiday dinners and walking in the Pride Parade, logging and editing footage, and, lastly, participating in film screenings. Below is an interview with one of the residents that addresses her feelings about being a woman:

JESSICA: Being the woman of the millennium means that I can make my breasts as big or as small as I want to on a daily basis. I can use whatever bathroom I want. I don't consider myself a chick with a uh, because I go to sleep as a woman, I wake up as a woman, I take a shower as a woman, I do everything as a woman, so I'm the woman of the millennium. Cuz I'm different, the men can have the best of both worlds with me, right? Right.
[The group cheers] Yeah girl.

CHRISTINE: There you go, girl, there you go, this is what I call the woman of the millennium.

[We all stand around as Jessica explains to the group members and the camera how she makes her breasts using condoms.]

JESSICA: So, this is a titty. It's just water. I like to layer mine with two condoms. These are latex condoms, they're the strongest.

[Jessica takes her breasts out to show all of us what they look like, demonstrating her morning routine, carefully putting one then the other into her bra. She then gets up to show us how when she walks, they bounce up and down.]

JESSICA: Look, they jiggle and move, just like yours, Becky.

Conclusions

Social service providers have begun to offer groups to transgender and gender variant youth in a variety of community settings. These groups help to validate, through the process of sharing, the life experiences of gender variant adolescents. The sharing of experiences and feelings within groups through discussion or structured activities (i.e. watching movies, art projects, and field trips) facilitates the adolescent's development of decision-making and interpersonal skills. In addition, the group provides support to its members around safer sex, alcohol and drug use, relationships, gender identity, sexual orientation, dating, education, and employment.

Practitioners, educators, and policy-makers must continue to challenge each other to confront the large spectrum of gender identities. It is important that social work research and literature begin to focus on practice strategies for transgender and gender variant youth that promote wellness and harm reduction. Social service providers in and out of the transgender community must communicate areas of need and contribute their insight and practice experience to the literature.

Social workers must offer an environment that is free from judgment and personal bias. By practicing one of the basic tenets of social work practice – meeting their clients where they are at – practitioners can begin to provide services that address the physical and emotional needs of these youth. Social services for transgender and gender variant youth should include crisis intervention and housing (either permanent or temporary), free or subsidized medical and mental health services, case management services to assist in advocating for benefits and clients' rights, educational services, employment training, and recreational activities.

Group-work practice with transgender and gender variant teens offers group members a counterforce to the isolation and rejection that many in this population experience. The social work profession is a pioneer in providing concrete services to gender variant youth and their families. Future work must begin to challenge the notion within the psychological, psychiatric, and medical professions that gender identity disorder is a mental illness. The social work profession has become a model for providing services to the transgender and gender variant community because of its policy and practice which state that "there is considerable diversity in gender expression and identity among our population and people of diverse genders should be afforded the same respect and rights as any other person" (NASW, 2000).

References

Brandler, S. and Roman, C. (1991). *Group Work: Skills and Strategies for Effective Interventions*. New York: Haworth Press.

Malekoff, A. (1997). *Group Work with Adolescents: Principles and Practice*. New York: Guilford Press.

NASW (2000). Transgender and gender identity issues. In *Social Work Speaks*. Washington, DC: NASW Press.

Schwartz, W. (1976). Between client and system: Mediating function. In R. Roberts and H. Northen (Eds.) *Theories of Social Work with Groups*. New York: Columbia University Press.

Social work practice with transgender and gender variant youth and their families

Ken Cooper

Introduction

There is, inevitably, one question that has welcomed each of us into family life: "Is it a boy or a girl?" The question is not asked of us, of course. It is assumed that the answer is simple and apparent. Someone looks at our genitalia and decides. Are you a boy or a girl? The answer to this question is assumed to be definitive, outside of our power, and it will shape much of our future life. It is believed to be a given, predetermined; and it is a binary. Boy or girl. Few of us ever question the assignment that was made at birth. Fewer still ever question the meaning of the question. Must we be a boy or a girl? Are these the only two options? Are they mutually exclusive and clearly distinguishable, and do I have a choice in the matter?

There is probably no aspect of working with the transgender community that is more striking than the discovery of the range and diversity of human sex and gender. For any individual, whether we identify as transgender or not, this can be confusing, frightening, intimidating, exhilarating, and difficult. In a world that insists on the duality and consistency of sex and gender, coming to understand the transgender individual can be challenging for all involved. For transgender individuals and their families, and for social workers, there is little support in understanding and shaping a life that transcends this duality. As a result, social workers may often feel as their clients do – adrift in a sea of the changing and seemingly unknowable possibilities. Furthermore, they may find little help in understanding these possibilities by examining the literature available to them.

Written from a medical rather than a social perspective, the literature tends to pathologize gender variance and almost exclusively assumes a "transsexual" model. This, unfortunately, can act to limit understanding of the diversity of transgender lives. While some transgender individuals desire to "transition" from one sexed body to another by means of hormones, electrolysis, and surgery, not all do, and fewer still have the economic ability to do so. Even more importantly, an increasing number of transgender individuals are choosing to identify as neither male nor female and are claiming unique contours of sex and gender that offer new and unlimited possibilities. Understanding the nature of these possibilities requires a language that challenges the cultural assumptions of sex and gender. The language and literature of transgender existence has been emerging over the past decade as the transgender community grows and we begin to think beyond the binary of male and female, man and woman, masculine and feminine (Allen, 2003; Bornstein, 1994; Feinberg, 1997; Wilchins, 1997).

The term "transgender" is relatively new, and even within the past ten years has changed (see Davis' introductory chapter in this book). Each of these ways of being transgender presents a different set of relationships to the individual's sense of themselves as a sexed and gendered person. Finding the "best fit" in terms of individual and family relations requires being open to and exploring the multiple meanings of sex and gender for us and our relationships. The exploration of these options requires not only that we turn inside and unravel complicated feelings about who we are, but that we examine and enter into dialogue with others about how we are perceived.

Sex and gender shape the ways in which we relate to others and how they relate to us. The "father" who reveals his understanding of himself as a woman, and the "daughter" who insists on wearing boys' clothes and being referred to by the pronoun "he", are not simply expressing their innermost sense of self but are reestablishing their relationship to the world. For families this can be difficult, confusing, and painful. When the medical and psychiatric literature describing the experience of transgender individuals focuses on individual dysphoria, discomfort, unhappiness, and family unrest, it is not surprising that families ask themselves where they went wrong. Social workers working with the families of transgender individuals often discover that they have entered into a dialogue concerning things they themselves only marginally comprehend.

This chapter explores social work practice issues with transgender persons and their families. Exploring some of the common myths and beliefs regarding sex and gender identity will assist the social worker in helping the family understand and adapt to new ways of being, along with their transgender members.

Sex, gender, attributes, and roles

It is impossible to understand the gender variant family member without drawing distinctions between sex and gender and articulating some of our assumptions about them. Sex refers to the biological status of being a male, a female, or intersexed. Since the mere existence of intersexuality is commonly denied by our society and surgically removed from our culture, reference to our sex generally means being either male or female. Gender, on the other hand, refers to the social role we play. Generally this implies a sense of ourselves as a man or a woman. Gender is "read" by others on the basis of social expectations and gender attributes that we convey. While the range of "acceptable" attributes for "man" and "woman" varies from culture to culture, it is generally assumed that masculine attributes appropriately belong to men, and feminine attributes appropriately belong to women. The cult of gender remains so entrenched in our culture that displays of inappropriate gender attributes, such as femininity in men and masculinity in women, are commonly met with outright violence both inside and outside the family (Mallon, 2008).

In Western culture, it is believed that we were born distinctly male or female and therefore will grow up to be a man or a woman. It is also commonly assumed that it is "natural" that being of one or the other sex leads one to the development of the corresponding gender (that is, that because I was born a male, I am a boy who will become a man). Our gender training and segregation begin from our earliest days as people respond to us and treat us as a boy or a girl. Even infants are assigned pink or blue blankets according to their assigned gender. Almost every aspect of our lives is shaped, if not determined, by our gender assignment. Demonstrating gender traits or identity that challenge expectations commonly evokes the reaction that something is wrong with us.

Seeing each other *through* the lenses of gender (Bern, 1993), families tend to assume that they know and understand each member's sex and gender, and expect that it will remain consistent with their understandings of gender. But despite these cultural prescriptions, our wider experience tells us that neither sex nor gender is bipolar, inevitably correlated, and invariant. Helping families to understand and adapt to the transgender member often requires that the social worker assist them in examining gender – looking *at* the lenses of gender, not simply *through* them (Bern, 1993). There is no telling at what point in the life cycle the individual will come to a transgender identity and in what unique fashion it will manifest. Looking at some ways of the ways of being transgender such as intersexuality in infants, gender variation in children, transsexuality in adolescence and adults, and some new gender options being explored in the transgender community may help families understand and grow along with their transgender member.

Intersexuality in infants

At birth we are assigned a gender based on some observation about our sex. In short, this generally means that if the baby has a penis then it is a boy, and if it has a vagina then it is a girl. The presence of a penis or vagina, however, is only one of many biological criteria indicating sex and is not always consistent with other criteria. Hormones, chromosomes, and internal reproductive organs can also act as indicators of sex in the infant.

When infants are born with ambiguous or hermaphroditic genitalia, then surgery (known as virilization) is generally performed to more clearly articulate the child's sex as recognizably male or female. This is currently accepted practice because it is assumed that *all* children *must* be either male or female. Because medicine cannot currently reproduce through surgery a fully functioning penis, more than 90 percent of children whose genitals are altered at birth are assigned female genitalia. Combining this with attitudes that equate maleness with an "adequately" sized penis means that parents of newborns with "micro"-penises are often encouraged to submit their children to sexual reassignment surgery.

Current estimates are that 1 in every 1,500 to 2,000 births show ambiguous or hermaphroditic sex characteristics (Intersex Society of North America, 2007). For most of these children, their intersexed past is hidden from them, often resulting in feelings of confusion and maladjustment as they grow older. Some female-to-male-identified transgender individuals have discovered that they were assigned the sex of female as a result of ambiguous sex characteristics at birth, as the following case illustrates. In her 1999 profile of transgender individuals, Mary Boenke tells us the story of Max, who was raised as a female from birth and came out as a lesbian while in college. Although Max was female-identified in college, "she" knew that when she was born, the doctors could not tell whether she was a boy or a girl and had performed surgery that had left her with a vagina that was scarred and painful. She knew her body was different from other women's bodies and felt that she couldn't hide it, yet didn't know how lesbian women would respond to her intersex status. As an adult, sexual activity for Max was difficult and painful both physically and emotionally. During her college years she became involved with another woman and together they set out to understand her intersexed body. During the four months that they spent examining her infant medical records, Max began questioning her female sexual assignment and battled unwavering depression and suicidal ideation. Finally, she and her lover began attending support groups for intersexed individuals. There they met other people like Max and began to break down some of their stereotypes and expectations regarding Max's female body and lesbian identity. Max has now begun the process of transitioning to a male-identified gender role and as a result feels a greater sense of control over his life.

While only a small percentage of adults who will later identify as transgender are intersexed at birth, it is an important field of research for two reasons. First, it underscores our cultural bias toward understanding sex and gender as an irrefutable binary, and second, it is the first arena where parents will be asked to interfere with the natural diversity of sex and gender in their children. Dr. Ann Fausto-Sterling (1993, p. 13) has argued that rather than the two sexes we believe to exist, "there are many gradations running from female to male; and depending on how one calls the shots, one can argue that along the spectrum lie at least five sexes – and perhaps even more." In recent years, the Intersex Society of North America (ISNA) has evolved to help intersexed individuals and their parents understand and cope with the experience of being sexed in a way that is largely misunderstood in Western society. In the past, infant genital surgery has been the assumed treatment for intersexed children, but the ISNA has begun to question the wisdom of that prescription. Its position is that parents need to be informed that in most cases there is no evidence that infant genital surgery is either necessary or beneficial and that there is significant evidence that it may result in pain, depression, suicidal feelings, and social or sexual dysfunction. Many intersexed individuals argue that genital surgery should be postponed until children are old enough to make decisions for themselves. Encouraging parents to raise an intersexed child is, of course, very difficult, given the lack of support and understanding currently evident in society. Intersexed individuals need protection, support, and understanding. Only with truthful information about their intersexed children can parents begin to advocate for their children's needs in schools and other settings.

Gender variation in children

Every aspect of our lives is permeated with situations where we are asked to identify our gender. Purchasing clothing or toys and even whether you are encouraged to stand or not while urinating are controlled by signs and forms that demand a choice: Are you a boy or are you a girl? It is often difficult for family members to comprehend and support the transgender individual because we lack the language to discuss the complexities and varieties of ways of being sexed and gendered.

It is commonly accepted that gender identity develops in children by the age of 3, when most identify themselves as either boys or girls. Because it is popularly assumed that there is a "natural" relationship between sex and gender, children who question their birth assignment are pathologized and labeled "gender dysphoric." Experience tells us that there is not always a correlation between sex and gender identity, and anthropological studies indicate that numerous cultures allow for a wide variety of gender variant identities and social roles (Denny, 1997; Williams, 1997). Nonetheless, families may often feel confused, angry, or guilty when a child or adolescent demonstrates transgender behavior or identity.

Furthermore, owing to misinformation and a lack of education regarding sex and gender options, transgender people and their families may mistakenly be advised that treatment for "gender identity disorder" is their only option in dealing with the discomforts of raising a non-traditionally gendered child. According to the American Psychological Association (1980), gender identity is the sense of "knowing" what one's gender is, and gender role is the public expression of that identity. The APA's belief that gender "dysphoria" is an illness complicates the process of coming to self-knowledge for gender variant children and their families. Parents will unfortunately be surrounded by social pressure and professional advice that insists that something is wrong with their child. Because of this, childhood is most often a difficult period for gender variant children and their parents. There is virtually no social support in most institutions for the gender variant child, and the parent who attempts to negotiate accommodations for the child will commonly meet misunderstanding, incredulity, and resistance.

In such an environment, it is often the child who is blamed for their failure to adapt to gender norms. Often the child will respond with depression, anxiety, fear, anger, low self-esteem, self-mutilation, and suicidal ideation. Unfortunately, this is often taken as further evidence that something is wrong with the child. Rather than focus on the systems that will not allow the child to develop in their own natural way, treatment usually focuses on the child's "maladaptive" gender identity.

"Gender identity disorder" (GID) first appeared in the American Psychological Association's *DSM*-III in 1980. GID is described as an "incongruence between assigned sex (i.e. the sex that is recorded on the birth certificate) and gender identity." *DSM* goes on to describe a broad range of gender variant behaviors that may be observed in individuals, and insists that "in the vast majority of cases the onset of the disorder can be traced back to childhood." Preposterously, GID is considered a disorder even though "some of these children, particularly girls, show no other signs of psychopathology" (APA, 1980).

The introduction of GID in Children into the *DSM* came as the result of a United States government-funded experiment on gender variant boys that took place in the 1970s. These studies found that very few "feminine" boys will go on to become transsexuals, but that a high percentage of them (one-half to two-thirds) will become homosexual (Burke, 1996). GID was added to the *DSM*-III in 1980 following the removal of homosexuality as an illness from that volume (Bern, 1993). The addition of GID in Children to the *DSM* is justified in the name of preventing transsexualism, but focuses instead on modifying gender variant behavior and may all too easily be used to "treat" future homosexuality. Pauline Parks, a transgender activist, argues that every psychiatrist who diagnoses GID in a patient merely by virtue of his or her transgender identity is complicit in the manipulation and control of transgender people and their bodies. In diagnosing someone with an "illness" that he or she does not have, the psychiatrist engages in behavior which is "not only unethical but... constitutes medical malpractice" (Parks, 1998). Children are particularly vulnerable to suffering medical injustices in the name of treating gender identity disorder. Social workers can and should provide parents with a broader-focus, alternative model of gender, and expertise that might not be provided by other helping professionals.

Given the level of medical, cultural, and social misunderstanding that gender variant children will endure, it is not surprising that many will develop social isolation, depression, and self-esteem problems. Instead of being helped with these difficulties, children who are diagnosed with GID are often treated with brutal aversion therapies intended to adjust their gender orientation (Burke, 1996; Scholinski, 1997). Social workers should assist parents in resisting these treatments outright. Treatment for depression and associated conditions should not attempt to enforce gender-stereotypical behavior.

Transsexuality

When Christine Jorgenson went to Denmark in 1952 for her sex-change operation, she became the first internationally famous transsexual. Her case, which was widely covered by the media, popularized the notion of transsexuals as being "trapped inside the wrong body," and indicated a hormonal and surgical solution to an "aberrant" condition that was causing the transsexual individual great psychological pain. Often transsexuality is the only framework families have for understanding transgender lives. In 1966, Dr. Harry Benjamin published *The Transsexual Phenomenon*, which did a great deal to heighten awareness of transsexuals and to underscore that it was a female as well as a male phenomenon. Nonetheless, Dr. Benjamin's book still emphasized transsexualism as an aberration or illness.

Characteristic of transsexuality is the desire to alter the body through hormones and surgery to more appropriately match the individual's gender identity. Because we live in a world that assumes a binary of sex and gender that assumes "man" or "woman" to be our only choices, this kind of surgery is often designated "sex reassignment surgery." Contemporary transgender activists have suggested that "genital reconstruction surgery" is a more accurate description because it more precisely describes the nature of the intervention.

Individuals seeking sex reassignment enter into a complicated relationship with the medical and psychiatric establishments that act as "gatekeepers" to the medical procedures. Dr. Benjamin's institute developed the *Standards of Care* that are used to determine the appropriateness of an individual's desire for sex reassignment surgery, and that supposedly provide controls to insure that individuals do not rush into surgery that they may later regret.

Coming to the decision to seek hormonal and surgical body alteration is indeed a difficult decision to make. Rather than simplifying the process, the medicalization of transsexuality often complicates this decision. The medicalized and pathologized notion of transsexuals presupposes that one must be very uncomfortable with one's body in order to seek out sex reassignment surgery so that one is in fact "rewarded" for one's psychological pain and discomfort. Many transsexuals fear that if they do not register the appropriate amount of discomfort with their bodies they will not be approved for surgery. This acts to reinforce notions of transsexuality as an illness that has a medical and surgical treatment.

Sex reassignment surgery may be a difficult topic for families to talk about. Literature that is intended to inform them may frighten them by pathologizing the transsexual individual. Social workers can help families by normalizing and reframing the desire of transsexuals to alter their bodies. Wendy Chapkis has suggested that we all alter our bodies to more accurately match our gender identities:

> [N]early everyone attempts to reshape their anatomy to bring it more comfortably close to the sex and gender ideal. Most women shave their legs and underarms because it is not only unfeminine, it is somehow unfemale to be hairy. The mustached woman will almost certainly contemplate a change of anatomy through depilatories or electrolysis to avoid being addressed as "sir," to rid herself of the confusing sensation of stubble, to ease the mixed signals. A small chested woman may receive breast implants to help her feel more womanly. A short man may wear elevator shoes and a small man devote himself to body building to create a more "manly" physique. All are trying to fix a conflict between social and sexual identity and anatomical reality.
>
> (1986, p. 155)

What the transsexual does to alter their bodily appearance, according to Sandra Lipsitz Bern (1993), is different only in degree (and direction) from what "normal" people do to match their bodies to their gender identities. By helping families understand how we all create gender through manipulation of our bodies, our clothing, and the gender clues we convey, social workers can help them accept and accommodate the transgender member. The choice to alter one's body can and should be framed as an act of empowerment over one's life rather than as a surgical solution to an uncomfortable situation.

Parents may often find themselves facing questions of transsexual identity during the child's adolescent years. Often the onset of puberty will bring about a feeling of crisis in the transgender individual because they find their bodies changing in ways that do not match their gender identities. Transgender teens may feel betrayed, isolated, shameful, and bewildered by the changes occurring in their bodies. These feelings may be accompanied by a sense of panic and immediacy that these changes must be stopped. Transgender teenagers will often feel confused about their sexual orientation, and are frequently subject to harassment and humiliation by their peers and by adults during this time. Teens who identify as transgender will need protection and support as they come to terms with their sexual and gender identity. It is often during these years that those who go on to be transsexual will begin contemplating sex reassignment surgery, and they will often express frustration at their lack of access to immediate treatment. Support groups where they can meet others like themselves, share frustrations, and explore ways of coping can be extremely helpful at this time. Because many teens will have a complete absence of transsexual role models, it is particularly desirable that transsexual teens have access to individuals who have gone through the surgical procedures who can help put perspective on the process for them. Support and social groups can help the transgender individual sort through their feelings about their sex and gender and help them in coming to an understanding of themselves in relation to transgender identity and transsexuality.

At a residence for gay, lesbian, and transgendered youth in New York City, I met Jaleeka, a 15-year-old Dominican male-to-female transsexual. While her family consider her too young to begin hormones and too poor to consider surgery, she is quite certain that she will begin the transition as soon as she can legally do so. Before meeting other transsexuals, Jaleeka was perceived as a young gay male and she was in conflict with her family, who did not consider homosexuality a viable option. Jaleeka found herself depressed and suicidal. Jaleeka knew that she had always thought of herself as a girl but she had never met another transsexual. When she first learned of transsexuality, she came to see herself as a "straight" woman who needed surgery in order to have the body she desired. She grew her hair, began dressing in woman's clothes on a full-time basis, and assumed a girl's role in the family. For her family, this transition was easier and more understandable than accepting an effeminate, homosexual son.

Social workers may be cautious in supporting transsexuality as an alternative to the stigma of homosexuality. Nonetheless, a supportive and non-judgmental environment may help transsexual teenagers come to terms with their gender identity. Not only did Jaleeka benefit from support groups where she met transsexuals who had been through sex reassignment surgery, but her parents benefited enormously both from contact with postoperative transsexuals and their parents.

Even those individuals who are interested in sex reassignment surgery will find it difficult to obtain. Most insurance companies explicitly exclude hormone therapy and sex reassignment surgery. Furthermore, this is a highly regulated medical industry whose benefits may or may not be awarded to an individual, depending on the recommendation of a so-called gender specialist. Often, gender specialists are just the opposite of what the term implies, offering little perspective on the way gender operates in society and distilling options down to "passing" as the "opposite" gender. Many transgender individuals find themselves poorly understood by these "gender specialists."

> There is a growing number of people who are diagnosed as gender dysphoric, but for one reason or another are not deemed good candidates for sex reassignment. Gender identity programs can turn down applicants for many reasons – age, a history of psychiatric illnesses, homosexuality, fetishism, sadomasochism, a criminal record, inability to tolerate hormones, a medical history of cancer, possessing a face or body that the surgeon believes will never pass muster as a member of the gender preference ("somatically inappropriate"), poverty, employment in the sex industry, a refusal to aspire to be a feminine woman or a masculine male, or uppitiness.
>
> (Califia, 1997, p. 169)

Whether by choice or by circumstance, many transgendered people are discovering that "transitioning" is not an option for them. One result is that an increasing number of individuals reject the notion that one must "transition" and "pass" as the opposite gender in order to blend in with the binary gender system. Growing awareness of the range of gender options between male and female has revolutionized transgender politics and increased gender options available to us.

New gender options

While the advent of sex reassignment surgery in the 1950s offered new possibilities for gender variant individuals, it also solidified an understanding of transsexuality that fed rather than dispelled common myths regarding sex and gender. It did little to dispel the notion that the binary gender system was a natural phenomenon. It ignored the possibility that an individual might have a healthy relationship to their transgender status, or that there might be a wide variety of ways of being sexed and/or gendered that may or may not include body alteration.

Increasingly, transgender individuals are coming to understand their lives as outside of the sex and gender binary and are discovering that this understanding increases the options available to all of us. Some choose not to undergo bodily transformation, but to dress and live their lives in differently gendered roles. Cross-dressers or male-bodied women, for example, may inhabit a male body but live dressed in and occupying the social role of women. Gender-blenders may incorporate physical and cultural characteristics of both genders in a way that feels comfortable and appropriate to them. Many transgender people have discovered that some forms of body modification such as breast reduction or hormone therapy may result in just the right amount of male or female characteristics, and thus may choose not to undergo genital reconstruction surgery. Gender-blenders, she-males, or he-shes are representative of this kind of sex and gender mix. "Transvestite" has traditionally been a term for individuals who maintain their original sex and gender identities but attain sexual gratification from dressing in the clothing of the opposite sex, but today the term may refer to individuals who prefer the clothing of the "opposite" sex for any of a variety of reasons. New sex and gender variations are being discovered or invented each day by individuals who are exploring their own unique needs.

The understanding that we do not need to trade one gender for another but can find or invent a mix that is just right for us has revolutionized the possibilities for transgender living. New gender possibilities will increase the need for adaptations within the family because of the way these gender possibilities confront our "knowledge" of sex and gender as a binary system.

It should not matter to the social worker whether the transgender individual decides to be male, female, or somewhere in the middle. However, in helping families work through the challenges of transition, we can encourage new forms of relationships that will support change and maximize freedom of choice.

Family transitions

Coming to understand a family member's transgender identity can be a difficult and confusing experience. The nature of our relationship with a son, daughter, wife, husband, mother, father, sister, brother, aunt, or uncle is intricately woven into what we believe we know about the consistency of gender. Learning to reframe a relationship with the family member who has begun to question or redefine their gender status may result in difficult and confusing alterations in the structure of the family. Understanding and accommodating these changes in family relationships is challenging at best, and often family members experience the same confusion, guilt, anger, pain, and disappointment that the transgender family member has already struggled with. Family members need time to grieve for the loss of a relationship as they understood it, and they need support and education in building a new relationship based on an unfamiliar gender dynamic (Brown and Rounsley, 1996; Lesser, 1999).

Social workers may help the families of transgender individuals by encouraging them to explore the meaning of gender in their relationships. They must also be prepared to deal with what may be a family's guilt, embarrassment, or shame about having a transgender family member.

Families may find it difficult to adjust to the use of new pronouns, or the use of a new name for a family member. But for many this is the first step in altering the terms of a relationship. The person who was a "son" may feel strongly that his parents should refer to her as their "daughter." The family member who forgets and uses the wrong pronoun may discover that they have caused pain without intending to do so. Whatever the circumstances, social workers should not underestimate the transition that is required from family members in adapting to a new relationship. The mother of a "heterosexual son" who must come to grips with the fact that she now has a "lesbian daughter" may feel betrayed by her own child.

Alternatively, family members may accept the newly gendered member without altering some basic terms of the relationship. Noelle Howey, for example, is a playwright whose father has transitioned to female. In *Dress Codes: Of Three Girlhoods – My Mother's, My Father's and Mine*, Howey (2003) tells how she learned to refer to her father as a woman and use the pronoun "she" when speaking of her but still recognized this woman as her father. Adjusting to new gender and familial relationships will take time, and social workers can provide support by offering reassurance to all family members that this transition can happen.

Forming families

Transgender individuals will, of course, form relationships and families of their own. Forming relationships requires honesty, acceptance, and understanding. Nonetheless, many professionals have encouraged their clients to hide their transsexuality and "pass" as their new gender. Gender clinics have even encouraged transsexuals to make up life histories that would validate their new gender identity. Transsexualism, as Kate Bornstein points out, is the only condition for which the recommended therapy is to lie:

> When I was growing up, people who lived cross-gendered lives were pressured into hiding deep within the darkest closets they could find. Those who came out of their closets were either studied under a microscope, ridiculed in the tabloids, or made exotic in porn books, so it paid to hide. It paid to lie. That was probably the most painful part of it: the lying to friends and family and lovers, the pretending to be someone I wasn't.
>
> (1994, p. 177)

Needless to say, the perpetuation of this perspective made dating and romance difficult if not impossible for many transgender individuals. As transgender individuals develop a broader, healthier, and more honest understanding of the meaning of their lives, they discover the need for partners who understand and are supportive of their transgender bodies.

Much of the literature about transgender people in relationships has focused on the difficulties: wives in turmoil when their husbands come out to them as cross-dressers or transsexuals who fear being "discovered" by their lovers. However, as the transgender community grows in self-aware-ness, new bodies of literature are emerging that speak to successful and honest relationships between transgender people and their partners (Boenke, 1999; Boylan, 2003; Califia, 1997). Often, these relationships must transcend the gender-based sexual orientation of our culture. The wife who comes to accept her husband as a woman, or the lesbian whose partner transitions to male may find that their relationship and sexual ori-entation can no longer be contained by the categories of "gay" or "straight." Pat Califia (1997) has suggested that there is a broad range of individuals who may prefer some form of transgenderism in their partners and that this group may be a sexual minority in their own right. For many, involvement with a transgender partner may offer an edge of excitement and discovery in both the social and the sexual arena that may draw them to these partners.

Increasingly, transgender individuals are beginning to form primary rela-tionships with each other. These relationships, which transcend contemporary notions of hetero- and homosexuality, may open doors for all of us in contemplating other ways besides gender in which our sexuality may be organized. Sylvia Riviera was a female-identified drag queen who played an important role in the Stonewall Rebellions. While she has always been attracted to men, in later life she found herself in a relation-ship with a male-to-female transsexual. This relationship surprised her and, because she was legally still a man and her partner legally a woman, they planned their wedding.

> I never thought that I was going to get into the situation of marrying somebody, but I'm very happy. I don't plan on getting a sex change as my partner has already done. But I feel that both of us being transgen-der, we understand what the other has gone through... we just want to be ourselves. And she's a great person for me.
>
> (Riviera, 1999, p. 49)

Building community, building family

How we define the family is vital because, as Hartman and Laird have pointed out, it is in defining the family that we define what models and social policies are stimulated and endorsed, for what families social polices are developed, and "even more basically... who is considered 'normal' and who is labeled 'deviant'" (Hartman and Laird, 1983, p. 110). The family should be, of course, a source of support, nourishment, and stability for each of its members. Given the wide variation in human circumstance, it naturally follows that family would take on a wide variety of forms. The strength of the family resides in its function rather than its form. Nonetheless, as a culture we frequently fret about what has become of "the family," and much public discussion of "the family" focuses on a rather narrow structural view of what constitutes family. The family occupies a prominent place in our public discourse and, as Hartman and Laird (1983, p. 112) point out, it is one topic that "sends people running to their philosophical battle stations."

In 1996, Congress passed almost unanimously, and President Clinton unhesitatingly signed, the "Defense of Marriage Act" (DOMA). This act, which was hastily thrown together and pushed through Congress by "pro-family" forces that felt threatened by the growing recognition of same-sex unions, defines marriage as strictly between "one man" and "one woman." The intention of the law is clear: that there should be governmental recognition of only one form of family. The ease with which the DOMA was passed underscores that it is not just the religious right wing that is vested in limiting the individual's options in forming families; rather, the conservative political agenda of so-called family values is a potent, and dangerous, mainstream dogma. The DOMA has no interest in supporting families; instead, it seeks to maintain a narrow definition of the family. It rewards and reinforces participation in a heterocentric family structure.

It is perhaps an indication of the invisibility of transgender people that the crafters of the DOMA did not deem it necessary to define a "man" and a "woman." This means that transgender individuals often find themselves in unusual (and sometimes even advantageous) circumstances in relation to the law. In some states, birth certificates are relied upon to assure that partners seeking a marriage license are "one man, and one woman." This loophole has allowed for the marriage of a gay male couple where one partner is a female-to-male transsexual. Mary Boenke (1999) tells of Mitch, who is a female-to-male transsexual attracted to other men. When he and his partner went to apply for a marriage license they were told that only gender-mixed couples were granted licenses and that birth certificates were necessary to prove gender. While Mitch had legally changed his driver's license from female to male, state law did not allow changes in birth certificates. He was therefore able to produce a birth certificate that showed that he was a woman, and he and his partner were granted a marriage license. In 1999, they may have been the only gay male couple legally married in America.

Limiting the ways in which we think about and define family constrains our ability to create family. As transgender people grow into new relationships, many discover that the traditional family is no longer a safe or supportive place for them. This, however, does not decrease their needs for belongingness, intimacy, interpersonal connectedness, and all of the day-to-day resources that belonging to a family can provide. The transgender person who wishes to live fully their transgender identity needs forms of family that will support and nourish their existence. Families provide economic support and interdependence, foster a sense of emotional connectivity, stability, and belongingness, help develop our capacity for intimacy, and provide for a sense of generativity (Hartman and Laird, 1983). The function and benefits of family are evident in differing degrees in a wide variety of social structures available to us. Recognition and reinforcement of structures that provide for the needs of transgender individuals may result in new and more communal forms of family.

In the film *Paris is Burning* (Livingston, 1991), which focuses on young transgender inner-city kids who participate in the Harlem Drag Ball culture, it is the "house" that provides an alternative to their often dysfunctional families. Each "house" has a "mother," someone of legendary status in the Drag Ball scene, who helps her "children" in finding their own way through the culture. The children take the mother's name as their own, a symbol of their strong identification with the house to which they belong. The film portrays the ways in which the house culture provides them with intimacy, understanding, support, and a sense of belongingness as they struggle with their emerging gender identity and the many questions that it raises in their lives. Not enough studies have examined the usefulness of alternative family structures in the transgender community, and further studies of the house culture in particular may provide wider understanding of ways in which family function may serve in the lives of otherwise marginalized individuals.

The growing transgender movement has also proven to be invaluable in helping transgender individuals redefine themselves in relation to gender, in relation to family, and in relation to larger social structures. Lombardi (1999) have found that involvement in transgender organizations results in a strengthening of the individual's identity and results in an increase in activities outside of club meetings as well. For individuals who have been told that they are "sick" and must hide their transgender status, these social structures provide acceptance, support, encouragement, education, and understanding. Transgender social networks empower transgender individuals to free themselves from the control of the medical establishment and establish new forms of relationships and families that support them and their transgender identities. They create a hospitable niche for the transgender individual where they can begin to explore the nature of their transgender lives, and find meaning in new relationships that may not fit the traditional definitions of family. Family is too important to us to be narrowly defined by blood, kinship, or constricting legal parameters. In building community and reaching out to others, transgender people are actively creating family in ways that support, encourage, and celebrate transgender lives.

References

Allen, M. P. (2003). *The Gender Frontier*. Heidelberg, Germany: Kehrer Verlag.
American Psychological Association (1980). *Diagnostic and Statistical Manual of Mental Disorders* (3rd ed.). Washington: APA.
American Psychological Association (1994). *Diagnostic and Statistical Manual of Mental Disorders* (4th ed.). Washington: APA.
Benjamin, H. (1966) *The Transsexual Phenomenon*. New York: Julian Press.
Bern, S. L. (1993). *The Lenses of Gender*. New Haven, CT: Yale University Press.
Boenke, M. (1999). *Trans Forming Families: Real Stories about Transgender Loved Ones*. Imperial Beach, CA: Walter Trook.
Bornstein, K. (1994). *Gender Outlaw: On Men, Women and the Rest of Us*. New York: Vintage Books.
Boylan, J. F. (2003). *She's Not There: A Life in Two Genders*. New York: Random House.
Brown, M. and Rounsley, C. A. (1996) *True Selves: Understanding Transsexualism for Family, Friends, Co-workers and Helping Professionals*. San Francisco: Jossey-Bass.
Burke, P. (1996) *Gender Shock: Exploding the Myths of Male and Female*. New York: Bantam Books.
Califia, P. (1997) *Sex Changes: The Politics of Transgenderism*. San Francisco: Cleis Press.
Chapkis, W. (1986) *Beauty Secrets: Women and the Politics of Appearance*. Boston: South End Press.
Denny, D. (1997) Transgender: Some historical, cross-cultural and contemporary models and methods for coping and treatment. In B. Bullough, V. Bullough, and J. Elias (Eds.) *Gender Blending*. Amherst, NY: Prometheus Books.
Fausto-Sterling, A. (1993) The five sexes: Why male and female are not enough. *The Sciences*, March/April, 12–22.
Feinberg, L. (1997). *Transgender Warriors: Making History from Joan of Arc to Denis Rodman*. Boston: Beacon Press.
Hartman, A. and Laird, J. (1983). *Family-centered Social Work Practice*. New York: Free Press.
Howey, N. (2003). *Dress Codes: Of Three Girlhoods – My Mother's, My Father's and Mine*. New York: Picador.
Intersex Society of North America (2007). *Intersexuality: Frequently Asked Questions*. Retrieved May 25, 2008 from the World Wide Web: http://www.isna.org/faq.
Lesser, J. G. (1999). When your son becomes your daughter: A mother's adjustment to a transgender child. *Families in Society 80* (2), 182–189.
Livingston, J. (Director) (1991). *Paris is Burning* [film].
Lombardi, E. L. (1999). Integration within a transgender social network and its effects on members' social and political activity. *Journal of Homosexuality* 37(1), 109–126.
Mallon, G. P. (Ed.) (2008). *Social Work Practice with LGBT People*. New York: Routledge.

Parks, P. (1998). *Are you a Gender Psychopath? Finding Common Cause in the Battles Against Homophobia and Transgenderphobia.* Lesbian and Gay New York, November 15, p. 16.

Riviera, S. (1999). I never thought I was going to be a part of gay history. *New York Times Magazine,* June 27, p. 49.

Scholinski, D. (1997). *The Last Time I Wore a Dress.* New York: Riverhead Books.

Wilchins, R. A. (1997). *Read My Lips: Sexual Subversion and the End of Gender.* Ann Arbor, MI: Firebrand Press.

Williams, W. (1997). The transgender phenomenon: An overview from the Australian perspective. *Venereology, 10*(3), 147–149.

Chapter 9

Legal advocacy on behalf of transgender and gender nonconforming youth

Cole Thaler, Flor Bermudez, and Susan Sommer

Introduction

Most young people in Western society take for granted such basic givens of civic life as having a birth certificate, school records, and first driver's license that accurately reflect their gender and name.[1] But for transgender and gender nonconforming young people, these "givens" can pose enormous legal obstacles. Even something as mundane as entering a public rest room can pose a dilemma for transgender people. The legal hurdles facing transgender youth who seek respect for their gender identity and expression in many walks of life can be daunting – but need not be insurmountable. This chapter outlines legal issues commonly faced by transgender and gender nonconforming young people and the growing range of rights and strategies to allow them to be respected for who they are.

The personal and social nuances of transgender or gender nonconforming identity vary as widely as human beings themselves. Legal protections and challenges for transgender people are considerably more standardized, but often vary from state to state or even city to city. Agencies, courts, and legislatures have established procedures and principles that affect transgender lives in a variety of ways. An overview of such information follows, but transgender and gender nonconforming youth and their advocates should be sure to consult legal authorities in their jurisdiction to learn more about the procedures and protections in place.

Gender transition is not a standardized process that all transgender people experience in the same way. Each transgender person undertakes particular changes in identity and appearance that are appropriate for that individual. The World Professional Association for Transgender Health (WPATH)'s *Standards of Care* – therapeutic guidelines written by transgender health experts – confirm that gender transition is an individualized process. First drafted in 1979 and updated five times, most recently in 2001, the *Standards of Care* articulate the professional consensus regarding health care for all transgender people (adults as well as youth). While hormone therapy and sex reassignment surgery are medically necessary procedures for a number of transgender people, others will complete their transition without undergoing any physical modifications. Furthermore, the WPATH Standards recommend that an individual undergo a "real-life experience" – that is, that he or she live as a member of the target gender in all aspects of life – for several months *before* receiving hormone therapy or surgery. Failure to treat a transgender person in accordance with gender identity thus can interfere with an important therapeutic process. Regardless of the components of an individual's gender transition, respect, and recognition for gender identity, should never be predicated on whether certain medical interventions have been performed. Teachers, social workers, employers, landlords, lawyers, and others who interact with transgender young people should not ask invasive questions about anatomy (or worse, demand proof of medical procedures) before using terms of address preferred by the transgender person and otherwise treating them in accordance with their gender identity. Many transgender youth have a legal name that does not correspond with their gender identity, and prefer to use a name and a pronoun that better reflect their sense of themselves as male or female. This fundamental principle should inform all interactions with, and advocacy on behalf of, transgender clients.

Name changes and identity documents

Transgender people seeking to change their legal names and government-issued identity documents to align with their gender identity must frequently find their way through a complicated thicket of rules and procedures. Many of the relevant laws, regulations, and policies vary depending on the transgender person's state of residence or state of birth. Minors seeking to navigate the maze of identity documentation issues may encounter additional hurdles, but most challenges can be overcome through thoughtful and educated advocacy.

Name changes

Many transgender people choose a new first name that aligns with their gender identity. However, having a preferred name that is different from one's legal name can lead to a host of problems. For example, school officials will often refuse to change the name in a student's records or on a student ID until the student can present a court order of legal name change. Discrepancies between the name someone is called and the name that appears on records, identity documents, job applications, paychecks, and other documents can have a range of consequences, from embarrassment to risk of physical harm due to undesired disclosure of transgender status. For these and other reasons, many transgender people eventually seek to formalize the preferred name by seeking a legal name change.

Although state laws regarding name changes vary, in most jurisdictions courts grant name changes to people who confirm that they are not seeking the change of name to defraud their creditors, evade law enforcement, or otherwise escape legal obligations. In most states, legal name changes are available only by filing a petition for legal name change in the court in the county where the person resides. Court procedures for legal name changes vary from state to state and sometimes among courts within a state. Some courts have pre-printed name-change forms for people seeking name changes to fill out and submit. Some courts require people seeking name changes to publish their name in a local newspaper for a certain number of weeks, and then present proof of publication to the court. This requirement may be waivable in some jurisdictions. Some courts require hearings in front of a judge before the name change is granted; others will grant them without hearings. It is standard for courts to charge filing fees, and there is typically a fee associated with publication, where that is required.

States also vary with respect to their rules for minors seeking name changes. Some states require the petition to be filed by a parent or guardian. Others may require the minor to present proof that his or her parents or guardians consent to the name change or have been notified of it. Transgender youth seeking name changes should call the clerk's office in the court in their county to inquire about relevant procedures.

Although a number of states formerly recognized common-law name changes – that is, names that become legal through usage alone – the number of states that do so is diminishing. State and federal trends towards standardization and electronic storage of data have contributed to this change. People who have obtained valid common-law name changes in the past may run into problems when seeking to change their names on identity documents such as passports, because government agencies typically request proof of a court-ordered name change before they will amend their records. People should consult their state's laws to learn what is permissible in their state.

Generally, it should not be necessary to retain a lawyer in order to obtain a legal name change. This is a common legal procedure, and many courts (particularly in urban areas) provide a relatively streamlined process, sometimes even posting the necessary forms on their website. However, minors, individuals in state custody, individuals with criminal records, and others with special circumstances might need added help from an attorney to ensure that they are fully informed of their rights.

Unfortunately, some transgender people find themselves in front of biased or uninformed judges who require the transgender person to present a different kind of evidence than is required of other petitioners, such as medical evidence that confirms that their anatomy "matches" their desired name. Courts that impose such heightened burdens are commonly motivated by the belief that the general public has an interest in knowing what sex a person "really is," or that gender transition has not occurred until genital anatomy is surgically changed. Name-change denials based on such reasoning are almost never supported by law and are typically over-turned (*In re Guido*, 2003; *Matter of Eck*, 1991; *In re McIntyre*, 1998). In some jurisdictions, community groups have established low or no-cost name change clinics for transgender people. For example, in New York City both the West Village Trans Legal Name Change Clinic and the Transgender Legal Defense and Education Fund's Name Change Project assist transgender people seeking legal name changes. Court fees and pub-lication costs for name changes may amount to several hundred dollars.

Identity documents

To facilitate living in the preferred gender, many transgender people seek at some point to change the name and sex designation on their govern-ment-issued identity documents. These documents include driver's licenses, birth certificates, passports, and Social Security records. As a rule, govern-ment agencies will change the name on documents upon presentation of a court order of name change (see the previous subsection). There is greater variation in rules and policies for changing the sex designation on identity documents, but, with few exceptions, such changes are possible.

Rules for changing the sex designation on *state*-issued documents such as driver's licenses and birth certificates vary by state. For more information on state birth certificate laws and policies, see Lambda Legal's website at http://www.lambdalegal.org/our-work/issues/rights-of-transgen-der-people/sources-of-authority-to-amend.html. Individuals must seek new driver's licenses in the state in which they live, and new birth certificates from the state in which they were born. Most agencies that issue birth cer-tificates require some form of medical evidence before they will change the sex designation. For example, a Nebraska law provides that a new birth certificate will be issued "[u]pon receipt of a notarized affidavit from the physician that performed sex reassignment surgery on an individual born in this state" (Neb. Rev. Stat. § 71–604.01, 2005). In general, people can obtain new or amended birth certificates by providing medical documenta-tion that tracks the language in the governing law or policy. Other states will not amend the sex on birth certificates without presentation of a court order confirming that an individual's sex has been changed. It is advisable to obtain legal assistance or consultation before filing petitions seeking such orders, especially for minors, who may not be able to present evid-ence of having undergone gender reassignment treatment.

Departments of motor vehicles similarly vary in their requirements for changing one's sex designation. For example, the Alabama Department of Public Safety requires submission of documentation from a physician attesting to the success of sex reassignment surgery. The California Department of Motor Vehicles requires a medical doctor or hospital to fill out a form offering their professional opinion about the transgender individual's gender identity.

The two *federal* documents that transgender people most commonly seek to amend are passports and Social Security records. The sex designation on passports can be changed upon presentation of medical evidence confirming that sex reassignment surgery has been performed. Sex on Social Security records can be amended upon presentation of a letter from the surgeon or attending physician verifying that sex reassignment surgery has been completed. New or amended naturalization certificates, United States Permanent Resident Cards ("green cards") or employment authorization documents can be obtained by submitting medical documentation establishing the new gender. To learn more about changing information on federal documents, visit the websites of the National Center for Transgender Equality (http://nctequality.org/Issues/Federal_Documents.html) or Immigration Equality (http://immigrationequality.org/template.php?pageid=171).

Transgender people seeking identity document changes should be mindful of several potential pitfalls. First, at the time of writing, three states refuse to issue new birth certificates with an amended sex under any circumstances. These states are Tennessee, Ohio, and Idaho. Second, a number of states that do amend sex do not issue a new, "clean" birth certificate, but will cross out the old sex or stamp "Amended" in the margin of the document, or otherwise indicate on the face of the document that information has been changed. This can pose a challenge to transgender people who do not want their amended birth certificate to reveal their transgender status. Third, variations often exist in how state agencies interpret or apply their policies. Some employees are simply unaware that policies exist and will deny such requests or will demand documentation or evidence actually required by the governing statute, regulation, or policy.

Fourth, some states have amended their interpretation of policy to be more restrictive. For example, Illinois recently changed its birth certificate policy to require individuals to present evidence that their sex reassignment surgery was performed by a surgeon licensed to practice in the United States. Fifth, recent years have seen a nationwide trend toward greater standardization of identity documents. These measures, purportedly intended to combat terrorism and immigration violations, have a direct effect on transgender people. The most prominent example of this trend is the federal Real ID Act, a 2005 law that establishes federal standards for driver's licenses, essentially converting the driving license into a national identification card. The Real ID Act and its regulations mandate the inclusion of gender on driver's licenses, but do not disturb states' discretion to set policies for changing gender. The Real ID Act mandates that states confirm the identity of individuals seeking to obtain or renew driver's licenses, requires states to retain and store documents presented by people seeking licenses, and creates a nationwide database of driver's license information. The Real ID Act's identity document provisions are scheduled to take effect in 2011, and a number of states have passed laws or resolutions opposing it. Its full effect on transgender people is as yet unknown.

Finally, there are a number of other documents or records on which transgender people may seek to change their name and (where applicable) their sex. The ease of securing such changes will vary. Such documents may include school transcripts or diplomas, public assistance records, bank accounts, human resources records, credit cards and utility bills, voter registration records, deeds or leases, insurance policies, loans, and professional licenses.

Advocacy for transgender youth regarding employment, housing, and public benefits

Employment

As of the date of writing, 12 states and the District of Columbia have passed laws explicitly prohibiting employment discrimination on the basis of gender identity. Those states are California, Colorado, Illinois, Iowa, Maine, Minnesota, New Jersey, New Mexico, Oregon, Rhode Island, Vermont, and Washington. Hawaii has enacted a gender identity non-discrimination law that applies only to housing and public accommodations, not to employment. Dozens of cities and counties have passed similar protections. Considered in the aggregate, this web of protections means that more than a third of people in the United States live in jurisdictions with explicit transgender protections. This rate is growing by leaps and bounds; similar laws are pending in a number of other states. No federal law currently prohibits employment discrimination on the basis of gender identity, but advocates seeking passage of the federal Employment Non-Discrimination Act (ENDA) are striving to pass a version of that law that includes gender identity protections.

Even in jurisdictions where there is no explicit protection on the basis of gender identity or expression, transgender employees may be protected by existing laws. A significant number of state and federal courts have held that laws against sex discrimination protect individuals who are discriminated against on the basis of their gender identity and expression, including transgender people. These rulings frequently cite a 1989 US Supreme Court case, *Hopkins v Price Waterhouse* (1989), which held that an employer discriminated against a female employee when it denied her a promotion because she was not "feminine" enough. The Supreme Court held that discrimination due to the failure to conform to an employer's sex stereotypes of masculinity or femininity is a form of sex discrimination. Transgender litigants have built on this doctrine in a variety of lawsuits and jurisdictions, with encouraging results (see *Smith v City of Salem*, 2004; *Enriquez v West Jersey Health Systems*, 2001; *Lie v Sky Publishing Corp.*, 2002). Other courts have declined to apply the sex stereotyping analysis, but have nevertheless ruled that discrimination on the basis of transgender status is sex discrimination per se (*Schroer v Billington*, 2006).

Still other courts have ruled in favor of transgender litigants under state disability laws, finding that transsexualism or gender identity disorder meets the statutory definition of disability (see *Doe v. Bell*, 2003; *Enriquez v W. Jersey Health Sys.*, 2001). Notably, such claims are not viable under the federal Americans with Disabilities Act, which contains an explicit exclusion for transvestism, transsexualism, and gender identity disorders (42 U.S.C. § 12211(b), 1990).

In addition, it is rapidly becoming the best practice in the workplace to enact non-discrimination policies that include gender identity and expression. To date, over 500 corporations have adopted such policies (Human Rights Campaign, 2007). This reflects a growing understanding among corporate employers that the most significant consideration in hiring is an employee's skill, not his or her gender identity. Employers who have adopted such policies often explain that broad non-discrimination policies attract the most qualified employees.

Despite these numerous sources of protection, transgender employees may face a variety of challenges in the workplace. Vulnerability to discrimination often begins as early as the job application process, when a transgender applicant must consider what name to write on the job application. In general, of course, job applicants should refrain from stating anything false on an application. An affirmative misrepresentation could serve as a justification for future termination. Transgender job applicants might also wonder how to dress or appear during a job interview. Potential employers may learn of an applicant's transgender status through a background check, or by calling references who know the applicant under a different name or pronoun. New employees typically must present personal identification in the course of filling out tax and other forms, and sometimes the presentation of that documentation leads to a disclosure of their transgender status. Some transgender employees feel comfortable trusting their employer's human resources department to keep their transgender status confidential, but such confidentiality is not always maintained.

Transgender employees who begin their transition during the course of employment (as opposed to starting a new job after transition) face an additional set of considerations. They must decide how to come out to coworkers, how to address any dress code or rest-room concerns, how to designate their sex on health insurance forms, and sometimes how to confront harassment or discrimination.

146 Cole Thaler, Flor Bermudez, and Susan Sommer

Complicating workplace matters even further, some employers receive "no match" letters from the Social Security Administration (SSA) when the sex of an employee, as reported by the employer, does not match the sex designated in SSA records. The purpose of the "no match" letter system is to notify employers when their employees may have provided false information. However, these letters sometimes reveal an employee's transgender status and jeopardize that person's employment.

Transgender youth seeking employment should be aware of this variety of challenges and hurdles that their identity or expression may present. The increase of transgender visibility over recent years means that many employers are becoming educated about transgender issues, and the fact of having a transgender employee (especially at larger workplaces) is rapidly becoming a non-issue. Nevertheless, employees often find themselves in the position of providing basic information about gender transition and nonconforming expression to employers. Many transgender employees successfully navigate these issues through frank, respectful discussions with employers, supplemented with materials about applicable legal protections. Transgender youth who believe that they are being discriminated against by their employer should contact Lambda Legal for assistance.

Housing

Transgender people frequently report feeling unsafe, unstable, or otherwise dissatisfied with their housing situations (see, for example, Xavier, 2000). Individuals seeking housing may find that bureaucratic procedures are complicated owing to inconsistent identity documents, legal names that are different from a preferred name, references who know them by another name or pronoun, and background or credit checks that produce conflicting gender-related information. Furthermore, just as transgender people sometimes find themselves the targets of coworkers' bias and prejudices, so too the hostilities of neighbors and landlords can sometimes disrupt the peaceful enjoyment of property. Transgender people may even run into problems in the course of paying rent or a security deposit because they have not yet been able to change the name on their checking account.

Housing discrimination against transgender people can have a spiraling effect. Rates of homelessness in the transgender community are high, owing to pervasive bias and harassment (see Transgender Law Center and National Center for Lesbian Rights, 2003). Many transgender youth are kicked out of their homes by family members after coming out, or run away from abusive situations. Homeless shelters are frequently segregated by sex and do not treat transgender residents with respect, leaving some transgender people with few options. Transgender students seeking appropriate campus housing often face misunderstanding and misclassification.

The vast majority of laws and ordinances prohibiting discrimination on the basis of gender identity apply to housing as well as employment. As in the employment context (see the previous subsection), protections on the basis of sex may also prove helpful to transgender people who are discriminated against in the housing context. A New York City court held in 2003 that the city's housing discrimination law prevented a group home facility from requiring a transgender girl to wear masculine clothing (*Doe v Bell*, 2003). Transgender youth facing housing discrimination are encouraged to seek legal advice about the protections offered in their jurisdiction.

Public benefits

Transgender people seeking to enroll in public assistance programs must often navigate a complicated maze of bureaucratic and administrative hurdles that are only made more daunting by gender nonconforming expression and by identity documents that appear to contradict the person's appearance or that present inconsistent name or sex information. Transgender youth seeking public benefits should expect to encounter misunderstanding when dealing with a system that is, at best, designed to enforce strict eligibility criteria and flag inconsistencies, and that is increasingly reliant on automation. As with agencies that issue identity documents, transgender youth may find that agency employees and case managers are unfamiliar with relevant policies or with transgender issues in general. The framework of public benefits programs varies from state to state, and individuals seeking to change their name and sex designation in public assistance records should be prepared to inquire about relevant policies.

Transgender youth seeking coverage for transgender-related health care through state Medicaid policies should be aware that a significant number of states exclude Medicaid coverage for gender transition and related treatments. Efforts to challenge these exclusions through advocacy, litigation, and grassroots organizing are under way in a number of states. Consultation with an attorney is important to determine the scope of Medicaid coverage in your state.

Advocacy for transgender youth in schools

An increasing number of students in college, high school, middle school, and even elementary school and preschool express a gender identity that does not conform to expectations of the sex assigned at birth, and schools are learning to accommodate these students. College and university campuses are increasingly fertile sites of transgender advocacy and organizing, and many primary and secondary school districts are formulating their own transgender student policies and practices. As in the workplace and housing contexts, a growing number of states are expanding non-discrimination or anti-bullying laws to protect transgender students. Even in states without explicit protections, some courts have held that transgender students are protected under Title IX of the federal Patsy T. Mink Equal Opportunity in Education Act and constitutional free expression theories.

Colleges and universities

The Gender Public Advocacy Coalition recently reported (Gender PAC, 2007) that over 150 colleges and universities have passed non-discrimination policies covering gender identity and expression. In addition to the adoption of non-discrimination policies, campus activism has focused on identifying and sharing information about gender-neutral rest rooms on campus and increasing the number of such rest rooms. For example, a growing number of colleges and universities list maps of single-occupancy, gender-neutral rest rooms on their websites specifically to promote access for transgender and gender nonconforming students. Transgender advocates have addressed gender-based housing assignments, changes to names and sex designations in student records, inclusion of transgender care under student health insurance policies, promoting campus safety and eliminating hate crimes, educating faculty and staff on transgender issues, and expanding institutional programming, training, and support for transgender students (see Beemyn, 2005).

Primary and secondary schools

High schools, middle schools, and even elementary schools and preschools are becoming increasingly aware of transgender issues, owing to a growing number of students who express gender nonconforming or transgender identity, often with parental support. Several school districts, including the Los Angeles Unified School District and the San Francisco Unified School District, have enacted comprehensive and thoughtful written policies for respectful treatment of transgender youth. In addition to adopting a general policy of non-discrimination, schools must ensure that any incident of discrimination, harassment, or violence is promptly investigated and all appropriate corrective actions are taken. Students who are perceived as gender nonconforming (including many gay and lesbian students) are particularly vulnerable to harassment and bullying, and school districts that fail to curtail such behavior have been held accountable by courts (see *Nabozny v Podlesny*, 1996).

Some of the issues that come up in the primary and secondary school context overlap with college and university issues. For example, transgender students often prefer to be addressed by a name and/or pronoun that corresponds with their gender identity, often without having obtained a court order or without changing their official records. Schools will often accommodate a transgender student who has not yet obtained a legal name change by including a notation in that student's records indicating the preferred name. School personnel should comply with all applicable privacy and confidentiality rules and should not disclose a student's transgender status to others unless they have a specific need to know. Confidentiality is particularly important when a transgender student enrolls in a new school as a member of the preferred gender and classmates or teachers are not aware of the student's transgender status.

Some schools have gendered dress codes that create restrictions about hair length or style of clothing (e.g. no miniskirts or halter tops for girls). Where such policies exist, transgender students should be permitted to comply with the dress code associated with the sex with which they identify. Transgender students may encounter some unwillingness on the part of school administrators to allow them to dress in accordance with their gender identity. A transgender student in Massachusetts won a lawsuit against her school district, which had mandated that she dress in a "masculine" way (*Doe v Yunits*, 2000). The court ruled that the transgender girl's expression of her deeply rooted female identity was constitutionally protected expression and reflected "her quintessence." Notably, this ruling came from a court in a state without an explicit gender identity non-discrimination law. Other transgender students have successfully engaged in informal advocacy with school districts in order to be allowed to attend school in the clothing that corresponds with their gender identity. Providing school authorities with accurate information about being transgender can help dispel misconceptions and lead to respectful treatment of a transgender student.

No transgender student should be forced to use a rest-room or locker-room facility that conflicts with his or her gender identity. Many school districts appropriately permit transgender students to use rest-room facilities that correspond to their gender identity. Transgender students seeking access to appropriate facilities often negotiate compromise solutions with school administrators, such as using a single-occupancy rest room in a nurse's office or administrators' suite. No student should be compelled to use a single-occupancy facility, however. Locker-room accommodations sometimes include the creation of a private area in or near the locker room (e.g. an area separated by a curtain) or a separate changing schedule (using the locker room before or after other students). Transgender and gender nonconforming students should be provided with the same opportunities to participate in physical education as all other students, including participation in gender-segregated physical education classes and athletic activities in accordance with their gender identity. Transgender students who meet resistance about participation on athletic teams are often successful in resolving disputes on a case-by-case basis that results in an outcome making the most sense in the particular circumstances.

A variety of other gender-based practices and policies are common in school contexts. These include, for example, gender-based housing on school trips, graduation gowns that are color-coded by gender, and even school bus seating requirements based on gender. In light of the proliferation of transgender protections, schools would be well advised to follow the guiding principle that transgender students should be treated in accordance with their gender identity.

Advocacy for transgender youth in healthcare settings

Healthcare access is a major site of vulnerability for all transgender people, and particularly those, such as youth, with other characteristics that locate them in relative positions of powerlessness. In 2004, the National Coalition for LGBT Health released *An Overview of U.S. Trans Health Priorities*. That publication lists 13 issues that affect transgender health and well-being, including lack of health insurance and underinsurance, healthcare provider hostility and insensitivity, and a range of ancillary health threats including depression and suicide, substance abuse, violence, and HIV/AIDS. Transgender healthcare advocates around the country are coming together to challenge insurance exclusions, share information regarding trans-friendly providers, conduct trainings, and otherwise promote transgender health. In addition, an annual transgender health conference takes place in Philadelphia, and a number of communities have established grassroots transgender health organizations and periodic transgender health and resource fairs. Examples include the Minnesota Transgender Health Coalition (http://www.mntranshealth.org/) and the Transhealth Information Project (http://www.preventionpointphilly.org/services/services-trans.html).

Many transgender people find that their access to transition-related health care is contingent upon receiving a diagnosis of gender identity disorder (GID), a diagnosis included in the American Psychiatric Association's *Diagnostic and Statistical Manual of Mental Disorders* ((DSM*-IV*), 2000). The *DSM*-IV lists "Gender Identity Disorder of Childhood" as a distinct diagnosis from adult GID. Some transgender people and allies oppose the inclusion of GID in the *DSM*-IV, owing to a belief that gender identity-related distress arises from societal misunderstanding and should not be designated as a health condition, particularly a stigmatized mental health condition, with roots in the individual. Limiting access to treatment based on diagnosis also raises concerns in light of the number of transgender people without reliable access to health care or who may benefit from treatment for gender transition but who do not satisfy all of the diagnostic criteria. Others point out that framing clinically significant gender identity distress as a health condition allows healthcare providers to conceptualize and legitimize treatments to alleviate that distress. Regardless of diagnostic labels, it is critical that transgender people and others questioning their gender identity have access to supportive mental and medical healthcare practitioners with expertise in treating transgender patients.

The World Professional Association for Transgender Health (WPATH), an international professional organization for transgender care providers, publishes *Standards of Care* for the treatment of gender identity disorders (WPATH, 2001). These guidelines outline a set of therapeutic recommendations for sex reassignment. WPATH's *Standards of Care* emphasize a flexible, individualized approach. A number of courts and agencies have recognized GID as a serious health condition and have accepted WPATH's *Standards of Care* as a reflection of medical consensus on sex reassignment.

In children and adolescents diagnosed with GID, the *Standards of Care* note that puberty-delaying hormone treatments may be appropriate as soon as pubertal changes have begun, and that masculinizing or feminizing hormone therapy may be appropriate as early as age 16, preferably (although not necessarily) with parental consent. A growing number of medical studies recognize the effectiveness of early medical intervention for transgender youth (Smith *et al.*, 2001). In addition, a growing number of courts in the United States and beyond affirm the medical necessity of sex reassignment treatments for transgender youth (see *Re Alex: Hormonal Treatment for Gender Identity Dysphoria*, 2004; but see *Mariah L. v Admin. for Children's Servs.* (2008), reversing a New York County Family Court order that required the New York City Administration for Children's Services to arrange for sex reassignment surgery for a transgender young person in foster care).

Transgender youth seeking transition-related care may face the hurdle of being told that they cannot consent to healthcare provision on their own. A parent or guardian can consent to health care for youth under 18. Providers may provide transgender care if a parent or guardian agrees or a court has ordered treatment. In addition, transgender youth can consent to their own health care if they are emancipated or in other circumstances that vary by state. For example, in New York mature minors may also be allowed to consent to treatments affecting their own health. Mature minors are people under 18 who are given decision-making capacity under a legal doctrine that recognizes them as mature enough to appreciate the consequences of their actions.

Finally, many private health insurance policies exclude coverage of transgender care (as do all Medicare and many Medicaid policies). Sometimes these exclusions are misinterpreted and misapplied to deny coverage for other forms of gendered care (such as pap smears for transgender men or prostate exams for transgender women) or even routine, ungendered care (flu shots, X-rays for fractures) that is falsely determined to be transgender related just because a transgender person is receiving it. However, as transgender awareness grows, advocates are experiencing increased success in advocating with insurance companies and employers to create some forms of coverage for transgender care.

Advocacy for transgender youth in foster care

Transgender youth commonly enter the foster-care system or become homeless after they have been rejected, neglected, or abused by their birth families and have stopped attending school because of harassment (Woronoff *et al.*, 2006, pp. 80–101). Once in the foster-care system, transgender youth face added burdens because they are at especially high risk of being targeted for harassment and violence. For example, transgender youth have been beaten by other residents while staff watched; rejected by foster parents, staff, and other residents because of their gender identity and expression; sexually assaulted; and forced to undergo conversion therapy (Gilliam, 2004).

Transgender youth in state foster care have a number of civil rights guaranteed under the US Constitution. These include the right to equal protection, which requires that they be provided with placements and services and protection from harassment on the same basis as other youth. In addition, transgender young people have the right under the First Amendment to have their gender identity acknowledged and accepted (see *Canell v Lightner*, 1998, p. 1214). The due process guarantee of the Fourteenth Amendment gives all young people in state custody the affirmative right to protection from harm. This right to safety includes the right to appropriate services, medical care, and safe placements. State constitutions may provide additional protections.

In addition to the legal protections available under the US Constitution, transgender youth in foster care may also be protected by state and local non-discrimination statutes and ordinances (see Estrada and Marksamer, 2006). For example, some transgender people have successfully argued that state non-discrimination laws that require reasonable accommodation for people with disabilities apply to those diagnosed with GID, and that denying transgender people the right to dress in ways that are consistent with their gender identities is discrimination based on disability (*Doe v Bell*, 2003). A select number of jurisdictions have LGBT anti-discrimination laws or regulations that are specific to foster-care settings. For example, in 2006 California passed a state law that prohibits discrimination in the foster-care system on the basis of sexual orientation and gender identity. Most recently, in January 2008 the Texas Department of Family and Protective Services implemented a Bill of Rights of Children and Youth in Foster Care, establishing a right to fair treatment regardless of sexual orientation or gender identity. It is important to note, however, that although transgender youth have the rights outlined above, there is still a long way to go for these rights to be fully understood and enforced.

Transgender youth in foster care can advocate on the basis of these constitutional, state, and local rights for safety in their placements and respect for their gender identity and expression. This means that transgender young people in government care should be allowed to express their sense of themselves as male or female, although that expression may not coincide with the sex assigned to them at birth. Accordingly, transgender youth should be referred to by the names and pronouns they choose and that best reflect their gender identity, rather than by the name on their birth certificate or the pronoun that matches the sex assigned to them at birth. Transgender youth in foster care also have the right to express their gender identity through clothing and grooming (see, for example, *Doe v Yunits*, 2000).[2] In *Doe v Bell* (2003), a young transgender female in state care challenged a group home's prohibition against her expression of her female gender identity in ways that did not conform with her assigned sex, even though she had a GID diagnosis. The court held that the New York City Administration for Children's Services (ACS) was required to make reasonable accommodations for her transgender status and had to permit her to dress and otherwise present herself in ways consistent with her female gender identity.

The affirmative right to safety held by transgender youth in state care and custody imposes a corresponding duty on the state to provide protection from physical, sexual, and psychological harm (see *DeShaney v Winnebago County Dep't of Soc. Serv.*, 1989, p. 201 n.9; *B.H. v Johnson*, 1989, p. 1395). Foster-care professionals have the responsibility to take immediate steps to address anti-transgender harassment in their facilities and to prevent it from happening. The right to safety should also include the right to receive counseling to help a transgender young person who has been negatively affected by parental rejection or abuse because of his or her gender identity or expression. The right to safety can also be invoked to prohibit the subjecting of transgender youth to so-called reparative therapies purporting to change their gender identity, given that these types of therapies are ineffective and extremely damaging to a transgender young person's emotional well-being (Woronoff *et al.*, 2006, pp. 80–101).

Transgender youth should also receive an individualized assessment of whether they most appropriately should be placed in congregate care facilities in accordance with their gender identity rather than their assigned sex (Woronoff *et al.*, 2006, pp. 80–101). Similarly, bathrooms, locker rooms, and dressing areas within these facilities must be made appropriate and safe for transgender youth. Placement decisions should be made on a case-by-case basis, taking into account the safety and needs of the particular young person, with respect to their gender identity. Some foster-care agencies may cite laws or regulations saying that children over a certain age cannot be placed with "opposite"-sex children. However, the sex of a transgender youth should be recognized to be that with which they identify, not the sex assigned at birth. Although at the present time transgender youth commonly are placed according to their assigned birth sex rather than their gender identity, often at risk to their safety, a growing number of foster care agencies around the country now make individualized placements that respect a transgender youth's gender identity.

Transgender youth also have the right to safe, supportive, and competent medical care, including transition-related care that can range from hormone therapy to sex reassignment surgery. This treatment is usually contingent on a diagnosis of GID and requires parental consent, which may present an issue for youth in foster care who are under the age of 18 (see "Advocacy for transgender youth in healthcare settings," p. 151). Thus, as a practical matter transition-related medical care may be difficult to access. In *Mariah L. v Admin. for Children's Servs.* (2008), the New York City's Administration for Children's Services refused to pay for sex reassignment surgery (SRS) for Mariah L., a 20-year-old transgender youth in the custody of ACS, on the grounds that it was experimental treatment for which Mariah did not qualify. The Appellate Division held that there was evidence that SRS is the generally recognized successful treatment for GID. On remand, the New York Family Court ordered ACS to pay for and provide Mariah with sex reassignment surgery. However, the Appellate Division reversed the Family Court order directing ACS to arrange for Mariah to have SRS, concluding that the "Family Court Act § 255 cannot be read as permitting Family Court to order ACS to arrange for a child in its care to receive specific medical or surgical care, since such an order would denigrate from ACS' statutory authority" and that the "Family Court does not have subject matter jurisdiction to review ACS' refusal to arrange for petitioner to have sex reassignment surgery."

Given the added hurdles transgender youth face in school, accessing identity documents, employment, housing, obtaining health care, and the other areas discussed earlier in the chapter, it is crucial that transgender youth receive additional support from foster-care providers as these youth prepare to transition to independence. Transgender youth in foster care are encouraged to contact Lambda Legal for resources and legal assistance.

Advocacy for transgender youth in juvenile justice settings

Alarming numbers of transgender youth find themselves in a cycle of being forced to leave home by disapproving parents, receiving unsafe placements in foster care, fleeing to the streets, and resorting to illegal activities in order to survive. This cycle sadly increases the likelihood that transgender youth will enter the juvenile justice system (Woronoff *et al.*, 2006, pp. 80–101).

Transgender youth, especially youth of color, who congregate in public places may face police harassment and selective enforcement of "quality of life" offenses.

Transgender youth in juvenile detention and correctional facilities frequently are subjected by staff and other residents to taunting, physical and sexual harassment and abuse, and violence. Some facilities automatically classify and house transgender youth as sex offenders or isolate them. The vast majority of correctional and detention facilities do not have policies or training that address harassment or discrimination based on sexual orientation; even fewer have policies addressing gender identity. It is therefore crucial that during the adjudicatory process, attorneys advocate for placements within the juvenile justice and delinquency systems that are safe for transgender youth and that their clients receive competent, sensitive health assessments and treatment as part of their disposition.

Unlike adult prisoners, children in the custody of the juvenile justice system have not been convicted of crimes, and the state has no legitimate interest in "punishing" them. For convicted adults, conditions of confinement violate the US Constitution when they amount to "cruel and unusual" punishment as proscribed by the Eighth Amendment. For detained youth, who are entitled to more protection than incarcerated adults, most courts analyze their conditions of confinement claims under the federal Due Process Clause of the Fourteenth Amendment. Transgender youth have the right not to be placed in conditions that amount to punishment. While some restrictions on the freedom of young people within these institutions are necessary for safety purposes, these restrictions must be "reasonably related" to a legitimate government interest. If not, they are inappropriate punishment (see Estrada and Marksamer, 2006, p. 428 n.53). Transgender youth in the juvenile justice system have the right to reasonably safe conditions, including the right to reasonable protection from physical and sexual harassment and aggression by other juveniles or staff. Transgender youth also have the right to be free from unreasonably restrictive conditions of confinement and should not be placed in isolation simply because of their gender identity or expression (Woronoff et al., 2006, pp. 80–101).

Detention and correctional facilities should develop policies that address safe placements for transgender youth. These youth should not automatically be placed in correctional facilities according to their birth sex, but rather, facilities should find an appropriate placement that will provide a particular transgender youth with the most safety and ability to express their gender identity (Woronoff et al., 2006, pp. 80–101). Although transgender girls wear feminine clothing, use female pronouns and names, and may already be transitioning and showing female secondary sex characteristics, they are almost always housed in boys' facilities. Transgender girls are particularly vulnerable to violence and sexual assault in correctional facilities. In addition, every facility must have a sound classification system for identifying and protecting the safety of transgender youth. Transgender youth should not be inappropriately placed with an aggressive population, with known sex offenders, or with other youth who display anti-LGBTQ (lesbian, gay, bisexual, transgender, and questioning) behaviors and attitudes (Lambda Legal, 2006).

Transgender youth in detention and correctional facilities have the right to adequate medical and mental health care (see Estrada and Marksamer, 2006, pp. 429–431). Facilities must provide general medical services for both prevention and treatment as well as medical services specific to transgender youth. If juvenile justice professionals know of a transgender youth's significant mental or medical health needs related to a possible diagnosis of GID, they should take the necessary steps to address them and should follow the instructions of the youth's treating physician. In 2006, Lambda Legal sued the New York Office of Children and Family Services (OCFS) on behalf of a transgender young person who had been abruptly terminated from her physician-prescribed feminizing hormones and disciplined for expressing her female gender identity while in OCFS custody (*Rodriguez v Johnson*, 2006). The parties reached a favorable settlement that included monetary damages and a commitment by OCFS to evaluate its policies to improve its ability to support and protect transgender young people in its care.

On March 17, 2008, OCFS issued its new LGBTQ Youth Anti-Discrimination Policies and Guidelines (PPM 3442.00). These policies and guidelines cover important issues relevant to transgender youth such as staff training on LGBTQ issues, notification to all youth in OCFS facilities and after-care programs regarding the policy, and placement transfers for LGBTQ youth who feel unsafe in their current placements. The guidelines also contain more specific guidance to accommodate transgender youth, including initiation and continuation of hormone treatment; choice of clothing, hair, and other personal grooming that matches the transgender youth's gender identity; use of preferred names and pronouns; individual bedrooms and bathroom facilities for transgender youth; and the possibility for transgender youth to choose whether male or female staff conduct body searches when required.

Similarly, in 2005 three teenagers who either identified as or were perceived to be lesbian, gay, bisexual, or transgender brought suit in federal court against the Hawaii Youth Correctional Facility (HYCF) after being verbally, physically, and sexually harassed and threatened while in the facility. One plaintiff alleged that other young people in the facility regularly exposed themselves to him, pressured him for sexual favors, and acted out violently toward him. The court ordered HYCF to adopt policies and procedures "that are appropriate to the treatment of lesbian, gay, and transgender youths, that set standards for the conduct of youth correctional officers and other staff, and that provide on-going staff training and oversight." The court also noted that placing LGBT youth in isolation simply to separate them from their abusers "cannot be viewed in any reasonable light as advancing a legitimate non-punitive governmental objective" (R.G. v Koller, 2006). In the fall of 2007, the HYCF released an anti-LGBT anti-discrimination policy. The policy firmly prohibits discrimination as well as physical and verbal harassment against youth who are or may be perceived as LGBT, imposes an affirmative duty on all state employees to protect LGBT youth from discrimination and harassment, requires individualized classification and housing decisions that take into account LGBT youth's safety, prohibits isolation of LGBT youth as a means for keeping them safe from discrimination, and mandates LGBT competency training for direct care staff and service providers (Hawaii Youth Correctional Facility Policy, 2007).

Advocacy for transgender youth in homeless shelters

Transgender youth become homeless primarily because they have had to run away from their families or foster-care placements after their physical and emotional safety has been jeopardized, they have been thrown out of their homes for being transgender or gender nonconforming, or they have aged out of the foster-care system. Too often, transgender youth are misunderstood and mistreated, even harassed, assaulted, or raped by the staff and other residents at temporary homeless shelters and youth transitional living programs (Lambda Legal, 2006). When these facilities refuse to accept transgender youth, or fail to treat them in accordance with their gender identity, these youth are put in an untenable situation: they must either stifle their authentic gender identity in order to access services and treatment, to the detriment of their overall well-being, or they must live on the streets.

When a transgender youth who identifies and presents as female is placed in a male shelter facility, she faces increased risk of abuse and rape. Furthermore, sex-segregated bathrooms, locker rooms, and dressing areas within these facilities are often inappropriate and unsafe for transgender youth. Transgender youth who are unsafe in shelters are more likely to run away. On the streets, they frequently find a thriving, oftentimes dangerous, black market for cross-sex hormones and other medical procedures that they may use to align their physical bodies with their gender identities. Those providing care and services to homeless transgender youth should link these youth with appropriate medical service providers in their communities to reduce the risk that they will take their health care into their own hands on the streets (Lambda Legal, 2006).

It is critically important that all youth homeless shelters take immediate steps to ensure the safety of transgender youth. Every agency providing shelter care and services should adopt and enforce trans-inclusive non-discrimination policies, provide training on transgender and gender nonconforming issues for all staff, and have a clear policy of zero tolerance for harassment, discrimination, and violence against transgender and gender nonconforming youth (Lambda Legal, 2006).

Some homeless shelters in a few jurisdictions have adopted policies for transgender access that make clear that transgender people should be treated in accordance with their gender identity – in other words, transgender females should be permitted access to the same facilities as other females, and transgender males should be permitted access to the same facilities as other males. These policies often include some flexibility based on the transgender person's safety and privacy considerations. For example, in 2002 the Boston Public Health Commission's Homeless Services program issued protocols and guidelines designed to improve services for transgender guests. Those guidelines provide in part that "[t]ransgender men and transgender women should be accommodated according to their gender identity and use the corresponding facilities to the fullest extent possible given safety considerations." Even jurisdictions where such policies exist must be monitored to make sure that all staff†members are in compliance and receive periodic training. Community members or local organizations may be able to provide training on transgender access issues for the facility's staff. The National Gay and Lesbian Task Force published a useful training guide on shelter access for transgender people called *Transitioning our Shelters* (n.d.).

Advocacy for immigrant transgender youth

Immigrant transgender youth eligible to adjust their immigration status face special obstacles. The assistance of a knowledgeable immigration lawyer is imperative, as immigration law can be quite complex and quick to change. Immigration officials often will not understand transgender identities and expressions, asking inappropriate questions about one's sex life or questions about "coming out," a concept that might not translate to other cultures (National Center for Transgender Equality and Transgender Law Center, n.d.). Officials can be ignorant of the rights of transgender individuals and refuse them services that they are due.

The Real ID Act of 2005 gives great discretion to the immigration official performing the initial interview for asylum, allowing the officer to request additional supporting evidence and making it harder for an appellate court to overturn a negative decision. Although a credible story of persecution was sufficient in the past to achieve asylum, officials can now ask a transgender applicant to provide additional evidence from the very government that perpetrated the discrimination (National Center for Transgender Equality and Transgender Law Center, n.d.). This is a significant burden, as the applicant might not have any official documentation or other hard evidence showing persecution. The Real ID Act could also cause transgender people to be "red-flagged" when they begin to change gender markers on various forms of ID, as various identification databases will be integrated and disparities between an applicant's gender markers will trigger additional scrutiny (Sylvia Rivera Law Project, n.d.).

An individual who has undergone gender transition should be able to have their immigration file and documents reflect their current gender (US Department of Homeland Security, 2004). Generally, the applicant must provide documents indicating that sex reassignment surgery has been performed. Name changes can also be obtained, but require a court order and should be completed before naturalization. Birth certificates, notes from doctors, court orders, and other supporting documents should be gathered and kept safe for proof of name or gender change as well as supporting evidence in asylum claims (Sylvia Rivera Law Project, n.d.).

The decision to apply for asylum can be difficult, as applying for asylum alerts the authorities to an undocumented immigrant's presence and results in deportation if asylum is not granted (Sylvia Rivera Law Project, n.d.). Asylum must be applied for within one year of the youth's last entrance into the United States, though extensions can be given in extraordinary situations or if the youth already has a student visa (Lambda Legal and Immigration Equality, n.d.). Asylum is granted if it can be proved that a transgender applicant has been, or has a reasonable fear of being, persecuted by the applicant's home government or by those whom the government has been unwilling or unable to control (Immigration Equality and Transgender Law Center, n.d.). It is important to maintain as much documentation as possible about past persecution as well as documents about involvement in or identification with LGBTQ groups (Immigration Equality, n.d., *LGBT/HIV asylum manual*). One can also claim asylum on grounds other than gender identity (see Pfitsch, 2006), such as sexual orientation or HIV status (National Center for Lesbian Rights, n.d.). For example, if a transgender woman's government persecuted her as being an effeminate gay man, she might still gain asylum even though she was persecuted for being a member of a group with which she does not actually identify (Immigration Equality, n.d., *Asylum*; see *Hernandez-Montiel v Immigration and Naturalization Service*, 2000).

Without a valid asylum claim, an undocumented transgender youth may have limited options for adjustment of status except for family-based petitions, including marriage, or employment-based petitions, if they are eligible. However, immigrants who entered the United States without inspection are rarely eligible for adjustment of their status while they remain in the United States, and are subject to a ban of up to ten years if they leave the country. Thus, undocumented transgender youth who entered without inspection face additional curtailment of their rights and an uncertain legal landscape.

Although transgender youth may not immediately be considering marriage, it is important for them to be aware of the possible ways the government will consider marriages of transgender individuals in the context adjustment of status. In 2004, the Department of Homeland Security established a policy of denying any application based upon marriage when at least one member "claims to be transsexual" (US Department of Homeland Security, 2004). However, in 2005 the Board of Immigration Appeals ruled that if the marriage is recognized as valid in the state in which it was performed, then it will be recognized for immigration purposes. Accordingly, entrance through marriage now depends upon whether the marriage was performed in a state that recognizes a transgender person's marriage to a person of a different sex (*In re Lovo*, 2005). Although this victory clears a path for certain individuals, those who live in states that do not recognize such marriages are likely to face challenges. One should not assume that if a state refuses to recognize a transgender woman's gender identity, her marriage to a woman will be considered as a different-sex relationship by the state and honored for immigration purposes. The law is often complex on this point (Immigration Equality and Transgender Law Center, n.d.). Also, many immigration officers may not be informed of this decision, as the Department of Homeland Security has not updated its official policy regarding transgender marriage (Immigration Equality and Transgender Law Center, n.d.).

Notes

We give special thanks to Jeff Rakover, Legal Assistant, and Christopher Benecke, Legal Intern, for their contributions to this chapter.

1 "Sex" typically refers to the biological features that distinguish males and females, while "gender" refers to the societal roles and expectations associated with each sex.
2 *Doe v Yunits* held that a transgender student had a First Amendment right to wear clothing consistent with her gender identity and that treating a transgender girl differently than biological girls was discrimination on the basis of sex.

References

American Psychiatric Association (2000). *Diagnostic and Statistical Manual of Mental Disorders* (4th ed. text revision). Washington, DC: APA.
Americans with Disabilities Act, 42 U.S.C. § 12211(b) (1990).
B. H. v Johnson, 715 F. Supp. 1387 (N.D. Ill. 1989).
Beemyn, B. G. (2005). Making campuses more inclusive of transgender students. *Journal of Gay and Lesbian Issues in Education*, 3(1), 77–87.

Boston Public Health Commission, Homeless Services. (2002). Retrieved February 12, 2008, from http://www.transgenderlaw.org/resources/transprotocol.pdf.

Canell v Lightner, 143 F.3d 1210 (9th Cir. 1998).

DeShaney v Winnebago County Dep't of Soc. Serv., 489 U.S. 189 (1989).

Doe v Bell, 194 Misc.2d 774 (N.Y. Sup. Ct. 2003).

Doe v Yunits, 2000 WL 33162199 (Mass. Super. 2000) *aff'd sub nom. Doe v Brockton Sch. Comm.*, 2000 WL 33342399 (Mass. App. Ct. 2000).

Enriquez v W. Jersey Health Sys., 777 A.2d 365 (N. J. Super. Ct. 2001), *cert. denied*, 785 A.2d 439 (N.J. 2001).

Estrada, R. and Marksamer, J. (2006). Lesbian, gay, bisexual, and transgender young people in state custody: Making the child welfare and juvenile justice systems safe through litigation, advocacy, and education. *Temple Law Review* 79, 415–438.

GenderPAC (2007). *Gender Equality Index for Universities and Schools.* Retrieved February 12, 2008, from http://www.gpac.org/genius/policies.html.

Gilliam, J. (2004). Toward providing a welcoming home for all: Enacting a new approach to address the longstanding problems lesbian, gay, bisexual, and transgender youth face in the foster care system. *Loyola of Los Angeles Law Review* 37, 1037–1063.

Hawaii Youth Correctional Facility Policy. 1.43.04. (2007). *Non-Discriminatory, Developmentally-Sound Treatment of Lesbian, Gay, Bi-Sexual and Transgender (LGBT) Youth.*

Hernandez-Montiel v Immigration and Naturalization Service, 225 F.3d 1084 (9th Cir. 2000).

Hopkins v Price Waterhouse, 490 U.S. 228 (1989).

Human Rights Campaign (2007). *Corporate Equality Index.* Retrieved February 12, 2008, from http://www.hrc.org/issues/ceihome.asp.

Immigration Equality and Transgender Law Center (n.d.). *Immigration Law and Transgender People.* Retrieved February 12, 2008, from http://transgenderlawcenter.org/pdf/Immigration%20Law%20-%20English%20fact%20sheet.pdf.

Immigration Equality (n.d.). *Asylum.* Retrieved February 12, 2008, from http://www.immigrationequality.org/template.php?pageid=173.

Immigration Equality. *LGBT/HIV Asylum Manual.* Retrieved February 12, 2008, from http://www.immigrationequality.org/manual_template.php.

In re Guido, 1 Misc. 3d 825 (Civ. Ct. N.Y. Co. 2003).

In re Lovo, 23 I and N Dec. 746 (BIA 2005).

In re McIntyre, 715 A.2d 400 (Pa. 1998).

Lambda Legal Defense and Education Fund (2006). *Getting Down to Basics: Tools to Support LGBTQ Youth in Care* [brochure]. New York: Lambda Legal.

Lambda Legal Defense and Education Fund and Immigration Equality (n.d.). *Sexual Orientation and Immigration: The Basics.* Retrieved February 12, 2008, from http://www.immigrationequality.org/uploadedfiles/Sexual_Orientation_and_Immigration_Lambda_Booklet.pdf.

Lie v Sky Publishing Corp., No. 013117J, 2002 WL 31492397 (Mass. Super. Oct. 7, 2002).

Mariah L. v Admin. for Children's Servs., No. 1407, 2008 WL 2024979 (N.Y. App. Div. May 13, 2008).

Matter of Eck, 584 A.D.2d 859 (N.J. App. Div. 1991).

Nabozny v Podlesny, 92 F.3d 446 (7th Cir. 1996).

National Center for Lesbian Rights (n.d.). *Immigration Project* [brochure]. Retrieved February 12, 2008, from http://www.nclrights.org/site/DocServer/immigration_english.pdf?docID=1401.

National Center for Transgender Equality and Transgender Law Center (n.d.). *The Real ID Act: Bad Law for our Community.* Retrieved February 12, 2008, from http://transgenderlawcenter.org/pdf/Joint%20statement%20-on%20the%20Real%20ID%20Act%20-%20final.pdf.

National Coalition for LGBT Health (2004, August). *An Overview of U.S. Trans Health Priorities: A Report by the Eliminating Disparities Working Group.* Washington, DC.

National Gay and Lesbian Task Force (n.d.). *Transitioning our Shelters.* Retrieved February 12, 2008, from http://www.thetaskforce.org/downloads/reports/reports/TransitioningOurShelters.pdf.

Neb. Rev. Stat. § 71–604.01 (2005).

Pfitsch, H. (2006). Homosexuality in asylum and constitutional law: Rhetoric of acts and identity. *Law and Sexuality 15*, 59–89.

R.G. v Koller, 415 F. Supp.2d 1129 (D. Haw. 2006).

Re Alex: Hormonal Treatment for Gender Identity Dysphoria (2004) 297 Fam. L.R. 168 (Austl.)

Rodriguez v Johnson, No. 06-CV-00214 (S.D.N.Y. 2006).

Schroer v Billington, 424 F. Supp.2d 203 (D.D.C. 2006).

Smith v City of Salem, 378 F.3d 566 (6th Cir. 2004).

Smith, Y. L. S., Van Goozen, S. H. M., and Cohen-Kettenis, P. T. (2001). Adolescents with gender identity disorder who were accepted or rejected for sex reassignment surgery: A prospective follow-up study. *Journal of the American Academy of Child and Adolescent Psychiatry 40*, 472–481.

Sylvia Rivera Law Project (n.d.). *Your Immigration Rights: Trans Immigrants in New York.* Retrieved February 12, 2008, from http://www.srlp.org/documents/kyr.immigration.pdf.

Transgender Law Center and National Center for Lesbian Rights (2003). *Trans Realities: A Legal Needs Assessment of San Francisco's Transgender communities.* Retrieved February 29, 2008, from http://transgenderlawcenter.org/tranny/pdfs/Trans%20Realities%20Final%20Final.pdf.

United States Department of Homeland Security. Interoffice Memorandum, April 16, 2004. Retrieved February 12, 2008, from http://www.srlp.org/documents/immigration_info_marriages_tran.pdf.

World Professional Association for Transgender Health. (2001). *Standards of Care for Gender Identity Disorders* (6th ed.). Retrieved February 12, 2008, from http://wpath.org/Documents2/socv6.pdf.

Woronoff, R., Estrada, R., and Sommer, S. (2006). *Out of the Margins: A Report on Regional Listening Forums Highlighting the Experiences of Lesbian, Gay, Bisexual, Transgender, and Questioning Youth in Care.* Washington, DC: Child Welfare League of America; New York: Lambda Legal Defense and Education Fund.

Xavier, J. (2000). *The Washington, DC Transgender Needs Assessment Survey.* Retrieved February 12, 2008, from http://www.gender.org/resources/dge/gea0.

Chapter 10

A call for organizational trans-formation

Gerald P. Mallon

Introduction

Several of this book's contributors have enumerated the needs of transgender youth and identified the obstacles that youth-serving agencies face in addressing their needs. This final chapter, using case examples from several nationally known transgender-affirming agencies, offers recommendations on agency philosophies concerning the reality of transgender youth and additionally offers suggestions on ways to create safe, welcoming, and nurturing environments.

The dilemmas faced by transgender youth and their families are clear (Feinberg, 1993; Israel and Tarver, 1997; Scholinski, 1997). Youth-serving agencies, already challenged by many substantial issues, tend to exhibit a range of sensitivities to transgender youth. At one extreme, some agencies openly discriminate against transgender youth; at the other extremity, there are those that are affirming in their approaches and strongly advocate for their needs. Most youth-serving agencies fall somewhere in the middle. Some youth-serving agencies initiate good faith efforts to become more affirming, but this usually occurs when they come across their first openly transgender youth. In many cases, such efforts are initiated because the transgender youth is seen as a "problem." Unfortunately, a more proactive stance in preparing for working with diverse groups of youth rarely takes place without some type of precipitating incident.

Youth-serving agencies come into contact with transgender youth for many of the same reasons that they see other youth: family conflict, the health or mental health of the youth (see Bockting *et al.*, 2006), school problems, or the need for an out-of-home placement. The scope of these issues with respect to a transgender identity requires that all youth-serving agencies become knowledgeable about and sensitive to the needs of transgender youth. The vulnerability of transgender youth, particularly at times when they come to the attention of youth-serving agencies, is yet another reason that youth providers should be prepared for working with this population. The most inopportune time to increase one's knowledge about a service population is when they arrive at the agency in a crisis and are in need of immediate assistance.

Case I

Green Chimneys Children's Services, initially designed to meet the needs of groups of heterosexually oriented children and youth aging out of foster care toward independence, is an excellent example of a mainstream child welfare agency that has been transformed into a gay-, lesbian-, and transgender-affirming organization. Established in 1947, Green Chimneys Children's Services was conceived, designed, and administered by heterosexually oriented professionals. The agency received financing from private sources to fund its efforts; however, public monies were also a major source of support of all of their programs.

In 1987, however, partly because of the hiring of an openly gay and lesbian staff member, Green Chimneys Children's Services took a bold step out of the child welfare closet and moved forward by reaching out to provide leadership in child welfare for another unique and underserved population: gay, lesbian, bisexual, transgender, and questioning (GLBTQ) children and youth, and families affected by issues of sexual orientation. Gay, lesbian, and transgender professionals were comfortable in working with GLBTQ adolescents, and began to openly address issues, challenge heterocentric policies, and design programs that insured a better fit for gay and lesbian young people and their families. With this new influx of GLBT-identified staff, the agency's culture, previously heterosexually oriented, began a process of transformation as the staff openly embraced GLBTQ adolescents into their array of diversity. In reflecting on this transformational process, one professional from that program made these observations:

> We just decided that we had gay kids and that we did good work with them and we would continue to provide care for them. We made a conscious decision not to discriminate. Initially, we were referred and accepted a number of self-identified gay kids; their orientation was not the issue, their needs fit the mission of the program and they were accepted. Then we began to earn a reputation for being an agency which would take gay kids and then we started to get calls for every gay kid that came through the system. I think at certain points in time the agency was uncomfortable about being stigmatized as "the gay agency" but for the most part they have been very supportive of our efforts. Our openness to accepting gay kids unfortunately has not been the norm.
>
> (Mallon, 1998, pp. 101–102)

In taking such a bold step out of the child welfare closet and moving forward to respond to the needs of GLBTQ youth and families, Green Chimneys has had to participate in a major shift in its organizational culture. Because Green Chimneys Children's Services was the first mainstream child welfare agency in the United States to openly address and respond to the needs and to work toward developing program options that would provide a continuum of care for GLBTQ children, youth, and their families, the organization's administration has provided leadership, but the transformation was not always painless.

Green Chimneys and GLASS (Gay and Lesbian Social Services) have both struggled with being more closely monitored in very different ways by state authorities. Such close scrutiny can be stressful to the operation of a program, but also to program staff who may feel that they are under constant watch. This is, unfortunately, a very real consequence of developing GLBTQ affirming programs. Additionally, not all agency staff were affirming or accepting at first. Religious and cultural biases played a large role in their level of discomfort. A major commitment to on-going training for all levels of staff and maintaining the stance that Green Chimneys has always served youth and families who were most needy, helped to change the organization's culture.

Even though a transgender youth might still raise an eyebrow if she or he attends a function on Green Chimneys' main campus, they are always treated with dignity and respect by the staff and residents. Staff in all program areas of the agency are aware of the NYC program's commitment to GLBTQ youth and affected families, and while not all staff fully comprehend the needs of these youth, the NYC branch of the agency continues to educate them and help them move toward acceptance.

In transforming themselves from heterocentric institutions to inclusive environments that affirm and recognize the uniqueness of GLBTQ adolescents, agencies like Green Chimneys had to confront the heterocentrism and strict requirements of gender conformity in their conceptions of GLBTQ youth. Such a transformation entails a process of discernment in scrutinizing their own organizational functions, in examining their boards and policy-making bodies, in reviewing the openness of their staff members toward issues of gender and sexual orientation, and in evaluating their relationship to the GLBTQ communities.

Creating a trans-affirming culture

Efforts to increase sensitivity to transgender youth cannot be sustained in an environment that does not explicitly encourage such undertakings. As agencies struggle to demonstrate their commitment to diversity, they must also be willing to include gender orientation into that diversity continuum. In doing so, they begin the work necessary for creating a safe and welcoming environment for *all* clients, not just trans youth. Once this affirming environment is established, and the organization's culture begins to shift to clearly include transgender concerns, it become possible for youth workers to learn about, advocate for, and provide affirming services to transgender youth (see White Holman and Goldberg, 2006a, b).

While it is a reality that some agency administrators and board members might object to specific transgender sensitivity awareness or programs specifically gears toward the population, no one should take exception to overall approaches designed to increase worker competence in working with clients who are underserved. Inherent in all change efforts are the realities of the political consequences of the change efforts (Grise-Owens *et al.*, 2004). Such changes can also be viewed as new opportunities for the organization (Dutton, 1992). Organizational paradigm shifts, such as I am suggesting here, can in the long run offer more effective services for children, youth, and families in need (Sawyer and Woodlock, 1995).

Trans-forming the organization's culture

Transformation is a powerful word, but nothing less is needed to create programs that are responsive to the needs of trans and gender-different youth. Appreciation of diversity and a knowledge of the organization's idiosyncratic culture (Kets de Vries and Miller, 1984) are key elements in this process. The examination of an organization's commitment to diversity is a common twenty-first-century theme for all youth-serving agency administrators. Diversity approaches in organizations have utilized various components to increase worker competence in meeting the needs of a variegated client population, including in-service training, non-discrimination policies, participating in culturally specific celebrations, advocacy, client/staff groups that explore diversity, and efforts which encourage a climate that welcomes all people. A transgender approach could be integrated into any one of these areas. A community-based youth center commemorating Latino History Month with a pot-luck dinner representing dishes from various Latino countries could just as easily celebrate Pride month by inviting a speaker to discuss the events that led to the civil rights struggle for trans persons.

Youth-oriented agencies must also be first and foremost committed to creating a safe environment for all youth. The enactment of a zero tolerance policy for violence, weapons, emotional maltreatment, slurs of all types, and direct or indirect mistreatment conveys to all clients that their safety is a priority. A clearly articulated stance against violence of all types, including verbal harassment, sends an important message to all youth. It says we will take responsibility for keeping you safe and you will not be blamed by anyone for being yourself. Those who offend are the ones who will be dealt with, because their behavior is unjustified.

Third, all youth benefit from youth workers who are open, honest, and genuine. Everyone benefits from philosophies that indicate an agency's willingness to address difficult issues head-on. Giving clients and staff permission to raise controversial topics signals that all people associated with the agency will be treated with respect and dignity.

It is only through intentional and deliberate organizational cultural shifts – true transformation that a climate supportive of and affirming toward trans youth can be developed (Schorr, 1988). Several agencies across the United States and in Canada have been successful in creating organizations where trans youth are welcomed, feel safe, and have their needs met. Such organizational trans-formation does not take huge amounts of money, tremendous time commitments on the part of staff, or other expensive overtures. It does, however, take commitment from board members, administrators, and other key organizational players, including the youth and their families.

Other youth-serving agencies, particularly those where there is a "correctional" component to services provision – juvenile justice facilities and juvenile detention facilities – continue to struggle, especially around issues such as prescribed hormone use, pronoun usage, and name changes (see the work by White Holman and Goldberg's (2006a, b) on these issues). Juvenile justice facilities, unlike foster-care agencies, have very clearly stated and codified rules of conduct and behavior. In some facilities, youth wear uniforms, are locked in their rooms at night, are not permitted to leave the facility for home visits, and are shackled when they are brought to court hearings or any other out-of-facility activity. Youth placed in these settings are sentenced by the courts to serve time for adjudicated criminal offenses, and freedoms of many types are restricted by virtue of the nature of this type of residential facility. Although most juvenile justice and detention facilities still continue to struggle with some of the issues that are important to trans youth and may not come to a complete resolution about how to address these issues, such systems and their staff can be challenged to move toward including content on respectfully addressing the needs of trans youth in their in-service and pre-training sessions and move toward the creation of trans-affirming environments for the youth with whom they work. One such example of a system that has been moving toward trans-affirming practices under the leadership of Commissioner Gladys Carroin is the New York State Office of Children and Family Services Department.

Case 2

In 2002, the New York State Office of Children and Family Services, Department of Rehabilitative Services (OCSF DRS), charged with safely maintaining adjudicated youth in 32 facilities around the state, made a conscious effort to become a more trans-affirming program. The agency had struggled with how best to provide affirming care for trans and gay youth, and how to incorporate training and policy changes into their system. The OCFS DJJOY administration hired a consultant (this writer) to meet with key state-level administrators to begin an open and frank discussion about how their organizational transformation could begin. After initial discussion, it was decided that the consultant would conduct a training with key state staff administrators. From this initial training the sessions were expanded to be piloted at several of the agency's key facility sites, first with those facilities that were already identified as gay-affirming, and then with other, larger facilities. After conducting three sessions and fielding pointed questions from the direct care staff and facility managers, it was decided that stand-alone training without practice guidelines to support the staff in the facilities was inadequate to transform the system.

Over a period of several months the consultant worked with OCFS DJJOY staff and administrators and attorneys to craft a publication entitled "Guidelines for good practice with LGBT youth." These guidelines clearly addressed issues such as safety, name usage, medical care, mental health care, and procedures for staff to utilize in working with LGBT youth. After a great deal of discussion and editing, the guidelines were approved by the administration and it was decided to resume training with staff. The consultant provided the initial LGBT overview training and utilized the good-practice guidelines as the second part of the training process. All OCFS DJJOY staff at all levels of employment were required to participate in these training sessions. Once staff completed the training, they were given copies of the guidelines and had opportunities to ask questions about them. It was clear from OCFS, however, that the implementation of the guidelines was non-negotiable; they were to be viewed as the approved guidelines for good practice in all New York State OCFS DJJOY programs. The guidelines are periodically revised, and changed when necessary, and all staff are trained in good practice with LGBT youth in New York State OCFS DRS facilities – a major change in organizational culture and a major move toward creating affirming environments for all youth in these facilities.

Although mainstream youth-serving agencies can be transformed into trans-affirming agencies, in many cases, out of necessity, GLBT persons have designed their own agencies, to meet the needs of their own communities. The following is an organizational case example of one such agency in Los Angeles.

Case 3

Despite the fact that in 1979 Governor Jerry Brown had signed an Executive Order preventing social services agencies from denying services to gay, lesbian, bisexual, transgender, and questioning (GLBTQ) youth, youth-serving agencies in California still searched during the next five years for any way in which they could effortlessly handle these youth. Their answer appeared in 1984, when Teresa DeCrescenzo, whose career as a social worker and probation officer gave her first-hand experience of the poor fit that most GLBTQ young people endured in mainstream and publicly funded child welfare agencies, founded the GLASS program. In 1985, shortly after incorporation as a city, West Hollywood City Council voted to grant GLASS start-up funding in the amount of $55,000 to set up a six-bed licensed group home. Financing was difficult, some in the community responded negatively, and come election time, politicians who had originally supported the effort came under fire for their support. But the neonate agency survived.

By 1987, with the demand for child welfare placements increasing, the Los Angeles County Department of Probation asked the organization to open a second facility with a grant of $45,000. By this point, GLASS had already developed a solid reputation in the community. At the same time, the agency responded to the call to provide effective residential programming for HIV-infected youth. At the time when this subgroup was added to the organization's mission statement, HIV was seen as a gay disease. At present, the majority of HIV-positive youth living in GLASS programs are heterosexual (Greeley, 1994, pp. 114–116).

In 1989, the agency expanded its mission to include foster care and initiated a program that recruited, screened, trained, certified, and supervised foster parents. Although this agency's specific mission is to provide care for gay and lesbian adolescents in five group homes and in 135 foster homes, it does not discriminate against heterosexually oriented young people who live in the Los Angeles area. The agency employs GLBTQ and heterosexually oriented staff with special skills (they are usually people with a gay or lesbian sibling or family member). The board of directors is also representative of the client base. In many respects, GLASS is just like other child welfare agencies, but the key differentiating significance, which makes it gay and lesbian affirming, is that GLASS was conceived and designed, and key decisions were made by, gay and lesbian child welfare professionals.

A central theme in the organizing of the GLASS program was that the agency is first and foremost a child welfare organization run by and for GLBT people. It is an organization that has as its central mission to work with GLBTQ adolescents and their families within the context of a child welfare environment.

The following section outlines concrete strategies for creating trans-affirming environments in other youth-serving agencies that may or may not be child welfare focused.

Concrete strategies

Hiring supportive employees

An organization that is responsive to the needs of transgender youth must be staffed and administered by people who demonstrate a similar commitment to providing services that foster self-esteem and acceptance for transgender youth. To achieve this, the organization must aim to hire open-minded, supportive employees, including openly gay, lesbian, bisexual, and transgender (GLBT) professionals. Organizations must communicate anti-discrimination policies in hiring, and must be honest about recruiting and maintaining GLBT employees. Hiring openly GLBT employees sends a clear message that the agency is demonstrating its commitment to transgender youth. Although hiring GLBT staff is critical, it should not be assumed that every GLBT person is knowledgeable about working with transgender youth, or appropriate for working with them. All staff, regardless of sexual orientation or gender identification, should be assessed for their appropriateness in working with youth, and then educated about transgender youth, the problems that they experience in society, and how to intervene effectively with them. Hiring non-GLBT staff who are comfortable with and knowledgeable about trans people and open to being educated about working with this population is also an essential part of this process.

With increasing openness about sexual and gender orientation, clients often ask employees about their sexual and gender orientation. One agency, Green Chimneys Children's Services, has encouraged staff to be open about their orientation, whatever their orientation happens to be. Ambiguity about staff's orientation leads to mistrust in the youth. Once staff are clear, residents stopped playing the guessing games and started to do the work that they had come to the agency for in the first place.

One of the most positive outcomes of recruiting openly GLBT staff reported by several of the agencies was that staff turnover was at an all-time-low rate. Being able to be employed in an accepting atmosphere is a great employee benefit for transgender persons.

In-service training

In-service training integrated into the overall training efforts of the organization, as opposed to one-shot training deals, is critical in providing quality services to transgender youth and families. As with all issues of diversity, integrating real-life case examples into the training sessions can make the educational process come alive for workers. Helping staff to identify appropriate language, banishing the common myths and stereotypes that most people have about transgender persons, replacing the myths with accurate information about the population, and helping staff to create environments that suggest safety, are all good places to start. Training efforts should, however, be tailored to meet the individual needs of staff members from various disciplines (see Mallon, 1998).

Helping staff to identify resources in the community and to assess their own personal heterocentrism is also a key factor in the training process. Use of videos and guest speakers – especially transgender youth or their parents – can be particularly effective in getting the message across.

Transferring abstract information learned in training sessions into actual intervention techniques takes practice. Participation in a variety of experiential exercises assists staff members in beginning to develop a set of apt and unconstrained responses. Staff members in the training sessions should be intentionally exposed to situations that lead to self-reflection. For example, in one training program focusing on the maladaptive coping responses that can be associated with hiding one's sexual or gender orientation, the participants were asked at the start of the session to write their most personal secret on a slip of paper, to fold it, and to place it under the chair that they would be sitting on all day. Although they were never asked to share what they wrote, the message, which is that keeping a secret can be stressful and difficult, is powerful. In ensuing discussion, attitudinal change and understanding of the consequences of secrecy often begin to evolve.

Providing staff at the training sessions with written information, resources, and other materials insures that the educational process continues after the training session is finished. Training that includes ongoing sessions and follow-up, and not one-shot deals, is the most constructive.

Welcoming strategies

The creation of a physical environment that welcomes transgender youth, families, and prospective employees is as significant as staff training.

Again, these efforts do need not cost a great deal of money, but evidence of an affirming environment signals acceptance and safety.

The organization's waiting room is probably the most important place to start this process. Reading materials, symbols, and signs that specifically spell out the organization's attitude about respect for all people will be noticed and will help clients, their families, and employment applicants feel welcome.

Many agencies have posters hung in their waiting rooms that signal acceptance. Green Chimneys Children's Services has specifically developed nine colorful, gender-neutral posters that announce a gay/lesbian- or transgender-affirming environment. The messages that these send are intentionally subtle. National transgender organizations will also be able to provide youth-serving agencies with pamphlets and materials; others can be downloaded from the Internet.

The presence or lack of books focusing on transgender issues also conveys important messages. Hundreds of transgender-related books could also be purchased online using the services of either amazon.com or barnesandnoble.com.

Integrated policies and public information materials

An organization's commitment to transgender youth involves more than posters and books. Recognizing that the internal structure of the organization by way of its policies and public information materials may also need to be evaluated is critical (Egri and Frost, 1991). Training and educational efforts may assist staff in developing their competence in working with a service population, but practice guidelines, policies, and what the outside community knows about the organization may also need to be altered to effect real change (Bolman and Deal, 1991; Brager and Holloway, 1978; Grise-Owens *et al.*, 2004; Moss-Kanter, 1988).

Although transgender persons have experienced greater acceptance and understanding in the past 30 years, many organizations may still actively discriminate against transgender youth. In other cases, the organization's inattentiveness to the needs of transgender youth will send a clear signal that they are not welcome. A review of the organization's policies and public materials can assist it in consistently attempting to provide sensitive services to all youth.

Advocacy efforts

Recognizing that the environment outside the organization is often actively hostile to transgender youth, youth-serving agencies must be committed to external change and advocacy efforts as well. This means participation in an advocacy campaign to end discriminatory language in contracts and in human-services-related conferences. Affirming organizations must also be prepared to advocate for transgender youth in community schools, in local adolescent treatment settings, and in families. Further, organizations' leaders must also be prepared to work to educate local and state politicians and funders about the needs of transgender youth.

Conclusions

As we approach the second decade of the new century, social workers continue to play a critical role in developing young people. Youth work has historically had a cyclical interest in certain subjects: youth suicide, violence, substance abuse, and homelessness. All are worthwhile issues that require our best efforts, but the needs of transgender youth should not be viewed as the issue *du jour* of youth work; sexual and gender orientation issues are too vital to continue to be overlooked. A particular transgender client might trigger a plethora of attention at the time, only to fade from view when the next pressing issue presents itself. Dealing with transgender youth issues in an intermittent manner is a mistake. Organizations must continue to develop diligence in training, and assess their own ability or inability to respond to the needs of transgender youth and to address new approaches to competent practice with these youth and their families. For an organization to be consistently sensitive to the needs of its clients, efforts to create affirming environments and to transform existing ones must be realized. If organizations are guided by the same principles that embrace diversity, and can translate these into concrete action, transgender youth will be better served.

References

Bockting, W. O., Knudsen, G., and Goldberg, J. M. (2006). *Counseling and Mental Health Care for Transgender Adults and Loved Ones. International Journal of Transgenderism* 9(3/4), 35–82.

Bolman, L. and Deal, T. E. (1991). *Reframing Organizations: Artistry, Choice, and Leadership*. San Francisco: Jossey-Bass.

Brager, G. and Holloway, S. (1978). *Changing Human Service Organizations: Politics and Practice*. New York: Free Press.

Dutton, J. E. (1992). The making of organizational opportunities: An interpretive pathway to organizational change. *Research in Organizational Behavior* 15, 195–226.

Egri, C. P. and Frost, P. J. (1991). Shamanism and change: Bringing back the magic in organizational transformation. In R.W. Woodman and W.A. Pasmore (Eds.), *Research in Organizational Change and Development*, 6,175–221, Greenwich, CT: JAI Press.

Feinberg, L. (1993). *Stone Butch Blues*. Ithaca, NY: Firebrand Books.

Greeley, G. (1994). Service organizations for gay and lesbian youth. In T. DeCrescenzo (Ed.) *Helping Gay and Lesbian Youth: New Policies, New Programs, New Practices.* New York: Haworth Press.

Grise-Owens, E., Vessels, J., and Owens, L. W. (2004). Organizing for change: One city's journey toward justice. *Journal of Gay and Lesbian Social Services* 16(3/4), 1–15.

Israel, G. and Tarver, D. E. (1997). *Transgender Care.* Philadelphia: Temple University Press.

Kets de Vries, M. F. R. and Miller, D. (1984). *The Neurotic Organization: Diagnosing and Changing Counterproductive Styles of Management.* San Francisco: Jossey-Bass.

Mallon, G. P. (1998). *We Don't Exactly get the Welcome Wagon: The Experiences of Gay and Lesbian Adolescents in Child Welfare Agencies.* New York: Columbia University Press.

Moss-Kanter, R. (1988). When a thousand flowers bloom: Structural, collective, and social conditions for innovation in organization. *Research in Organizational Behavior 10*, 169–211.

Sawyer, D. A. and Woodlock, D. J. (1995). An organizational culture paradigm for effective residential treatment. *Administration and Policy in Mental Health* 22(4), 437–446.

Scholinski, D. (1997). *The Last Time I Wore a Dress.* New York: Riverhead Books.

Schorr, L. B. with D. Schorr (1988). *Within Our Reach: Breaking the Cycle of Disadvantage.* New York: Doubleday.

White Holman, N. and Goldberg, J. (2006a). Ethical, legal, and psychosocial issues for transgender adolescents. *International Journal of Transgenderism* 9(3/4), 95–110.

White Holman, N. and Goldberg, J. (2006b). Social and medical transgender case advocacy. *International Journal of Transgenderism* 9(3/4), 197–217.

Summary of recommendations for the clinical treatment of transgender and gender variant youth

Gerald P. Mallon

Comprehensive care

1   Complete care for transgender and gender variant adolescents must be considered in the context of a holistic approach that includes primary care as well as cultural, economic, psychosocial, sexual, and spiritual influences on health.

2   Mental health professionals typically play a primary role in providing and coordinating care of the trans adolescent. Involvement of clinicians from all disciplines (e.g. social work, family practice, pediatric endocrinology) is essential.

3   The non-specialist can facilitate peer and family interactions that help the transgender adolescent learn emotional and relational skills, including tools to recognize, express, and manage emotion; to resolve conflicts constructively; and to work cooperatively with others.

Clinical competence

1   Clinicians who diagnose and treat trangender and gender variant adolescents should have training in adolescent psychiatry and/or clinical psychology and/or clinical social work and experience in diagnosing and treating the typical issues related to adolescents, as well as specific expertise relating to transgender and gender variant identity development and gender identity concerns.

2   Therapists working with transgender adolescents must be accustomed to working with adolescents and be able to practice in a trans-affirming manner that includes the ability to discuss sensitive topics, including sexuality.

3   Regardless of the presenting issues, the clinician should be able to evaluate the impact of trans-specific issues on the adolescent's overall health and well-being, and incorporate this into the overall care plan.

4   Clinicians should be aware of the gender diversity among the local transgender/gender variant adolescent population as part of the

general sensitivity and awareness needed for any work with the trans-gender communities.

Facilitating discussion of transgender issues

1 Gender concerns may not always be obvious; techniques to facilitate discussion of transgender/gender variant issues should be used with all adolescents.
2 To promote awareness of transgender/gender variant issues and help give adolescents language with which to talk about their concerns. This includes creating a trans-affirming environment, which may include having trans-affirming reading materials and posters in the waiting room and office.
3 The clinician should emphasize a non-judgmental attitude, reassure the adolescent about confidentiality, and actively demonstrate trans-gender awareness and sensitivity.
4 A brief screening question about gender concerns should be incorpo-rated into the intake process for all youth, and not just for those who appear to be gender variant. A short normalizing statement should be used, followed by a simple question that can be answered without directly declaring transgender identity. For example: "Many people struggle with gender. Is this an issue for you?"

Determining the level of treatment needed for gender concerns

1 If an adolescent discloses concerns about gender, the clinician should explore the nature of the concerns, the impact on the adoles-cent's life, the adolescent's feelings about transgender identification, and related or coexisting factors contributing to the adolescent's distress.
2 For the adolescent who is confused, questioning, or unsure about gender issues, counseling by the non-specialist and referral to age-appropriate community resources are often sufficient.
3 Evaluation by a mental health clinician specializing in gender identity concerns is recommended if the adolescent:

- is so distressed about gender issues that health and well-being, rela-tionships, or school/work are negatively affected;
- expresses feelings of gender dysphoria, an aversion to aspects of their body associated with sex/gender, discomfort with gender iden-tity, or a wish to live as the opposite sex;
- is compulsively cross-dressing or compulsively pursuing validation of gender identity;

• has a coexisting or preexisting condition that complicates evaluation of gender concerns.

Differential diagnosis

1   The usefulness of a diagnosis of gender identity disorder (GID) or transvestic fetishism in treatment and care planning is a decision that should be made on a case-by-case basis, with care taken to distinguish both compulsive cross-dressing and GID from gender-variant behavior that is not intrinsically problematic.
2   The "distress" criterion of GID as defined in the *DSM*-IV-TR should not be applied to parents' distress that their child is atypical, or a child's distress about other people's transphobic reactions. These are societally caused situations that can be addressed by intervention with the parents focused on building acceptance for gender diversity, along with intervention for the adolescent to build resilience and address stigma issues.
3   Adolescents should not be diagnosed with GID solely because they display behaviors that are contrary to societal gender norms.

Assessment

1   An adolescent who presents with a wish for sex reassignment should be thoroughly assessed to determine the history of gender concerns and potential underlying or related problems. Ideally, parents or guardians will be involved in providing collateral information.
2   Assessment areas include the adolescent's general and psychosexual development, historical and current cross-gender feelings and behavior (including cross-dressing), school functioning, peer relations, family functioning, sexual experiences, sexual behavior and fantasies, sexual attractions, and body image.
3   The possibilities and limitations of sex reassignment and other kinds of treatment should be discussed both to give the adolescent accurate information about treatment options and to aid in assessment.
4   Distress relating to gender identity/gender dysphoria should be distinguished from confusion relating to sexual orientation, shame relating to cross-dressing or other stigmatized transgender behavior, transient stress-related cross-dressing, erotically motivated cross-dressing, gender concerns secondary to a psychiatric condition (e.g. schizophrenia), or adolescent experimentation.

Treatment planning

1   Strategies for management of a trans or gender-variant identity include a variety of means of acknowledging and incorporating the felt

identity into everyday life. These may (but do not always) include physiological changes and/or social role changes.

2   Physical treatment is not an option prior to puberty, although psychological treatment including (supportive) psychotherapy may be offered.

3   Adolescents who are confused about their gender or whose wish for sex reassignment seems to originate from factors other than a genuine and complete cross-gender identity should be offered psychotherapeutic treatment.

4   Potential psychological and social risk factors should be taken into account when considering the viability of sex reassignment. If psychological resiliency or adequate social supports are lacking, treatment may focus on creating the conditions that will be conducive to a more positive outcome for eventual sex reassignment.

5   Any coexisting psychopathology unrelated to trans identification should be appropriately treated, and psychosocial supports put in place prior to initiation of physical intervention.

6   In addition to the involvement of other clinicians, mental health professional involvement is a requirement for physical intervention in adolescence. Treatment should be thoughtfully and recurrently considered over time, with the consequences of sex reassignment as well as the wish for sex reassignment reconsidered and discussed again with each new developmental phase.

7   Care planning includes identification of resources the client can call on as they make the transition from adolescence to adulthood.

Psychosocial interventions

1   Psychosocial assessment should include evaluation of transgender adolescents' Home life, Education/employment, Eating, Activities, Drugs, Sexuality, Suicide/depression, and Safety (**HEEADSSS**). For the adolescent who has disclosed transgender identity, the standard HEEADSSS interview should be modified to include trans-specific content.

2   Services for transgender adolescents should be relevant and accessible to youth who are involved in the sex-trade industry. Involvement in the sex-trade industry should not be considered an exclusionary criterion for adolescents seeking sex reassignment, as this leaves youth who are financially dependent on the sex-trade industry unable to access care.

3   When discussing sexuality, clinicians should engage in frank and explicit discussion about the actual practices an adolescent is engaged in, rather than making assumptions about the gender of partner(s) or sexual activities. The transgender adolescent should be asked about preferred terms for genitals to ensure that sexual health discussion is respectful of self-defined gender identity.

4 For adolescents with intense frustration or distress about body image, in addition to a general screening tool for eating disorders it may be appropriate to inquire about excessively tight breast binding, wrapping of the penis/testicles, and compulsive or excessive exercise. Intervention may include exploration of transgender identity, transgender community involvement, and peer support.

5 Psychotherapeutic treatment can be helpful both for adolescents who are unsure of the direction they want to take and for those who have a clear wish to pursue sex reassignment.

6 Any form of psychotherapy offered to adolescents who are considering sex reassignment should be supportive. The purpose of therapy is to contribute to the well-being of the adolescent, not to achieve a specific outcome. Psychotherapy should not have the underlying goal of promoting conformity with gender norms.

7 For adolescents undergoing gender transition, psychosocial issues that tend to be impacted over the course of gender transition or to change as part of general adolescent development (e.g. relationships, sexuality, infertility, disclosure of transgender identity, body image) need to be revisited periodically.

8 Sexual health education should be offered as part of treatment.

9 Family therapists or family counselors should try to help parents determine realistic demands and to work on the development of healthy boundaries and limits. In some cases, it may be appropriate to involve a second clinician in work with parents to avoid compromise of the therapeutic alliance with the adolescent.

10 Psychotherapy for adolescents may be necessary during the whole sex reassignment period, including after transition.

Supporting transgender emergence in adolescence

1 For both questioning adolescents and those who already have a strong sense of self, the emphasis is on self-understanding rather than reaching toward a preset goal. The adolescent should not be pressured to try a form of gender expression they are uncomfortable with, but rather encouraged to try experimenting as a way of deciding who they are and what feels right.

2 Adolescents who are in early stages of questioning their gender orientation should be encouraged to explore identity without making decisions about transition or sex reassignment.

3 Experimentation with fluidity of gender identification and expression is encouraged if the adolescent has a generally stable core sense of self. If there are concerns about fragmentation of identity or if the process of experimentation seems to be increasing distress, referral should be made to an advanced mental health clinician with

experience in treatment of coexisting gender concerns and mental illness.

4   Adolescents who have already made a decision to pursue sex reassignment should not be dissuaded, but should be made aware of diverse possibilities for gender identity and expression (including but not limited to sex reassignment).

5   For the adolescent who has a clear and consistent sense of self, the next step in identity development is the identification of strategies to reconcile discrepancies between identity and daily life. Whatever options are considered, there should be thought as to how changes will realistically be integrated into daily life, and what reactions there might be by others.

6   The adolescent who is considering disclosure should be supported to think about the likely reactions of the people they are telling, and possible resources to help facilitate understanding and adjustment. When there are concerns about possible violence or eviction from the home, a crisis/safety plan should be included as part of the preparation for disclosure. Role-playing the disclosure with a skilled clinician can be a very useful strategy in this process.

Sex reassignment in adolescence

1   Parents or legal guardians must consent to and participate in medical intervention for a legal minor.

2   It is beneficial to make a plan for disclosure prior to gender transition in school, in a foster or group home, or in the workplace. This may include education and clinical advocacy from professionals.

3   Planning around "real-life experience" (RLE) must include consideration of the adolescent's safety and the relative risks and benefits of undergoing RLE. When an adolescent cannot cross-live full time as part of gender transition, the clinician must consider whether the inability to live full time in the desired role is simply a mature and reasonable accommodation of the limited socioeconomic options open to adolescents, or ambivalence about full-time cross-living.

4   To prevent use of hormones without medical assistance, adolescents who express the intention to pursue transition should be given information about options for care, including the process for hormone assessment. Assessment by a trans-competent pediatric endocrinologist should be sought for the adolescent who has disclosed use of hormones without medical assistance. Only a physician is qualified to prescribe hormones.

5   Older adolescents who are intending to pursue sex reassignment surgery should be informed of eligibility criteria according to the Harry Benjamin Standards.

"Real-life experience" (RLE)

1 "Real-life experience" (RLE) – living full time in the role the adolescent is "transitioning" to – allows the adolescent to experience directly the familial, interpersonal, socioeconomic, and legal consequences of gender transition, as well as the experience of living in a different role, prior to making irreversible changes.

2 During the RLE, the adolescent's feelings about the social transformation, including coping with the responses of others as well as management of disclosure in the school/workplace, is a major focus of counselling.

3 The timing of RLE depends on the adolescent's personality and life circumstances. RLE may take place at an early age, or after hormonal feminization/masculinization begins to take effect.

Endocrine therapy

1 GnRH analogues, also known as androgen blockers, may be prescribed by a physician to prevent development of secondary sex characteristics shortly after the onset of puberty if:

- throughout childhood the adolescent has demonstrated an intense pattern of cross-gender behaviors and cross-gender identity; *and*
- the adolescent has gender dysphoria that is significantly increased with the onset of puberty; *and*
- parents or guardians consent to and participate in the therapy.

2 Feminizing/masculinizing endocrine therapy typically does not begin until the adolescent is 16 years or older, and should be preceded by GnRH treatment (androgen blockers) regardless of the adolescent's Tanner Stage, with a gradual phase-out of GnRH agents as estrogen (MTF) or androgens (FTM) are phased in. (For a complete discussion of the Tanner Stages see Brill and Pepper, 2008, p. 206).

3 The mental health professional who is coordinating care should be involved with the adolescent for a minimum of six months prior to making a recommendation for the adolescent to begin hormonal feminization/masculinization, with the number of sessions during this six-month period depending on the clinician's judgment of what is needed to ensure that treatment is thoughtfully and recurrently considered over time.

Sex reassignment surgery

1 Sex reassignment surgery should not be performed before the age of 18.

2 A minimum of two years' "real-life experience" is necessary prior to

surgery in an older adolescent; that is, an 18-year-old who is felt to be a suitable candidate for surgery must have been cross-living since age 16 (or earlier).

Recommendations for future work

1 Ongoing research and collegial meetings are needed to further develop practice protocols for trans and gender variant adolescents.
2 Future work should include:

- practice protocols for care of gender variant children under 13 years of age;
- more detailed protocols for counseling of family members of adolescents;
- consumer and clinician information about the anticipated effects, adverse effects, and questions about long-term impact of androgen blocker hormones, as well as any effects of cross-sex hormones that are different in adolescents than in adults.

Acknowledgment

The author wishes to acknowledge that much of what is presented above is adapted from work by Annelou L. C. de Vries, Peggy T. Cohen-Kettenis, and Henriette Delemarre-Van de Waal in their work titled *Clinical Management of Gender Dysphoria in Adolescents* and by Catherine White Holman and Joshua Goldberg in their work titled *Ethical, Legal, and Psychosocial Issues in Care of Transgender Adolescents*.

Reference

Brill, S. and Pepper, R. (2008). *The Transgender Child: A Handbook for Families and Professionals*. San Francisco, CA: Cleis Press.

Index

Transgender Emergence: Therapeutic Guidelines for Working with Gender Variant People and their Families 17, 28
Transgender Health Program, Vancouver 28, 80
Transgender Law Center & National Center for Lesbian Rights 146
transgender terminology 1–2, 5, 15, 53, 123
Transgender Warriors: Making History from Joan of Arc to Dennis Rodman 28
transgenderphobia 33
Transhealth Information Project 150
transitioning 8–9; during the course of employment 145; definition 4; a non-standard process 139–40
Transitioning our Shelters 158
'transsexual men' 15
Transsexual Menace 5
Transsexual Phenomenon, The 128
'transsexual women' 15
Transsexualism and Transvestism as Psycho-somatic and Somato-psychic Syndrome 5
transsexuality 1, 5, 128–31
transvestite 1, 5–6, 132
True Selves: Understanding Transsexualism – For Families, Friends, Coworkers and helping Professionals 29

UCLA 76
universities and colleges, legal advocacy in 148

Valentine, D. 4, 55
van Goozen, S. H. M. 11, 12, 82
verbal harassment 91, 98, 157, 166

Vierling, L. 39
violence towards trans people 30, 60, 81, 98, 124; in foster care 152; in juvenile detention centers 155; in schools 30, 60; sexual 81, 157; in youth-service agencies 166–7
virilization surgery 125, 126
Volcano, D. L. 28

waiting rooms 172
Weithorn, L. A. 38
Wesson Oil 82
White Holman, N. 28, 80, 166, 182
Wicks, L. K. 55
Wilchins, R.A. 5, 14, 15–17, 22, 28, 54, 12
Williams, W. 126
Wilson, K. 57
Woodlock, D. J. 166
World Professional Association for Transgender Health (WPATH) 139, 151
Woronoff, R. 152, 153, 154, 155
Wren, B. 11

Xavier, J. 11, 146

youth-service agencies: *see* agencies, youth-serving

Zastrow, C. 58
Zevin, B. 13
Zucker, K. J. 42, 43, 57, 69, 71, 97